THE POLITICS OF ENGLISH SECOND LANGUAGE WRITING ASSESSMENT IN GLOBAL CONTEXTS

Reflecting the internationalization of the field of second language writing, this book focuses on political aspects and pedagogical issues of writing instruction and testing in a global context. High-stakes assessment impacts the lives of second language (L2) writers and their teachers around the world, be it the College English Test in China, Common Core-aligned assessments in the U.S., English proficiency tests in Poland, or the material conditions (such as access to technology, training, and other resources) affecting a classroom. With contributions from authors working in ten different countries in a variety of institutional contexts, the chapters examine the uses and abuses of various writing-related assessments, and the policies that determine their form and use. Representing a diverse range of contexts, methods, and disciplines, the authors jointly call for more equitable testing systems that consider the socioeconomic, psychometric, affective, institutional, and needs of all students who strive to gain access to education and employment opportunities related to English language proficiency.

Todd Ruecker is Assistant Professor of English at the University of New Mexico, USA.

Deborah Crusan is Professor of English at Wright State University, USA.

ESL & Applied Linguistics Professional Series

Eli Hinkel, Series Editor

The Politics of English Second Language Writing Assessment in Global Contexts
Ruecker/Crusan, Eds.

Research on Reflective Practice in TESOL
Farrell

Reflective Practice in English Language Teaching: Research-Based Principles and Practices
Mann/Walsh

Teacher Training and Professional Development of Chinese English Language Teachers: Changing from Fish to Dragon
Pawan/Fan/Miao, Eds.

Corrective Feedback in Second Language Teaching and Learning: Research, Theory, Applications, Implications
Nassaji/Kartchava, Eds.

Teaching Writing for Academic Purposes to Multilingual Students: Instructional Approaches
Bitchener/Storch/Wette, Eds.

Family Language Policies in a Multilingual World: Opportunities, Challenges, and Consequences
Macalister/Mirvahedi, Eds.

Handbook of Research in Second Language Teaching and Learning, Volume III
Hinkel, Ed.

Visit **www.routledge.com/education** for additional information on titles in the ESL & Applied Linguistics Professional Series.

THE POLITICS OF ENGLISH SECOND LANGUAGE WRITING ASSESSMENT IN GLOBAL CONTEXTS

Edited by Todd Ruecker and Deborah Crusan

Routledge
Taylor & Francis Group

NEW YORK AND LONDON

First published 2018
by Routledge
711 Third Avenue, New York, NY 10017

and by Routledge
2 Park Square, Milton Park, Abingdon, Oxon, OX14 4RN

Routledge is an imprint of the Taylor & Francis Group, an informa business

© 2018 Taylor & Francis

The right of Todd Ruecker and Deborah Crusan to be identified as the authors of the editorial material, and of the authors for their individual chapters, has been asserted in accordance with sections 77 and 78 of the Copyright, Designs and Patents Act 1988.

Library of Congress Cataloging-in-Publication Data
A catalog record for this book has been requested

ISBN: 978-1-138-09446-8 (hbk)
ISBN: 978-1-138-09447-5 (pbk)
ISBN: 978-1-315-10606-9 (ebk)

Typeset in Bembo
by Apex CoVantage, LLC

CONTENTS

PART III
Seeking Solutions: Assessing Better Locally and Internationally

FIGURES

TABLES

ACKNOWLEDGMENTS

We'd like to thank the contributors to this collection for their dedication to supporting language learners in a variety of contexts. We also thank them for believing in this collection from the beginning and their persistence in revising chapters throughout the process. We would also like to thank Naomi Silverman and Karen Adler, our Routledge editors; Eli Hinkel, the ESL and Applied Linguistics Professional Series editor; and Emmalee Ortega, our Routledge editorial assistant. Their encouragement, feedback, support, and guidance throughout this process helped us to bring this project to fruition. We thank those who have been supportive throughout this process, especially our families.

We dedicate this book to teachers and students throughout the world who are at the frontlines in navigating the politics of assessment in their institutions and classrooms. We hope this book positively impacts policy and practice in the contexts in which they teach and learn.

1

THE INTERSECTIONS OF POLITICS AND SECOND LANGUAGE WRITING ASSESSMENT

What We Know

Todd Ruecker and Deborah Crusan

Pennycook (2013) claims, "English and English language teaching seems ubiquitous in the world, playing a role everywhere from large-scale global politics to the intricacies of people's lives" (p. 4). Inextricably coupled with language teaching, perennially it seems, is language assessment. Whether it is the College English Test (CET) in China, Common Core-aligned assessments in the U.S., English proficiency tests in Poland, or material conditions such as access to technology, training, and other resources affecting classroom assessment in a variety of global contexts, assessment impacts the lives of L2 writers and their teachers around the world. Too often, assessment policies are imposed on teachers and their classrooms by those removed from these contexts, leading to policies that negatively impact the teaching and learning process, often demoralizing teachers and students in the process.

Let us provide an example from Todd's state of New Mexico in the United States. The latest governor appointed a secretary of education early in her term who has connections with a neoliberal reform group called Chiefs for Change (Layton, 2015), a group that aims to promote policies such as using test scores to evaluate teachers and as report cards for schools. In New Mexico, this has translated into student test scores accounting for half of a teacher's evaluation, creating an environment in which teachers are under intense pressure to teach to a particular test lest they face the possibility of losing their jobs. For a time, the state education department tried to issue a gag order preventing teachers from disparaging high-stakes standardized tests, but this did not hold up in court (Rivera, 2016). As Todd has documented elsewhere, high-stakes testing policies can have hugely negative impacts on schools with large numbers of English Language Learners (e.g., Ruecker, Chamcharatsri, & Saengngoen, 2015; Ruecker, 2013).

You (2004) has discussed ways the CET shapes writing instruction in China with this illustrative anecdote of a teacher leading students in exam practice. The teacher explained,

> I scored your writing according to a 15-point scale. If your writing could not pass (did not get a passing score), here is the *fanwen* (model essay) on the blackboard (for your reference). As you can see, this is a typical *san-duanlun* (three-paragraph format): introduction, disadvantages and advantages of holiday economy, and the author's own opinion.
>
> *(p. 101)*

You noted that the teacher "already had the 'correct' writing in her mind before she asked her students to write" (p. 101). The teacher continued offering suggestions to her students: "Students with lower proficiency should try to memorize some model writings, so you can write with much more ease. There are 34 model writings in this booklet. It would be better if you could memorize all of them" (p. 101).

As teachers of writing, researchers, and administrators interested in assessment, we are dismayed at examples like the ones mentioned above. We feel strongly that well-designed, context-driven assessment is a force for good in improving classroom structure and student learning. Having clearly defined goals, focused criteria, and informal and formal assessments can help a teacher and student constantly gauge individuals' progress so that teaching can be adjusted as needed to focus on a particular topic or theme. However, when politicians, big-money organizations, and distant administrators get involved and create poorly designed assessments and impose uninformed or heavy-handed penalties for low performance, the value of assessment gets distorted and has real potential to harm students and teachers.

As we will discuss a bit later, the policies of high-stakes testing have been well documented in the U.S. Further, as with much scholarship in second language writing and education, the work that gets published and disseminated is very much centered on English speaking countries like the U.S. Internationally, we don't know enough about various local English as a foreign language (EFL) contexts of assessment, such as material or policy conditions in particular schools, whether secondary schools, private language institutes, or institutions of higher education. For those reasons, we were driven to create a collection to address these gaps, a collection that brings together teachers and scholars working in and writing about a variety of contexts around the world, helping to build a picture of the challenges L2 writing teachers face in relation to assessment policies and practices.

In general, we have been disappointed in our field's aversion to engaging in political discussions, despite publication of works such as Matsuda, Ortmeier-Hooper, and You's (2006) *The Politics of Second Language Writing*. This may be due in part to the sensitive nature of this topic and the contingent nature of the positions of many of those involved in the teaching of writing around the world. If one challenges entrenched power structures, then there is the real risk of losing one's hard-earned position. Nonetheless, we have seen scholars make calls for more considerations of the sociopolitical contexts of writing and writing instruction. In a 2003 *JSLW* article, "Looking Ahead to More Sociopolitically-Oriented Case Study Research in L2 Writing Scholarship," Casanave noted that L2 writing scholars "are attending to social and political aspects of writing that in the past were not considered central either to writing process research or to textual studies of writing" (p. 86), while calling for more work on the sociopolitical contexts of writing instruction. In this article, Casanave raised pointed questions about assessment and L2 writing, such as

> What attitudes and strategies are taken by students, writing instructors, administrators, and evaluators who are involved in a particular competency exam system in a particular setting? How do particular exam requirements determine how students prepare and how teachers design class activities?
> *(p. 90)*

A Bit on Terms

While we were disseminating the call for proposals (CFP) for this collection, we regularly were asked, "What do you mean by the politics of assessment?" and once we explained, were warned that we might have trouble finding authors because of the sensitive nature of political decisions in particular contexts. While dictionary definitions typically tend to connect politics with "government," we are using this term broadly. On one level, we are concerned about the impact that national, state, and local governmental policies have on assessment. However, we also consider institutions, whether public or private, as governing bodies where policies are set at different levels, policies that impact those at other levels.

An important part of politics that the above dictionary definition doesn't explicitly address is power, an issue that has been taken up extensively by critical theorists such as Foucault (1977) and Bourdieu and Passeron (1977). In *Discipline and Punish*, Foucault depicted power as a force spread throughout society whose workings are not always implicit. Teachers and students are embedded in a "political field" shaped by the workings of individuals, corporations, and other organizations that in turn shapes the assessment practices in their classrooms. At the most extreme, we see instances where teachers are mandated to teach a scripted curriculum designed to get students to pass a particular test. In such an instance, they are subjugated through the imposition of penalties that can cost teachers their jobs or, in a student's case, success in an educational institution or acceptance for a particular job. One aspect of power not discussed as extensively by Foucault is the role wealth plays in shaping power structures; this is a concept that Bourdieu and Passeron (1977) captured through the concept of capital, which dealt with both social capital and economic capital, the latter of which Bourdieu and Passeron (1977) depicted as the most influential. In recent years, we have seen an increased role of big money involved in the shaping of assessments. With large foundations and corporations involved in the creation of tests and the textbooks behind them, these big money entities win contracts worth tens of millions of dollars, which essentially grants them carte blanche to define the teaching and learning processes in different institutions. Because tests affect the lives of and define the people who take them, we need to examine their uses and the consequences of those uses in society (Shohamy, 2001; McNamara & Roever, 2006) and their ties to power distributions in society. We aim to do that very thing with this book.

When we talk about assessment, we are often concerned with large-scale assessment since that is so frequently overtly political. However, we recognize that assessment is much more than that. For us, assessment is not only large-scale tests but also everyday practices in a classroom that enable a teacher to judge the progress of her students in order to provide additional guidance to help them develop and advance. For instance, depending on the information a teacher needs, a short timed writing assignment at the beginning of class can be used as an assessment as well as a larger research essay. In working towards an essay, there may be mini assessments, such as an annotated bibliography, an outline, and partial drafts of different components of the paper. All of these different assessments, micro or macro, are often shaped by the layers of political fields embedding teachers, classrooms, and students. For instance, if a teacher is required to teach towards a particular test, as in You's (2004) aforementioned example, then the type of writing students will be completing and being assessed on during the class will be inevitably shaped by the test. In another example, resource disparities, often a product of political decisions about school funding, may mean that teachers work with too many students, preventing their ability to prioritize feedback and revision in assessing writing, instead looking for a scoring system that will streamline the process as much as possible.

Politics in Education

In "Importing Composition: Teaching and Researching Academic Writing Beyond North America," Muchiri, Mulamba, Myers, and Ndoloi (1995) wrote, "Everyday academic work is still overwhelmingly determined by its national setting. The funding, the geography, the politics, the national ideology determine daily concerns like hours, class size, assessment, careers" (p. 194). Political forces at different levels have long played a role in shaping classrooms and the experiences of L2 writers within them. At the local level, we often see disparities between different schools and classrooms that shape the type of assessments teachers can do and the impact of those assessments on students. For instance, in the U.S., school funding is highly inequitable as it is mostly funded locally via property taxes. It has been well documented that schools in poorer neighborhoods tend to have lower quality facilities, larger class sizes, less qualified teachers, and higher concentrations of L2 learners (e.g., Turner et al., 2016). In a study of English teaching in Jordan, Al-Jarrah and Al-Ahmad (2013) similarly reported that a "shortage of qualified teachers and researchers, textbooks, school buildings, and facilities has been reflected negatively on the students' attitudes toward the learning situation" (p. 90). The authors also noted that university writing classes have at least 60–70 students in a writing class, with primary and secondary public schools regularly having class sizes of 50 or more. Similarly, we have had colleagues from Thailand report teaching university language classes with hundreds of students. As we all know, writing assessment takes time, and material conditions such as large class sizes and access to computers impact what a teacher can do. Ruecker et al. (2014) stated that a lack of time to provide feedback was one of the top challenges reported by teachers on an internationally distributed survey on the contexts of L2 writing instruction.

On the national level, we have seen governments regularly intervene in education systems for a variety of reasons. For instance, Prendergast (2008) documented the spread of English language instruction in Slovakia as part of a larger government initiative to be competitive in the international economy. Al-Jarrah and Al-Ahmad (2013) explained how English teaching mandates in Jordan came under opposition from various forces, including religious figures, who were concerned about the teaching of a non-Arabic language in the country. The existence of national policies to encourage or require the teaching of a particular language impacts the attitudes teachers and students bring to a particular writing task and assessment. As Reichelt (2005) noted, "EFL writing pedagogy in Poland, as well as in other non-English-dominant contexts, is shaped by the role English plays, local attitudes toward English, the history of English-language teaching, and other context-specific educational factors" (p. 226). Muchiri et al. (1995), Clachar (2000), and Leki (2001) have all documented the problems when teachers bring or are required to teach and assess explicitly in a western style. For instance, Clachar (2000) noted how teachers and students both struggled with the expectations posed by an "alien rhetorical style" (p. 80).

Perhaps the most commonly identified national interventions concerning L2 writing assessment concern national mandates of standardized, high-stakes tests. A Council of the Great City Schools (2015) study reported that U.S. students take 112 **mandated** standardized tests between pre-kindergarten classes and twelfth grade. In contrast, other countries administer three tests to students during that same time period. The impact of increased testing on L2 writers over the past few decades has been well documented. For instance, Booher-Jennings (2005) reported that English Language Learners in doubt of passing the test were often ignored or, even worse, increasingly placed into special education programs where they did not impact a school's overall grade. Ruecker (2013, 2015) has written extensively about how a school on the U.S.–Mexico border that was 40% English Language Learner (ELL) was forced to teach narrowly towards a particular state test, restricting the types of writing experiences students had during high school. Ruecker et al. (2015) reported that even the latest high-stakes standardized tests developed in the U.S. are rife with cultural bias and disproportionately harm schools with large numbers of ELLs.

Some scholars have documented the impact of high-stakes assessments in other countries. As cited earlier, You (2004) has explored how the CET has helped contribute to rote, reductive writing instruction in China. In what seems a nod towards positive washback, Reichelt (2005) explained how the new Polish Matura (the school leaving exam) was going to require writing whereas the older form of the test did not, thus increasing teachers' interest in writing instruction. As Leki (2001) noted, "In a spiraling interaction of mutual reinforcement, once writing becomes important in academic settings, it becomes subject to testing; once writing is tested, its importance is further augmented" (p. 199). However, Reichelt (2005) found that the emphasis on preparing students for exams, especially in Polish universities, meant that students were writing essays in the current-traditional mold that bore little relation to the practical, culturally situated contexts in which they would be writing in throughout their lives.

Coupled with too much testing is the issue of how we use the test scores (Crusan, 2006). Often, the powers that be place too much emphasis on one score on one test and use that single score to evaluate both teachers and students. Since we believe that the primary function of testing is to promote teaching and learning in the classroom, it is often difficult for us to support the amount of standardized testing that goes on in our schools, for it is not locally developed and the teachers and students who are most affected have no voice in its creation and/or administration. Further, the consequences brought on by these tests—the narrowing of students' writing experiences in school—can cause repercussions.

In several ways, the global standardized testing movement, especially regarding writing assessment, affects institutions of higher learning. In fact, "inferences drawn about test-takers' language abilities based on language test scores result in life changing decisions, for example, university admission, professional certification, immigration, and citizenship" (Fox & Cheng, 2016, p. 66). In particular, writing teachers complain that their incoming students commonly have the opinion that good writing has five paragraphs, with an introduction, three body paragraphs that present three different assertions regarding the topic and add shallow evidence for those assertions, and a conclusion that restates what has been stated in the previous paragraphs. They are taught standardized, formulaic methods to accomplish these tasks and rarely engage in the word play, genre analysis, and/or genre awareness-building activities that advance real literacy and writing ability, nor are they enlightened to the fact that everything cannot possibly be an essay—that this perspective on writing leaves out multitudinous genres such as letters, movie reviews, research reports, and proposals (Caplan & de Oliveira, 2016). But to engage in such linguistic knowledge construction—to understand that writing grows from many purposes (CCCC, 2016)—would sacrifice time devoted to learning the forms required by the standardized test. So when the new college student enters the composition classroom, writing teachers have the task of teaching them that the essay is not king, that other ways of writing are equally valid, that "there is no single format that is an adequate response to every rhetorical situation" (Caplan & de Oliveira, 2016, para. 5), rather than building on the skills they'll need to succeed in the complex writing assignments they'll face in their university careers.

A second way that institutions of higher education are affected by standardized, high-stakes writing assessment is in terms of placement and graduation testing. Placement tests such as the TOEFL and the ACCUPLACER (in the U.S.) have been argued about, researched, revised, and presented in various institutional iterations, including the mass writing assignment on the first day of freshman orientation, the online essay writing task, and directed self-placement. Since 1987, college students in China have had to pass the College English test, even if not English majors, in order to secure an undergraduate degree (You, 2010). For Korean students, the dreaded *Suneung*, the college entrance exam which includes an eight-page paper written in English, marks a high-stakes event that determines in which university they will study and, in some cases, their career path. Similarly, Japanese students face rigorous tests and enormous pressure, for these tests determine entrance into a university. In the same way, nine million Chinese students each year sit for the entrance exam to Chinese universities. All of these tests have English components and are described as grueling.

What Assessment Should Be

Whatever the advantages and disadvantages to assessment, be it large-scale or classroom, it is vitally important that teachers are prepared to assess the writing their students do and to also understand the impact of standardized tests, what they mean to the curriculum, and how they might influence their teaching. Further, in order to know what our students know and can do, we need to know how to do good assessment and how to interpret the results. When we mention the word *interpret*, we are not necessarily referring to the interpretation of numbers, although that can be one approach; instead, we're talking about looking at data (be it numbers or a set of paragraphs students have written in class) to determine what students know, what they need to know, what they need to know how to do. While commonly distorted by policy makers and institutional officials, assessment should be for one reason—to guide and promote teaching and learning. Once teachers have data about their students, they can then design their lessons and assignments around that knowledge, supported by what they know their students need. It is vitally important to remember that student *need*s should guide every class—and we recognize that at times that need is the need to pass a test—and the way to understand student needs is to gather data. However, we understand that large classrooms internationally raise obstacles in local, teacher-created assessment—as do administrative mandates. Further, there are important questions that we often ask, including: are teachers trusted to create their own assessments? Are teachers trained to create their own assessments?

One of the reasons for this book is to examine writing assessment internationally; however, since we see assessment and teaching as intertwined, it is vital to examine the connections between the two. As detailed above, many scholars have raised concerns over the impact of high-stakes tests on writing instruction in both ESL and EFL contexts. We saw how Reichelt (2005) and You (2010) revealed how teachers under pressure from high-stakes tests may be more likely to cling to a rather current-traditional stance in their teaching, directing very rote memorization-driven, teacher-centered instruction focusing on language forms. If writing instruction is reduced to focus on the subskills of writing, then locally designed classroom assessments may be as well, with teachers using multiple-choice grammar quizzes and calling it writing assessment. It is clear that there is work to do; hence, we offer this collection as a way to move forward.

The Collection

This collection has grown out of ongoing interests in the intersection of politics and assessment, interest that has emerged from our teaching and research interests in a variety of institutional contexts. Todd has spent extensive time in U.S. K–12 schools and has seen the impact of high-stakes standardized testing on L2 writers and their teachers. He has been frustrated in seeing how these tests are often sold under the guise of helping students when the reality is that they often water down writing instruction and limit the opportunities that L2 writers have to become prepared for college-level writing. At the college level, he has been concerned about the use of reductive, often computer-scored, writing placement tests as well as the increased push for standardized testing in postsecondary education overall. Throughout her career, Deborah has argued for the inclusion of stakeholders in testing decisions, whether it is at the primary, secondary, or tertiary level. She has championed the idea that all teachers should be assessment literate and should have taken courses that lead them in the examination of testing methodology, instructed them in the creation of reliable and valid assessment instruments for their own classrooms, provided them with arguments both for and against testing, and made them aware of the consequences of the assessments we mandate. In an effort to walk her talk, she successfully argued for a required assessment course in the MATESOL program in which she teaches and structures that class so that her students better understand the purposes of assessment; grasp key concepts and their underlying theories in the field of language assessment; create authentic assessment tasks in the classroom; understand that assessment is an integral part of teaching and learning but that it should be ancillary to both; and critically examine issues surrounding assessment and the consequences of assessment. What's more, she emphasizes writing assessment intensely, dedicating several weeks of the curriculum to its study; part of her rationale for the time spent on writing assessment is based on the jobs most of her students take. The programs in which they work are largely focused on writing for academic purposes.

In distributing the call for papers for this collection, we were particularly interested in gaining a global perspective beyond our own experiences of the intersections of politics and assessment in classrooms and schools. We distributed the call via a variety of listservs. We called for work that focused on different settings, ranging from elementary schools to private language institutes. We called for chapters that dealt with assessment politics locally, nationally, and internationally. In addition to full-length, research-based chapters, we also solicited vignette chapters, which provide a more personal take on a particular topic. We have scattered these throughout the collection. We were pleased to receive submissions from a variety of contexts around the world and were conscious to limit the number of chapters from U.S.-based contexts in order to create a collection that would put a variety of contexts into conversation with one another.

We have divided this collection into three parts. Part I: *Local and National Policy Contexts* includes four chapters and two vignettes that take a broader focus and look at ways in which policies in a particular country or across countries impact writing instruction and assessment in classrooms. Chapters discuss ways local policies impact writing instruction and assessment as well local initiatives seeking to affect change locally or nationally. Part II: *High-Stakes Assessment* includes four chapters and two vignettes that examine consequences of various governmental and institutional high-stakes assessment policies on the lives of teachers and students. Part III: *Seeking Solutions: Assessing Better Locally and Internationally* focuses on both U.S. and international contexts, populations such as students with disabilities and K–12, and topics such as writing across the curriculum, creative writing, and placement.

As evident from its title, Part I—*Local and National Policy Contexts*—includes chapters focused primarily on exploring the impact of national policies on assessment practices. In Chapter 2, Estela Ene and Katarzyna Hryniuk report on a transnational study (China, Mexico, and Poland), focusing on ways macro-policies such as high-stakes national exams impacted writing instruction in the different contexts. In Chapter 3, Theresa A. Orlovsky draws on her experience teaching in the U.S. and Mexico to discuss the importance of teaching context in the assessment of ESL and EFL writing. In Chapter 4, Luciana C. de Oliveira, Solange Aranha, and Fernando Zolin-Vesz take us to Brazil via an exploration of official documents that leads to proposing a framework to improve English and Spanish writing assessment using theories that position the assessment of writing as an essential element of literacy development. Chapter 5 moves us to Vietnam as Xuan Minh Ngo discusses the experiences of two English teachers to illustrate how national strategies, institutional policies, and logistic factors simultaneously shape and reshape their professional practice. In Chapter 6, Hadi Banat draws on his experience teaching at a local university and an American branch university in the United Arab Emirates to explore how English writing classrooms are impacted by local institutional policies. In Chapter 7, Fahimeh Marefat and Mojtaba Heydari discuss the disconnect between global exams such as the TOEFL and more local (albeit national) high-stakes tests in Iran, articulating considerations for the training of Iranian EFL teachers to address this gap.

Part II—*High-Stakes Assessment*—shifts to an examination of high-stakes writing assessment in a variety of contexts and ways in which these policies affect stakeholders. In Chapter 8, Muhammad M. Abdel Latif and Abdelbaset Haridy report on a study examining the impact of national curricular decisions on English writing assessment in high schools. In Chapter 9, Pornpimol Sukavatee and Bee Chamcharatsri describe the problems with English proficiency tests developed in-house at Thai universities. Chapter 10 by Aleksandra Swatek and Aleksandra Kasztalska examines the theoretical and ideological underpinnings of the written portion of the English Matura exam in Poland. In Chapter 11, Mira Bekar draws on her experience teaching in Macedonia to discuss the impact of that country's State Matura exam on English writing instruction. In Chapter 12, Benjamin Kremmel, Kathrin Eberharter, and Michael Maurer track how reform of a national exam in Austria instigated changes in classroom teaching and assessment practices of writing. The last chapter in this section—Chapter 14 by Gordon West and Bala Thiruchelvam—examines the effects of high-stakes testing policies in mandatory English language writing courses at a South Korean university and explores ways in which some instructors act as mediator between their students and educational authorities.

Part III—*Seeking Solutions: Assessing Better Locally and Internationally*—begins with Chapter 14 and Chenchen Huang and Xiaoye You's exploration of local teacher responses to national assessment mandates in China, resulting in teachers tailoring their curriculum to foster students' creativity and agency. In Chapter 15, Hee-Seung Kang delves into the complexities surrounding assessment of L2 writers in one writing across the curriculum (WAC) program and demonstrates how ethically and politically charged assessment is in the context of a WAC program in U.S. higher education. Chapter 16 by Natalie Nordby Chen and Renée Saulter draws on the experiences of the authors as test developers for Cambridge Michigan Language Assessments as they worked to develop accommodations on large-scale L2 writing assessments for students with disabilities. In Chapter 17, Betsy Gilliland, Katterine Pavez Bravo, and Andrea Muñoz Galleguillos discuss the development of a local portfolio evaluation system for English teachers in training to meet expectations set by national teacher certification requirements, arguing that local knowledge allows for the development of contextually relevant measures that support individual learners' agency while still fulfilling requirements for high-stakes assessment. In Chapter 18, Megan M. Siczek and Natalia Dolgova problematize institutions' reliance on generic and acontextual assessment practices as they document the evolution of a targeted usage-based diagnostic assessment procedure at a private postsecondary institution in the Eastern U.S. The collection closes with a chapter by Mark Chapman, Ahyoung Alicia Kim, Jing Wei, and Tanya Bitterman of the WIDA Consortium, which develops standards and assessments for English language learners in the U.S. Their vignette describes a focus on what students can do to optimize student opportunities to best demonstrate their written English language proficiency.

In building this collection, we believe that we have endeavored to raise awareness of the importance of writing assessment in global perspectives. Too often, assessment falls to the wayside; to bring it to the forefront—particularly in the global contexts considered in this book—entails effort, commitment, and not a little risk-taking. Within these chapters, authors have taken risks to uncover what is actually happening in terms of assessment in their context. It is our hope that these risks provide an intense examination of what is happening in international contexts in regard to the practices and challenges of writing assessment with an eye toward teacher training and policy reformation.

References

Al-Jarrah, R. S., & Al-Ahmad, S. (2013). Writing instruction in Jordan: Past, present, and future trends. *System, 41*, 84–94. http://dx.doi.org/10.1016/j.system.2013.01.016

Booher-Jennings, J. (2005). Below the bubble: "Educational triage" and the Texas accountability system. *American Educational Research Journal, 42*(2), 231–268. http://dx.doi.org/10.3102/00028312042002231

Bourdieu, P., & Passeron, J. C. (1977). *Reproduction in education, culture and society*. London: Sage.

Caplan, N., & de Oliveira, L. C. (2016, February 16). Why we still won't teach the 5-paragraph essay [Web log post]. Retrieved from http://blog.tesol.org/why-we-still-wont-teach-the-5-paragraph-essay/

Casanave, C. P. (2003). Looking ahead to more sociopolitically-oriented case study research in L2 writing scholarship: (But should it be called "post-process"?). *Journal of Second Language Writing, 12*(1), 85–102. http://dx.doi.org/10.1016/S1060-3743(03)00002-X

CCCC. (2016, February). Professional knowledge for the teaching of writing. Retrieved from www.ncte.org/positions/statements/teaching-writing

Clachar, A. (2000). Opposition and accommodation: An examination of Turkish teachers' attitudes toward Western approaches to the teaching of writing. *Research in the Teaching of English, 35*(1), 66–100.

Council of the Great City Schools. (2015). Student testing in America's great city schools: An inventory and preliminary analysis. Retrieved from www.cgcs.org/cms/lib/DC00001581/Centricity/Domain/87/Testing%20Report.pdf

Crusan, D. (2006). The politics of implementing online directed self-placement for second language writers. In P. K. Matsuda, C. Ortmeier-Hooper, & X. You (Eds.), *The politics of second language writing: In search of the promised land* (pp. 205–221). West Lafayette, IN: Parlor Press.

Foucault, M. (1977). *Discipline and punish: The birth of a prison*. London: Penguin.

Fox, J., & Cheng, L. (2016). Walk a mile in my shoes: Stakeholder accounts of testing experience with a computer-administered test. *TESL Canada Journal, 65*(32), 65–86.

Layton, L. (2015, March 10). Chiefs for Change education advocacy group is headed for more change. *The Washington Post*. Retrieved from www.washingtonpost.com/local/education/chiefs-for-change-education-advocacy-group-is-headed-for-more-change/2015/03/10/2e98a510-c73f-11e4-a199-6cb5e63819d2_story.html

Leki, I. (2001). Material, educational, and ideological challenges of teaching EFL writing at the turn of the century. *International Journal of English Studies, 1*(2), 197–209.

Matsuda, P. K., Ortmeier-Hooper, C., & You, X. (2006). *The politics of second language writing*. West Lafayette, IN: Parlor Press.

McNamara, T., & Roever, C. (2006). *Language testing: The social dimension*. Hoboken, NJ: Wiley-Blackwell.

Muchiri, M. N., Mulamba, N. G., Myers, G., & Ndoloi, D. B. (1995). Importing composition: Teaching and researching academic writing beyond North America. *College Composition and Communication, 46*(2), 175–198. http://dx.doi.org/10.2307/358427

Pennycook, A. (2013). *The cultural politics of English as an international language*. London: Routledge.

Prendergast, C. (2008). *Buying into English: Language and investment in the new capitalist world*. Pittsburgh, PA: University of Pittsburgh Press.

Reichelt, M. (2005). English-language writing instruction in Poland. *Journal of Second Language Writing, 14*(4), 215–232. http://dx.doi.org/10.1016/j.jslw.2005.10.005

Rivera, C. (2016, May 9). New Mexico PED agrees to end gag rule for testing. KRQE News 13. Retrieved from http://krqe.com/2016/05/09/new-mexico-ped-agrees-to-end-gag-rule-for-testing/

Ruecker, T. (2013). High-stakes testing and Latina/o students: Creating a hierarchy of college readiness. *Journal of Hispanic Higher Education, 12*(3), 303–320. http://dx.doi.org/10.1177/1538192713493011

Ruecker, T. (2015). *Transiciones: Pathways of Latinas and Latinos writing in high school and college*. Logan, UT: Utah State University Press.

Ruecker, T., Chamcharatsri, B., & Saengngoen, J. (2015). Teacher perceptions of the impact of the common core assessments on linguistically diverse high school students. *Journal of Writing Assessment, 8*(1). Retrieved from http://journalofwritingassessment.org/article.php?article=87

Ruecker, T., Shapiro, S., Johnson, E., & Tardy, C. (2014). Exploring the contexts of writing instruction in TESOL. *TESOL Quarterly, 48*(2), 401–412.

Shohamy, E. (2001). *The power of tests: A critical perspective on the uses of language tests*. Harlow, UK: Pearson Education Limited.

Turner, C., Khrais, R., Lloyd, T., Olgin, A., Isensee, L., Vevea, B., & Carsen, D. (2016, April 18). Why America's schools have a money problem. *National Public Radio*. Retrieved from www.npr.org/2016/04/18/474256366/why-americas-schools-have-a-money-problem

You, X. (2004). New directions in EFL writing: A report from China. *Journal of Second Language Writing, 13*(4), 253–256.

You, X. (2010). *Writing in the devil's tongue: A history of English composition in China*. Carbondale, IL: Southern Illinois University Press.

PART I

Local and National Policy Contexts

2

WORLDS APART, BUT IN THE SAME BOAT

How Macro-Level Policy Influences EFL Writing Pedagogy in China, Mexico, and Poland

Estela Ene and Katarzyna Hryniuk

Introduction

English as a foreign language (EFL) classrooms, as arenas in which the global and the local co-exist, reflect the complex status of English in the world. They empower by propagating English as the main means of global communication (or *lingua franca*) and access to global resources and opportunities. However, they contribute to the creation of a homogenized, "single global market which is supplanting the nation-state as the primary economic and political unit" (Fairclough, 2006, p. 15).

Despite the pull towards global homogeneity, distinctions among EFL contexts persist, due in part to the fact that global and national policies are conceptualized and enacted differently. Some have contended that "the principal locus of policy making remains the nation-state" (Haskell, 2002, p. 5), and that language policies, as a subcategory of national policy, reflect different national sociopolitical and economic goals. Most states promote English as the most important foreign language. However, they may also promote other foreign and local languages (Lo Bianco, 2002). For example, former Soviet republics or Québec, the Basque region, Catalonia, and other areas interested in preserving minority rights may prioritize local or minority languages over English. In multilingual states like Switzerland, the official languages of the country may be expected to be developed first (Haskell, 2002; Lo Bianco, 2002). Such circumstances lead to variation, across and even within nation-states, in when students begin and end studying English, for what purposes, and how achievement is assessed.

Assessment is particularly influential in English Language Teaching (ELT) because standardized examinations are often mandated through national policy. Large-scale, centrally administered achievement tests allow for comparability of students' performance in schools across a country or internationally. A positive washback effect is that certain writing—genres, for example, and their formal features—gets taught when it is required in high-stakes examinations (Crusan, 2010). A negative effect is that only the forms and task types tested are practiced. Such tests assess only subskills, as writing under time pressure does not reflect writing ability realistically, reliably, or fairly. Also, standardization hinders creativity, "ignoring the richness of culturally diverse backgrounds and neglecting the unique problems of students" (Crusan, 2010, p. 256). Yet, such tests determine students' further education and the focus of the EFL class.

The need to account for variability in teaching EFL/ESL writing across institutional and sociopolitical contexts has been emphasized by many (Crusan, 2010; Crusan, Plakans, & Gebril, 2016; Cumming, 2001; Ruecker, Shapiro, John- son, & Tardy, 2014; Spalding, Wang, & Lin, 2010). The value of research on variability across EFL contexts lies in that it promotes the critical evaluation of the mainstream, English-centered ideas that underpin the teaching and assessing of EFL writing (Donahue, 2009; Min, 2011). Additionally, such research fills in a long-standing gap in the scholarship on EFL writing that, if left unfilled, may "perpetuate stereotypes about practice and could limit valuable cross-context dialogue" (Ruecker et al., 2014, p. 402; also Cumming, 2003; Ene & Mitrea, 2013; Ortega, 2009; Silva, Leki, & Carson, 1997).

Philosophically, the concept that English is plurilithic (Pennycook, 2007) and its teaching should be, too (Hall, 2013), has emphasized the need to pay attention to local factors, because EFL contexts are different enough from one another to warrant dramatically different approaches to EFL teacher preparation and classroom teaching. Until now, researchers have investigated many EFL writing contexts one by one (see edited volumes by Cimasko & Reichelt, 2011; Manchón, 2009). Recently, large multinational surveys have been used to achieve a more inclusive representation of ESL and EFL writing contexts. Ruecker et al. (2014) explored the linguistic and institutional contexts of writing instruction in TESOL through a survey completed by 290 ESL and 111 EFL participants from Japan, Canada, China, Mexico, South Korea, and Thailand. Crusan et al. (2016) investigated the writing assessment literacy of 702 second language instructors from tertiary institutions in 41 countries. Still, there is a scarcity of research that directly com- pares different EFL contexts based on a common research question and method- ology in order to understand how EFL writing practices differ (or not) across the world, due to a variety of factors, including assessment policies.

Purpose of the Study

The purpose of this chapter is to explore the tenets of both homogeneity and variability in EFL contexts, particularly as related to macro-policy and its influ- ence on EFL writing pedagogy and assessment. Our goal is to address the current need in L2 writing for a clearer understanding of EFL contexts, representations of approaches to L2 writing, and implications for teacher development. The chapter offers insights from comparative research conducted in China, Mexico, and Poland, and focuses on the question:

> What is the impact of assessment, national, and global policy on EFL writing teachers' beliefs and practices?

In the sections below, we describe each context with respect to the status of English and assessment policies. Then, we present the results of our survey, interviews, and focus groups, and we discuss the results focusing on similarities and differences in teaching and assessing EFL writing in relation to national and global policy.

ELT in China

China has the largest English-learning population in the world. English is the most important foreign language for finance, business, travel, and academic success. In the 1990s, English began being taught in schools in third grade "wherever conditions permit[ted]" (Qixin, 2002, p. 228). The study continues through high school, and then for at least two years in college for English non-majors. Qixin (2002) has noted:

> there is no single document [mandating English competence] from the Ministry of Education. . . . Still, the Chinese government's strategy for foreign language education permeates the national curricula . . . at all levels. Approved and issued by the Ministry of Education, it is reflected in . . . required levels of proficiency in English, length of study and required courses.
>
> *(p. 228)*

English, alongside Chinese and mathematics, is tested when entering high school and college. In 1989, a writing task was added to the national college admission exam. At the tertiary level, there are three semesters of mandatory EFL, after which students take the College English Test (CET) Band 4. For this, students should be able to communicate easily in English, especially orally, and write short essays with personal opinion in at least 160 words, summarize literature, and write abstracts. The belief that admission into university guarantees upward mobility and personal honor has created a culture of testing, building up from the lower grades to the beginning of college (Cheng, 2008).

ELT in Mexico

In Mexico, "the mission of the National English Programme in Basic Education is framed by the needs of 'contemporary society . . . that demands citizens with the necessary competencies to face and incorporate into a globalised constantly changing world'" (British Council, 2015, p. 7). National standards of proficiency have been designed with attention to the European Union's *Common European Framework of Reference* (*CEFR*, Council of Europe, 2001). Basic education is divided into primary school (grades 1–6), junior high school (grades 7–9), and high school (grades 10–12). The Secretariat of Public Education (SPE) sets standards for English education, but the federal educational system is decentralized. Officially, since 2012, English instruction begins in pre-K (in year 3 of 3) and continues until twelfth grade; however, in practice many schools do not implement the programs due to funding shortages (Jimenez, 2008). Admission to the university does not take foreign language proficiency into account. There is great variation across the 31 Mexican states, caused by the fact that there is no real national policy for English, and the expansion of English education has been slow and uneven (Ramírez-Romero & Sayer, 2016).

ELT in Poland

Foreign language teaching in Poland is regulated by the Ministry for National Education, and it adheres to the *CEFR* (Council of Europe, 2001). Since Poland's admission to the European Union in 2004, the largest of many changes was the 2008 educational reform, which introduced a compulsory foreign language from the first grade. Most students (95%) choose to study English (Salski, 2016).

The Central Examination Commission oversees the design and administration of national, standardized English tests. At the end of primary school, a test checks learners' foreign language knowledge. Lower secondary school (grades 7–9) ends with a written exam for which the students can choose the A1 or A2 level of the *CEFR*. This assesses listening and reading comprehension, grammar and lexis, and language functions. In the A2 exam, learners write texts of 50–100 words (a letter, a news item, an email). High school (grades 10–12) also ends with a foreign language exam (part of the Matura exam). On the high school exit examination, all levels must complete a writing task. The high school exit exam substituted for university entrance exams in 2005. Its high-stakes nature motivates students to prepare for it meticulously. Learners can choose among written tests B1 (less advanced), B2 (advanced), or C1 level (for bilingual schools). At the lower level, learners write texts of 80–130 words (a letter, an email, blog news, etc.); at the more advanced level, texts of 200–250 words (a formal letter, an argumentative essay, an article, etc.). For bilingual schools, the examinees must write 300–350 words. At universities, students are required to pass an exam in a foreign language, which is usually English, at the B2 level, in order to graduate.

In sum, China, Mexico, and Poland share a similar view of the importance of English language skills in the globalized world. All have expectations of early and long exposure to the language, but in Mexico national policy and testing are less strict. ELT begins in kindergarten in Mexico, first grade in Poland, and third grade in China. Chinese and Polish high schoolers take an exit exam in English, while Mexican students do not. Chinese students take a national college admission test in English, while Mexican and Polish students do not. Finally, college English is mandated in China and Poland (where a foreign language is required and English is usually chosen), but not in Mexico.

Study Design

Instruments and Procedures

To determine the similarities and differences among different EFL contexts, as well as the influence of macro-level policy on EFL writing, we investigated comparatively the beliefs and practices of EFL writing teachers in China, Mexico, and Poland. Using instruments implemented in a similar study in Romania (Ene & Mitrea, 2013), the researchers conducted teacher surveys with 71 in-service teachers—15 from China, 14 from Mexico, and 42 from Poland. The survey consisted of close- and open-ended questions, including Likert-type scale items. The survey for the Polish group was administered a year after collecting data in China and Mexico. In China and Mexico, focus groups and follow-up interviews with willing participants were audio-recorded and transcribed before being analyzed. All of the participants were in the focus groups and seven from each group were interviewed. Interviews and focus groups were not conducted in Poland; instead, questions about national policy and globalization—topics that emerged in interviews and focus groups in China and Mexico, as well as the Romanian study—were added to the survey. For the Polish data, we also benefited from one of the researchers' emic perspective.

Analysis

The open-ended answers from the survey and the focus group and interview transcripts were analyzed qualitatively. The researchers read the responses and grouped them into themes, which were rank-ordered based on their frequency. For the Likert-type scale items, we counted the responses. For both the open-ended answers and the Likert-type items, we will report the number and percentage of respondents out of the total number of participants in each context who elected a certain theme or option.

Participants

The participants were in-service K–12 teachers of English enrolled in English departments at universities in China and Mexico, where one of the authors was on research and teaching visits, and in Poland, where the other researcher works. All were MA students except for eight (11%) Polish participants who were BA students. Ninety-three percent (or 14 and 13, respectively) of the participants in China and Mexico, and 86% (36) in Poland, were female. On average, the Chinese teachers had 12 years of English teaching experience, the Mexican teachers 9 years, and the Polish teachers 6.

Results

Classroom Practices

General Approach to Teaching EFL Writing

What is taught in English classes and how it is taught speaks to the status of English and EFL writing in the overall system. In terms of *what*, 46% (7) of the Chinese teachers reported teaching academic, persuasive essay writing, and professional letters and reports, respectively. Half of the teachers from Mexico also placed the academic essay at the top of frequently taught types of writing, and 28% (4) marked professional and business writing. In Poland, informal letter and email writing emerged as the genres most frequently taught (by 38% (16) of the participants), while academic writing—persuasive essays, research papers, summaries, and literary analyses—was marked by only 5% (2) of the teachers. The Polish teachers reported using no professional writing assignments, and no creative writing (narratives, poems, anecdotes, etc.), which the Mexican and Chinese teachers reported engaging with occasionally, to lighten up the load of academic assignments and allow the students to explore their creative side. An explanation for this is the fact that, although Poland has national assessments for English, the exams at the lower levels of education require informal personal writing, and only in the higher secondary and tertiary levels do academic essays become important. Thus, we note a clear alignment between the text types taught and the national curriculum/language policy of each country, as noted by Crusan (2010). In Mexico, where national exams are not mandated but English and academic writing have become more valued, the same alignment existed.

Teachers from all three groups engaged in effective instructional practices such as providing feedback, utilizing multiple drafts, and peer reviews. Sixty-four percent (9) of the Mexican teachers, 90% (38) of the Polish teachers, and 93% (14) of the Chinese teachers reported providing feedback on writing. Fifty-seven percent (8) of the Mexican teachers, 46% (7) of the Chinese teachers, and 40% (17) of the Polish teachers used peer reviews. Only 20% (3) of the Chinese teachers and 29% (12) of the Polish teachers required multiple drafts, compared to 57% (8) of the Mexican teachers. The use of multiple drafts was the least frequent practice, especially for the Polish and Chinese teachers. Overall, the Mexican teachers' approach came across as more methodologically balanced and diversified, while the Chinese and the Polish groups seemed more product-oriented and teacher-centered. In the focus group, the Chinese teachers were unanimous about what one of them expressed in her interview: "Correcting and telling the students what is right or wrong is a teacher's duty. . . . Our students do not trust other students to find their mistakes and show them the right way." Similar feelings were expressed in the Mexican focus group, one teacher eloquently noting: "We must write feedback on essays. The students depend on us."

In addition to the cultural belief that being a writing teacher equals providing feedback and that peers have limited ability to support others, all three groups named class size and workload as limiting factors. In all three contexts, a full-time teacher's load could amount to 40 hours of classroom teaching per week. The Chinese teachers, who could have multiple classes with as many as 40 students in each, stressed that it is "absolutely impossible" to implement process-oriented techniques with large groups, especially when buy-in from the students is low. The Mexican teachers felt similarly, but an interviewee (who had studied in the U.S.) pointed out: "It is important to try new techniques. Everything takes a lot of time, but we want the students to learn on their own, and I see sometimes that peer reviews and self-assessment can reduce the time I spend correcting." Large classes, workload, low pay, and limited professional development are known systemic problems that negatively impact teaching in China (Lee, 2010), Mexico (Ramírez-Romero & Sayer, 2016), and Poland (Reichelt, 2005).

Assessment

The assessment practices used by our participants reflected the prioritization of formal accuracy. When asked *What do you most focus on when evaluating student writing?*—Polish teachers answered grammar (50% or 21), vocabulary (36% or 15), and content (31% or 13). The Chinese teachers assigned more weight to correct grammar (70% or 10) and vocabulary (65% or 10). In the focus group, the Chinese teachers explained that they valued content and text organization, but that these could not be achieved without solid grammar and vocabulary. The Chinese teachers felt that their students did not lack ideas for their essays, but rather the grammatical and lexical issues stemming from the linguistic distance between Chinese and English made it difficult to express those ideas. The teachers from Mexico indicated concerns for grammar (49% or 6) and vocabulary (37% or 5) less than the Chinese group, and their interest in content and organization (67% or 9) was higher. The importance of grammar and lexis was similar in Mexico and Poland, despite their different national assessment policies, indicating the strong influence of linguistic factors on EFL teaching and assessment. Other aspects of writing, including style, register, and punctuation, were marked as important to assess by less than 20% of the teachers in all three contexts, so they will not be discussed.

We also asked the teachers what most influences the way they teach and assess EFL writing. In Poland, 31% (13) of the participants identified the national curriculum and, separately, the textbooks available, which in fact overlap, as textbook choices are pre-approved nationally. A teacher explained: "Teachers tend to focus on grammar, reading and listening skills rather than writing. There is no time to teach English-language writing during the class, as you have to follow the national curriculum." Indeed, other literature on ELT in Poland has acknowledged that oral skills receive the most attention throughout school (Salski, 2012), primarily due to the national curriculum. The next most frequent factor— for 29% (12) of the teachers—was students' needs and interests. Nineteen percent (8) of the respondents identified the Matura exam evaluation criteria as a determining factor. The Chinese and Mexican focus groups also claimed that student needs shaped their practices (76% (11) and 59% (8)). The Chinese group explained that their "students have to be ready for the [national] college English test," which they framed as a learner need. It is notable that this "need" is predefined by national policy and curriculum (as found in Romania by Ene and Mitrea (2013)), not personal goals, yet the two overlapped in the teachers' view. In contrast, for the Mexican teachers, the notion of student need was a more diffuse sense that the students should have, generally speaking, good English (writing) skills in today's world. This view reflects the influence of the global view that English is important. Finally, the teachers' familiarity with topics and genres mattered only for 24% (10) of the respondents in Poland, 19% (3) in China, and 22% (3) in Mexico. Cumulatively, our findings show that policy and curriculum are more powerful influences than individual factors such as teacher preparedness or student-voiced preferences.

Perceptions of the Value of EFL Writing

When asked to rank order the importance of the four skills, all of the participants placed speaking first, followed by listening, reading, and, lastly, writing. Large surveys of learners (British Council, 2015; European Commission, 2006) have indeed shown that they value more the ability to speak English, for both personal and professional purposes, while writing academically in English is only important for the professional and academic elites (Haskell, 2002). In Mexico, an interviewee shared that "students don't really care about English, and especially about writing, until they are older and start thinking about going to study in the U.S. or getting a good job." A Chinese teacher stated: "We don't really emphasize writing a lot. Our students don't really need it. Speaking is more important for communication. The curriculum starts to introduce writing to prepare for the [national] exam, and it's important to follow that." In Poland, as pointed out in the section above, the national curriculum and target exams set the pace of the classroom and shape most perceptions about the value of EFL writing skills. The influence of the national requirements is evident once more. Naturally, the perceived low value of EFL writing and the over-valuing of the types of writing included in national exams is bound to affect teaching practices—including the methods, content, and assessment, as shown above.

Perceptions of National Policy and Globalization

In China and Mexico, the interviewees spoke about the challenges of keeping up with the frequent education reforms, and a general sense of instability and disempowerment. One of the Chinese teachers observed: "Our country is trying to change, to advance, all the time. We have new rules, new textbooks, reform all the time. One must keep up." A Mexican teacher characterized educational reforms as frequently changing as "the flavor of the day. It can make you dizzy, but we do what we do—teach." Some noted that the importance of mastering English seemed overblown in the official discourse ("Not *everybody* wants to or needs to know English in reality," a Mexican teacher stated), and that it was important to equip the students with the skills needed in the global economy without "turning" them into native English speakers. A Polish teacher commented: "There is no point in speaking and writing fluently, but just so-so, just a communicative language." In the Chinese and Mexican groups, the participants wished for more stability in the educational system, smaller classes, and more professional development focused on EFL writing. They acknowledged that access to materials in English is easier than ever. Primed by their comments, we added related questions to the Poland survey. When asked what they wished their institution would offer them, the most frequent answer (from 38% (16) participants) indicated professional development in L2 writing and pedagogy. When asked what they wished their Ministry of Education would offer them, they made the same request, and a few respondents also marked better pay and smaller classes. We also asked how globalization affected the teaching of EFL writing. Except for one person, the Polish teachers had a positive perception of how it affected their work. They pointed out that the level of English is increasing as a consequence of access to more authentic, relevant materials; ease of communication outside one's local context, including through technology and the Internet; increased cross-cultural awareness; and improved teaching due to easier access to materials. The same desires and attitude towards the effects of globalization were documented in a similarly designed study in Romania (Ene & Mitrea, 2013), further attesting to the commonalities among EFL contexts.

Discussion and Conclusions

The goal of the study was to explore the similarities and differences in the beliefs and practices of EFL writing teachers in three different EFL contexts, to understand the extent to which they are unitary or diverse and how policy impacts ELT practice, especially in EFL writing. The three contexts explored were distinct geographically, linguistically, and culturally, as well as by orientation towards English language assessment policy. China and Poland implement national standardized assessments in English at crucial transition points in students' education, while Mexico does not. In all three settings, we found important similarities, including related to the influence of global linguistic priorities and national curricula for ELT. All three countries officially acknowledge the importance of English, first for spoken communication, and to a lesser degree for academic and professional writing. The English language curriculum balanced attention to these skills in the order in which they were prioritized above the classroom level. The teachers' view of the reduced importance of EFL writing correlated with this hierarchy. Where a national-level English exam is not (yet) required—meaning, in Mexico—academic and professional writing were prioritized by the K–12 teachers included in the study, in line with the national and global rhetoric that advocates the need for multilingual professionals in the global economy. Thus, in broad terms, we see EFL classrooms and the teaching of EFL writing as reflecting the global zeitgeist in general and national policy in particular. In this respect, the EFL world appears as unitary, despite contextual differences, in its response to the English-dominated, single global market (Fairclough, 2006).

In all three contexts, the long, firm reach of national policy was felt in specific terms. The evidence presented in this study supports the argument that "the principal locus of policy making remains the nation-state" (Haskell, 2002, p. 5; Lo Bianco, 2002). In Poland, where the national tests do not emphasize academic writing in the earlier years, the teachers reported not focusing on essays in their classes. In China, too, the types of writing tasks to be mastered for college admission were included in classroom practice. "Teaching to the test" and even to the eventuality of a test (in Mexico's case) occurred in all three contexts. The existence and effects of cultures of testing on classroom teaching have been noted before (Crusan, 2010; Cumming, 2001; You, 2010). Crusan (2010) in particular noted that while such cultures ensure that certain genres are taught, they also enhance the disconnect from learners' true needs, as these are shaped and defined from above, by the national curriculum. In her view, standardized tests should not be used exclusively. More locally developed assessment of writing and more teacher training in this area is needed. Our study seconds Crusan (2010), but it should also be noted that

> in some cases, it is very hard to identify any specific current or future needs a student might have for writing in English, beyond perhaps passing required exams. This might be especially true for secondary students [in Poland], whose future is unclear.
>
> *(Reichelt, 2013, p. 33)*

Especially in the lower levels of K–12, learners often feel no real need for EFL writing skills. Consequently, it is understandable that teachers rely primarily on national guidelines, as they provide—for what it's worth—a structure.

The specter of future tests influenced the teaching of EFL writing at classroom level. In China and Poland, the teachers' pedagogical choices were connected to what the students needed to be prepared for in national exams. This factor interacted with other linguistic and cultural factors in each country. To a significant degree, the teachers felt obligated to develop their learners' grammatical and lexical accuracy as a way to provide the means to express ideas. The linguistic distance between the L1s of the students and English in the contexts we explored correlated with the sense the teachers felt to focus on the formal aspects of EFL writing. In addition, commonly shared beliefs about teacher roles, where teachers are viewed as the source of all answers and are expected to perform the duty of providing corrections, enforced the tendency to focus on grammar and vocabulary when evaluating writing. Such interactions between the culture of testing and linguistic and cultural context are known to lead to more form-focused, teacher-centered practices in EFL (Ene & Mitrea, 2013; Lee, 2010; You, 2010). Ultimately, this is also indicative of another significant feature of EFL contexts, especially at K–12 levels, where learners learn how to write in English in order to learn the English language first, and only then in order to learn how to write (Manchón, 2009).

At a large, systemic level, the teaching of EFL writing in the three contexts explored here was also affected by the conditions for language teacher education and development as well as labor conditions. These limited the variety of pedagogical approaches the teachers used. In Mexico, teachers frequently rally in order to draw the governments' attention to the instability of their jobs, inhumane workloads with low pay, and scarcity of training and resources (Ramírez-Romero & Sayer, 2016). Arguably, and in concordance with the reported wishes of the teachers, Ministries of Education and other supervising bodies in each respective country should design curricula and policies that make it possible for teachers and students to perform at the desired levels. It is important to understand that, without decent working conditions, teachers' ability to give even more of their time or engage in continued professional development will remain limited (also see Lee (2010) and You (2010)).

An additional similarity between the contexts investigated here is that the relative value of EFL writing skills is low compared to other skills, in a similar way that it is relatively less important compared to ESL and university-level studies (Ruecker et al., 2014). Research from Romania (Ene & Mitrea, 2013) and Poland (Majchrzak & Salski, 2016; Reichelt, 2005; Salski, 2016) previously pointed out that an additional reason for deprioritizing the development of writing skills in EFL is that in these countries there is no strong tradition of teaching writing in the native tongue, except at the primary school level. Despite the fact that Poland has undergone many educational reforms over the last decades, the 2005 format of the Matura examinations caused a significant drop in writing practice even in Polish (Majchrzak & Salski, 2016), and there is a known negative attitude of learners and teachers towards the activity of writing itself (Salski, 2012).

With regard to globalization, it is notable that positive feelings about it were prevalent, and focusing on the opportunities afforded by this process to both teachers and learners of English. The teachers credited globalization for making it easier to find authentic language samples, native speakers to practice with, and many online materials in the target language. One may argue, like Pennycook (2007), that a more critical attitude towards globalization is desirable. It is possible that the participating teachers found it difficult to express criticism. However, it appears that, while in the "trenches," teachers prioritize teaching over fighting problems that are out of their immediate reach, such as linguistic imperialism (Ene & Mitrea, 2013). Further research is needed to explore this issue, as our study was limited in size and cannot claim to represent all EFL contexts.

Our study reinforces the realization that there exists a certain unity in the EFL world that co-exists with a high degree of diversity induced by localized policies, needs, and linguistic, cultural, and institutional factors. The most important ramification is for teacher training and development. The fields of Teachers of English to Speakers of Other Languages (TESOL) and second language writing would benefit from the development of not only research but also theoretical frameworks from EFL contexts. For a while now, we have been looking at ELT and EFL writing using ESL as a point of reference. It is realistic to expect that, from the existing populations of applied linguists from EFL contexts, a certain number should specialize in EFL writing in order to represent the field in the international arena, formulate theories, and provide the much-needed training for teachers in those contexts. Dissatisfaction with the importation of U.S.- and UK-based approaches and materials and the preferential consultation of experts from those countries has been expressed quite vocally in Mexico (Ramírez-Romero & Sayer, 2016). For Poland, too, researchers have noted the need for local expertise to develop (Reichelt, 2013; Salski, 2012). Ultimately, L2 writing research can only benefit from contributions from EFL contexts that more clearly define the theoretical propensities of different contexts. In the meantime, it appears necessary to provide training, in TESOL programs, focused on the specific needs and expectations teachers should be prepared for in EFL contexts.

References

British Council. (2015). *English in Mexico: An examination of policy, perceptions, and influencing factors.* Retrieved from https://ei.britishcouncil.org/sites/default/files/latin-america-research/English%20in%20Mexico.pdf

Cheng, L. (2008). The key to success: English language testing in China. *Language Testing, 25*(1), 15–37. https://doi.org/10.1177/0265532207083743

Cimasko, T., & Reichelt, M. (Eds.). (2011). *Foreign language writing instruction: Principles and practices.* Anderson, SC: Parlor Press.

Council of Europe. (2001). *Common European framework of reference for languages.* Retrieved July 15, 2015 from www.coe.int/t/dg4/linguistic/Source/Framework_EN.pdf

Crusan, D. (2010). Assess thyself lest others assess thee. In T. Silva & P. K. Matsuda (Eds.), *Practicing theory in second language writing* (pp. 245–262). West Lafayette, IN: Parlor Press.

Crusan, D., Plakans, L., & Gebril, A. (2016). Writing assessment literacy: Surveying second language teachers' knowledge, beliefs, and practices. *Assessing Writing, 28,* 43–56. https://doi.org/10.1016/j.asw.2016.03.001

Cumming, A. (2001). The difficulty of standards, for example in L2 writing. In T. Silva & P. K. Matsuda (Eds.), *On second language writing* (pp. 209–229). Mahwah, NJ: Lawrence Erlbaum Associates.

Cumming, A. (2003). Experienced ESL/EFL writing instructors' conceptualizations of their teaching: Curriculum options and implications. In B. Kroll (Ed.), *Exploring the dynamics of second language writing* (pp. 71–92). New York: Cambridge University Press. https://doi.org/10.1017/CBO9781139524810

Donahue, C. (2009). "Internationalization" and composition studies: Reorienting the discourse. *College Composition and Communication, 61*(2), 212–243.

Ene, E., & Mitrea, A. (2013). EFL writing teacher training, beliefs, and practices in Romania: A tale of adaptation. *The European Journal of Applied Linguistics and TEFL, 2*(2), 117–138.

European Commission. (2006). *Special Eurobarometer 243: Europeans and their languages.* Retrieved May 17, 2010 from http://ec.europa.eu/education/languages/pdf/doc631_en.pdf

Fairclough, N. (2006). *Language and globalization.* New York: Routledge.

Hall, C. J. (2013). Cognitive contributions to plurilithic views of English and other languages. *Applied Linguistics, 34*(2), 211–231. https://doi.org/10.1093/applin/ams042

Haskell, C. C. (2002). Language and globalization: Why national policies matter. In S. J. Baker (Ed.), *Language policy: Lessons from global models* (pp. 2–7). Monterey, CA: Monterey Institute of International Studies.

Jimenez, E. (2008, April). *Six Latin American countries: Creativity and innovation. The teaching of English in Mexico.* Paper presented at the 42nd Annual TESOL Convention and Exhibit, New York.

Lee, I. (2010). Writing teacher education and teacher learning: Testimonies of four EFL teachers. *Journal of Second Language Writing, 19,* 143–157. https://doi.org/10.1016/j.jslw.2010.05.001

Lo Bianco, J. (2002). Real world language politics and policy. In S. J. Baker (Ed.), *Language policy: Lessons from global models* (pp. 8–28). Monterey, CA: Monterey Institute of International Studies.

Majchrzak, O., & Salski, Ł (2016). Poland. In O. Kruse, M. Chitez, B. Rodriguez, & M. Castelló (Eds.), *Exploring European writing cultures: Country reports on genres, writing practices and languages used in European higher education* (pp. 151–164). Winterthur, SZ: ZHAW Zurich University of Applied Sciences (Working Papers in Applied Linguistics 10). https://doi.org/10.21256/zhaw-1056

Manchón, R. (Ed.). (2009). *Writing in foreign language contexts: Learning, teaching, and research.* Buffalo, NY: Multilingual Matters.

Min, H.-T. (2011). Foreign language writing instruction: A principled eclectic approach in Taiwan. In T. Cimasko & M. Reichelt (Eds.), *Foreign language writing instruction: Principles and practices* (pp. 159–182). Anderson, SC: Parlor Press. https://doi.org/10.1558/wap.v5i1.151

Ortega, L. (2009). Studying writing across EFL contexts: Looking back and moving forward. In R. Manchón (Ed.), *Writing in foreign language contexts: Learning, teaching, and research* (pp. 232–255). Buffalo, NY: Multilingual Matters.

Pennycook, A. (2007). The myth of English as an international language. In S. Makoni & A. Pennycook (Eds.), *Disinventing and reconstituting languages* (pp. 90–115). Clevedon, UK: Multilingual Matters.

Qixin, H. (2002). English language education in China. In S. J. Baker (Ed.), *Language policy: Lessons from global models* (pp. 225–231). Monterey, CA: Monterey Institute of International Studies.

Ramírez-Romero, J. L., & Sayer, P. (2016). The teaching of English in public primary schools in Mexico: More heat than light? *Education Policy Analysis Archives, 24*(84). http://dx.doi.org/10.14507/epaa.24.2502

Reichelt, M. (2005). English-language instruction in Poland. *Journal of Second Language Writing, 14*, 215–232. https://doi.org/10.1016/j.jslw.2005.10.005

Reichelt, M. (2013). English-language writing instruction in Poland: Adapting to the local EFL context. In O. Majchrzak (Ed.), *PLEJ_2 czyli Psycholingwistyczne Eksploracje Językowe* (pp. 25–42). Łódz, PL: Łódz University Press.

Ruecker, T., Shapiro, S., Johnson, E. N., & Tardy, C. M. (2014). Exploring the linguistic and institutional contexts of writing instruction in TESOL. *TESOL Quarterly, 48*(2), 401–412. https://doi.org/10.1002/tesq.165

Salski, Ł (2012). *Contrastive rhetoric and teaching English composition skills.* Łódz PL: Łódz University Press.

Salski, Ł (2016). EFL writing in Poland, where traditional does not mean current, but current means traditional. In T. Silva, J. Wang, J. Paiz, & C. Zhang (Eds.), *Second language writing in the global context: Represented, underrepresented, and unrepresented voices* (pp. 207–226). Beijing, CH: Foreign Language Teaching and Research Press.

Silva, T., Leki, I., & Carson, J. (1997). Broadening the perspective of mainstream composition studies. *Written Communication, 14*(3), 398–428. http://dx.doi.org/10.1177/0741088397014003004

Spalding, E., Wang, J., & Lin, E. (2010). The impact of a writing workshop approach on Chinese English teachers' beliefs about effective writing instruction. *Asian Journal of English Writing Teaching, 20*, 135–160.

You, X. (2010). *Writing in the devil's tongue: A history of English composition in China.* Carbondale, IL: Southern Illinois University Press.

3

VIGNETTE

The Importance of Context in Second Language Writing Evaluation

Theresa A. Orlovsky

"But what is your teaching context?" That's what I was asked repeatedly during my teaching methods class the first semester of my master's program. At the time, this seemed like just a required part of our assignments. As if we were filling out a form, we had to list who our hypothetical students were, where we were teaching them, and the reasons why they were learning English. These factors would then influence how we shaped hypothetical activities and classroom demonstrations. Four years and three different "contexts" later, I've realized how fundamental that initial question is. Moreover, I've realized how much more complex the answer can be.

Balancing Act

My second semester as a teaching assistant (TA) during my master's, I was assigned to a "cross-cultural" section of one the university's required undergraduate composition classes. The semester prior, my first time as the teacher-of-record, had already taught me a lot about being at the front of the classroom. Coming fresh off four years studying for a bachelor's degree in English with an emphasis in Writing, I had been eager to teach what I love. My students, nearly all native English-speaking (NES), first-year students majoring in STEM at a major four-year university in the midwestern United States, were less enthused. In order for either of us to have any success, I had to put myself mentally in their places. Even for NES students, I had to consider deeply who my students were, what their goals were for the class, and how best they would learn to become better writers.

Things became more complicated the following semester. "Cross-cultural" meant that 50% of the class was reserved for international students and the rest was left open to domestic students. I was thrilled. The chance to gain real experience teaching non-native English speakers (NNES) was a dream come true. But, although most in the class were still future engineers and scientists, the NES and NNES students had strongly different needs, backgrounds, and goals.

This was clear when it came to evaluating their essays. For instance, the NES often struggled with higher-order demands like having a clear focus and completely answering the prompt. The NNES, on the other hand, often did better with the big-picture ideas but struggled with organization and grammar. However, I had to use the same rubric, designed mainly for NES, to evaluate all of the students. Fortunately, the class curriculum, including the assignments and their rubrics, was part of the larger composition series that focused on rhetoric rather than form. Therefore, none of the five categories on the rubric counted more than another; all of the students, no matter who they were, had the chance to succeed.

Still another huge issue in assessing my students' writing was how to evaluate citations and penalize plagiarism. Over the three years I taught in our composition program, first as a TA and later as a lecturer, I tried different strategies for teaching citations, such as group discussions about the purpose of citations and in-class activities practicing how to cite various sources. I would warn students about the consequences of the plagiarism that could result from incorrect citations. My classes throughout the years, though not always officially "cross-cultural," still contained a nearly even number of international and domestic students. Every semester, the NES struggled with citations, but for most NNES, citing sources was a completely new cultural concept. Often, NNES students would turn in work missing in-text citations, Works Cited pages, or both. I had to consider, having warned students, was it fair then to mark them down or, in some cases, fail them for plagiarism?

Luckily, for at least one of the assignments, we had a student-teacher conference after students had written their first drafts. Rather than penalizing students immediately for leaving off citations or, sometimes even, copying word-for-word from sources, I used these opportunities to review citation guidelines with students. Many times, simply asking, "Are these your words or are they from a source?" would allow me to review and to emphasize the standards we learned in class in a more effective, personal setting. Having both the students and their papers directly in front of me allowed me to highlight errors on Works Cited pages or to remind students to respect their sources by including quotation marks around direct quotes. I would breathe a sigh of relief with the students that we had "caught these errors now," rather than in the final draft when they would have "a severe impact on their grade."

Community Learning

After completing my master's and while teaching as a lecturer, I also started teaching community ESL at a branch of the local community college. The four-skills practical English class was intended to help immigrant students integrate into their new lives, and the textbook encouraged them to pursue career-readiness tracks like becoming an HVAC repairman or a dental technician. However, since our location was in the same town as the university, my class was filled with a mix of visiting scholars and their spouses, Asian and Hispanic immigrants, and some refugees from Africa and the Middle East, most of whom had high levels of education in their home countries. This often allowed us to expand beyond the examples provided in the text, but the class still mainly focused on the immediate communicative needs of the workplace and community life.

Consequently, writing took on a much different approach than in my previous teaching context and was often limited to short in-class exercises in our textbooks. For instance, the last activity of the unit would ask students write about their personal experience with the theme, often incorporating the target grammar from the chapter as well. Giving the students a few minutes to respond, I wasn't sure what else to do but slowly walk around the room as they wrote. As students finished, I would stop at their desks and read through their responses. Initially, I wasn't sure what to correct or how to give feedback. In the university classes I was concurrently teaching, I was able to thoughtfully evaluate each student's writing with a set standard of evaluation. But in a non-credit ESL class, I was given little material beyond the text and very few guidelines for assessing the three-to-five sentence responses the students wrote.

Context gave the answer. Considering the setting and purpose of the class prompted me to employ a sort of "triage" method I had learned in my graduate studies. In a multi-skills class, we couldn't spend as much time solely on writing, so I came up with an informal hierarchy of errors to target quickly as I moved from student to student. First, I checked for basic errors in form, like starting sentences with capital letters and using ending punctuation. Then, I concentrated on errors that would impede intelligibility and those that were part of our grammar focus. As I was teaching a mixed class ranging from low beginner to low intermediate, different students had different needs. I could challenge the higher-level students by pointing out more complex errors, but I didn't want to discourage lower level students with too much red ink.

These strategies seemed to work well, but one particular incidence of using them had a strong impact on my future teaching and research. During the chapter about going to the doctor, students were asked to write about a time when they had to seek medical help. As per usual, I walked around the room, reading students' responses and pointing out small things that needed to be corrected until I reached one of my most memorable students. From a war-torn country in Eastern Africa, this student was almost always smiling. She spoke excitedly and fluidly, albeit with some mistakes, about her dreams for her future and the three low-paying jobs she was working to save up for them. Highly engaged in class, she was continually disappointed that she could not move up a level on the reading test that capped every eight-week session. That day when I read her writing, I began to understand why.

The student, always eager to improve, asked to me to read her response. But what was written on the page did not look like English to me. I asked the student to read to me what she had written, and as she read, I heard a very clear, well-formed response about the time she needed to have her appendix removed. On the page, however, it described how she had to have her "a pendus" removed, along with a variety of other invented spellings. I realized this student, whose native language used a different orthography, was having trouble connecting the sounds of English to its symbols. Somewhere, in the long time she been learning English, that fundamental step had been left out. Soon after, I quickly tried to find free or inexpensive resources for adult learners to work on those "bottom-up" strategies of literacy. Yet, most of the resources that were available were intended for elementary-aged learners in their first language. Nevertheless, I felt I had to do something and was soon bringing in exercises and activities that highlighted the relationships between sounds and spellings in English. Some students seemed bored by the exercises while others were enthralled—most notably, the student who inspired the activities. And, at the end of the semester, when she took her reading test again, she finally went up a level.

Higher Stakes

After three years of teaching at a U.S. university and one year at the community college, I was able to fulfill my dream of teaching abroad. For my third context, I was contracted as a visiting lecturer at a private, highly competitive university in Mexico that specialized in engineering and business. Although stereotyped to be full of rich kids, or "fresas," quite a few of the students were on scholarship. Notably bright and driven, they had varied experiences with English and were required to receive a minimum score on their exit English exam to graduate.

For years, the university had been using an institutional paper-based TOEFL but had recently switched to the Cambridge BULATS. Now, rather than just being tested on reading, grammar, and listening, students would also have to speak and write during the exam. The writing portion called for students to complete two specific tasks: first, a short email, and second, a letter or a report. My task was to teach a Business English class focused on communicating in a business setting in all four major skill areas. At the end of the semester, students would need an overall score of B2 on the Common European Framework of Reference (CEFR) scale on the exam in order to receive credit for the class and qualify for graduation. As in my last context, writing was only one of the skills we needed to focus on, but this time, stakes were incredibly high.

Our curriculum team decided it was best to assign writing assignments that aligned well with those the students would see on the exam. We also considered that, given the length of the semester and the breadth of topics we needed to cover, we could only give students about three writing assignments in the semester. In class, students worked through dynamic activities to analyze the three required genres, define their qualities, and write and evaluate examples as groups. Then they were given a sample prompt and a few days to write a response.

To evaluate their work, we followed the rubric provided by BULATS and assigned percentages to each CEFR score. For instance, a short email fitting the rubric's description for B2 could receive between an 80–89% but would need to be at least C1 material to garner a 90% or above. Indeed, we were very strict about each technicality in the rubric's descriptions. For instance, if a student wrote a report in the form of a letter, they were automatically given a B1, or between a 70–79% because the format was "inappropriate to task" (Cambridge, 2017). Students, concerned about their grades, grumbled about this system until we reminded them why we were holding them to such high standards. Both teachers and students had to do our best to anticipate how the Cambridge examiners would score the students' writing because, for some students, that could mean the difference between graduating the following week or not. That possibility created a tension between teaching the students how to pass a test with British-based standards and how to use English in their professional lives after graduation.

Each of my experiences over the past four years have shown me that the challenges of teaching and assessing a core skill such as writing can vary greatly depending on the context. In one context, evaluating second-language writing can mean assessing NES and NNES simultaneously while trying to meet the needs of both. In another, it can mean using a student's seemingly unintelligible work to unlock barriers in other skills, allowing her to move forward in life. And, in another, it can mean accompanying and encouraging students as they work to graduate from college in a country in which many don't go beyond the sixth grade. In short, teaching English as a second language can look like a lot of different things depending on where you are teaching, who you are teaching, and why you are teaching. It is game of variables, and changing any part of the equation can change the purpose, objectives, and the outcome. Contexts may change, but the desire to understand our students—who they are, what they need, and how we can help them succeed—must not. That must remain constant.

Reference

Cambridge English Language Assessment. (2017). *BULATS online writing assessment criteria.* Retrieved from www.bulats.org/sites/bulats.org/files/bulats_writing_markscheme.pdf

4

FOREIGN LANGUAGE WRITING ASSESSMENT AND BRAZILIAN EDUCATIONAL POLICIES

Luciana C. de Oliveira, Solange Aranha, and Fernando Zolin-Vesz

Writing assessment has been a focus of educational research in foreign language contexts. However, little is known about foreign language assessment in the Brazilian context and much less about foreign language writing assessment. This chapter addresses to what extent foreign language writing assessment has been included or not in Brazilian educational policy in Years 1–3 of high school.

We examine and discuss an official document that guides the teaching and learning of foreign languages in Brazil, especially English and Spanish, entitled Curricular Frameworks for High School Teaching (Orientações Curriculares para o Ensino Médio—OCEM; Brasil, 2006) and the guidelines to select school textbooks entitled the National Program of School Textbooks (Programa Nacional do Livro Didático—PNLD; Brasil, 2015). In addition, we propose a framework for the inclusion of English and Spanish writing assessment for the Brazilian educational context based on the theories that put assessment of writing as an essential element of literacy development and on our experiences in second and foreign language teacher education. Finally, we discuss principles of foreign language writing assessment that should guide assessment and instruction in high school classrooms.

Theoretical Framework

Teaching Writing Through Genres

Writing is an essential skill for elementary and secondary (K–12) students. Among the various approaches to teaching writing, genre-based approaches have become more widespread over the past several years, in several different parts of the world

(Aranha, 2009; Martin & Rose, 2008; Tardy, 2011). Genres can be defined as "recurrent configurations of meanings (. . .) that (. . .) enact the social practices of a given culture" (Martin & Rose, 2008, p. 6). In Brazil, many research studies have addressed the teaching of writing, especially based on genre and at the university level (Aranha, 2009, 2015; Meurer, Bonini, & Motta-Roth, 2005; Motta-Roth & Hendges, 2010; Meurer & Motta-Roth, 2002).

The concept of genre has guided the teaching and learning of languages in Brazil since the late 1990s with the publication of the National Curriculum Parameters (Parâmetros Curriculares Nacionais; Brasil, 1997), which was the major guide for educational activities in Brazil. Since then, and with the establishment and publication of the Curricular Frameworks for High School Teaching (Orientações Curriculares para o Ensino Médio), genres continue to influence the teaching of languages in Brazil, including Portuguese, English, Spanish, and other foreign languages (Motta-Roth, 2008).

Learning About Language

Literacy is not inseparable from formal knowledge and knowledge of the world (Britto, 2007). Thus, it is not possible to maintain the hypothesis that literacy is a specific competence conceived as a kind of abstract knowledge. That is why the concept of literacy implies what de Oliveira and Avalos (2018) call "learning about language" (p. 111).

Critical language awareness approaches, for example, emphasize how linguistic practices shape and are shaped by social relationships of power and highlight language as a significant aspect in learning content while drawing on discourses of power (Gee, 2002; MacDonald & Molle, 2015).

Learning about language, in the context of Brazil, includes exploring how language is used to make meaning in various contexts of use, including those in the school context. Analysis of texts in different genres allows for an exploration of thematic content, rhetorical organization and linguistic forms in various social and cultural contexts (Motta-Roth, 2008).

Developing Writing Assessment Literacy

Foreign language teachers need to develop what has been termed in the literature assessment literacy. Assessment literacy involves more than assessing students' work (Stiggins, 1995). Assessment literacy includes recognition of appropriate assessment, evaluation, and communication practices; using assessment methods to collect relevant information; communicating assessment results effectively; and using assessments to increase student motivation and learning by including students in the assessment process (Haught & Crusan, 2016; Mertler, 2009; Stiggins, 1995).

In the context of the teaching and learning of writing in a foreign language, teachers need to develop writing assessment literacy that would include what has been described above but in relation to writing instruction: recognition of appropriate writing assessment, evaluation, and communication practices; using writing assessment methods to collect relevant information; communicating writing assessment results effectively; and using writing assessments to increase student motivation and learning by including students in the assessment process, such as with peer reviews and feedback.

Status of Foreign Language Teaching in Brazilian Educational Policy

LDB (Lei de Diretrizes e Bases da Educação; Brasil, 1996), the national law for Education in Brazil, has been altered by the law number 13,415 in 2017. The revocation of the law changed two points of the previous version related to foreign language teaching: instead of a non-defining foreign language to be taught from K–6 on, whose definition was in charge of the local community, the alteration has established English as mandatory to be offered from the elementary to high school.

Another shift is related to Spanish and the inclusion of other languages in the curriculum. In high school, Spanish was mandatory to be offered from 2005 to 2017—although students' registration was optional according to the national law number 11,165. Other languages could also be offered depending on geographical location and local needs and decisions. Since the law was revoked by the national law number 13,415, other languages—Spanish preferably—can also be offered, depending on their availability, place, and time defined by the teaching system. However, students' registration remains optional.

These changes will certainly require some adjustments in educational policy. It is important to note that though this chapter describes what Brazil has been using as supporting guidelines for teaching in Years 1–3 of high school, currently a new document is being developed and considered. The BNCC (Base Nacional Comum Curricular; National Basis for Common Curriculum; Brasil, 2016) has the goal of achieving a common core curriculum to guide every school in the country. In the next section, we consider the main educational policy that is still ongoing.

Foreign Languages in Brazilian Educational Policy for High School

We examine the main educational policy, entitled Curricular Frameworks for High School Teaching (Orientações Curriculares para o Ensino Médio-OCEM), to show the areas of focus for foreign language teaching and learning, with specific attention to writing.

Curricular Frameworks for High School Teaching (*Orientações Curriculares para o Ensino Médio-OCEM*)

The Curricular Frameworks for High School Teaching (Orientações Curriculares para o Ensino Médio-OCEM) was published in 2006 by the Department of Policies for High School Teaching of the Ministry of Education. It is the official document that has been guiding teaching and learning in high school in Brazil. In relation to foreign languages, the document emphasizes a theoretical background beyond linguistic constructs, that is, the teaching of a foreign language should be centered on contextualized reading, writing practice, and oral communication based on the concept of citizenship. For example, this could take the form of discussing indigenous languages, gender issues, and linguistic differences. The concept of citizenship is a central point for understanding the document: the purpose seems to be an attempt to enhance citizenship through the teaching of a foreign language rather than to provide just a guide to propose what and how a foreign language should be taught at the high school level (Years 1, 2, and 3). Perhaps this political purpose is the reason why evaluation and assessment, pivotal to teaching and learning, seem to be neglected.

Since the concept of citizenship has such a central role in the discussion of teaching and learning a foreign language, "being a citizen" demands the comprehension of the position/place a person occupies in society. According to the document, being a citizen requires understanding of "de que lugar ele fala na sociedade? Por que essa é a sua posição? Como veio parar ali? Ele quer estar nela? Quer mudá-la? Quer sair dela? Essa posição o inclui ou o exclui de quê?" ["from what place does s/he speak? Why is s/he in that position? How did s/he end up there? Does s/he want to be there? Does s/he want to change it? Does s/he want to leave it? Does that position include or exclude her/him?"] (Brasil, 2006, p. 91).[1] This is the perspective from which the foreign language teaching may include the development of the "sense of citizenship." Therefore, according to the document, the teaching of a language is related to its educational value: it "goes beyond than just enabling the learner to use a specific language for communicative purposes only" (Brasil, 2006, p. 92).

In order to associate a sense of citizenship with the contextualized teaching of reading and writing a foreign language, the document proposes the concepts of literacy and multiliteracy, since these concepts allow the development of citizenship through reading and writing practices. In terms of reading, the concepts consider the reader as someone who "assumes a position or an epistemological relation with regard to values, ideologies, discourses, world perspectives" (Brasil, 2006, p. 98). According to the document, this assumption requires understanding of

> (1) how and for what purpose people use reading in their lives, (2) what reading has to do with the distribution of knowledge and power in a society, and (3) the type of reading development results a type of reader.
> *(Brasil, 2006, p. 98)*

Regarding writing as literacy, the document asserts that writing itself cannot be seen in an abstract way, that is to say, disconnected from the context of its uses and users. This argument is based on the comprehension that each language and each culture use writing in different contexts with different purposes. Thus, writing is defined as "a set of various sociocultural practices" (Brasil, 2006, p. 100). As writing is considered both practice and literacy, it concerns the production of a meaningful writing, of contextualized uses of the foreign language, such as writing and answering messages with other people through the Internet, since "the advent of computing and the Internet have a great influence on the writing activity expansion" (Brasil, 2006, p. 121).

Since the Curricular Frameworks for High School Teaching seem to focus their theoretical background on the relationship between the concept of citizenship and the teaching of a foreign language, the absence of an explicit mention of evaluation or even assessment sounds more or less expected. The document clearly enhances the notion of "being a citizen" and the comprehension about the position/place a person occupies in society through teaching/learning a foreign language. Next, we examine the National Program of School Textbooks guidelines as they take into account what the Curricular Frameworks state.

The National Program of School Textbooks—PNLD (Programa Nacional do Livro Didático) Guidelines

The National Program of School Textbooks (PNLD—Programa Nacional do Livro Didático) is a document that establishes the curricular guidelines of school textbooks that are endorsed by the government to be used in public schools. Every author, and consequently, every publisher, who wants their material to be published and used by students in public schools are supposed to follow these ground rules. In 2015, the last call for the selection of school textbooks for high school, which occurs every three years, the document supported the choice of two books for Spanish courses and four for English in the high school level. The critical analysis of the chosen materials was based upon criteria widely discussed and shared among scholars involved in the evaluation process and has been used since the beginning of the establishment of the high school guidelines. Although the Curricular Frameworks do not explicitly determine the contents teachers should approach, let alone the assessment practice they should hold, we believe these guidelines may be useful for determining the framework we are suggesting to help teachers and schools in this crucial aspect of teaching/learning; that is, to assess the development of learning and, consequently, evaluate pedagogical practices and content.

Citizenship is a key factor in all arguments developed to instruct teachers who will choose the material to be used in their classes and was fundamental for determining the selection of books by the board of scholars and teachers, appointed by the Ministry of Education (MEC) based on unknown criteria. According to

Brasil (2015), this board is appointed by the Coordenação Geral de Materiais Didáticos (COGEAM; General Coordination of Pedagogical Materials), which is responsible for the evaluation and selection of the books submitted to the PNLD.

According to the document, the building of citizenship will be possible if one uses materials that

> allow the discussion about socially relevant questions; allow access to multiple literacies and discourse genres produced in different spaces and times; allow, fundamentally, the development of a critical reader, able to go beyond the decoding of texts; offer access to situations that improve speaking and writing, through the comprehension of production and circulation and their own social purposes.
>
> *(Brasil, 2015, p. 7)*[2]

The criteria included reading as a macroskill to promote critical literacy; however, every collection must have audio CDs and Internet resources as supporting materials. During the selection process, the board is guided by an assessment form that determines the aspects that should be considered in order to favor one collection and disregard the other (22% selected and 78% disregarded in 2015). Detailed information about every topic was pinpointed because it was the second time that foreign languages as a discipline in high school was subjected to PNLD guidelines.

Therefore, the evaluation of school textbooks considers various factors related to the skills of listening, speaking, reading, and writing. The guidelines show a focus on reading and building citizenship. Reading and writing are emphasized as core skills. We highlight here the ones that relate to the teaching of writing, as it is presented in the PNLD guidelines:

- "Considers variety of discourse genres, realized through verbal, non-verbal, and verbal-visual language, used in different expressions in the foreign language and the national language."
- "Promotes activities of writing production that consider it as an interactive process, that requires definitions of communicative patterns (who, for whom, and for what objectives), supported by an understanding of writing based on conventions related to context and genres and involves re-writing of the same text."
- "Prioritizes activities that give reading and writing production activities a central role in the foreign language teaching and learning process in high school."
- "Proposes assessment and self-assessment activities that integrate different aspects that make up language studies at this level, looking to complement discursive and linguistic knowledge and cultural aspects related to the expressions and comprehension of the foreign language."

(p. 11–13)

The guidelines above mention genres as a tool for achieving the competences proposed and also consider types of activities. The only mention of assessment can be found in the fourth bullet, which includes self-assessment as a possibility (among others not mentioned). The guidelines also predict that both national and foreign language should be considered and suggest intertextuality as a strategy to achieve interdisciplinarity.

The evaluation form used to assess the school textbooks was composed of two parts. Part A is of interest because it includes writing production and linguistic elements in its nine subdivisions (subsections IV and VI, respectively). The board was supposed to answer the questions to assess the quality and adequacy of materials:

- "In reference to writing production, does the collection: promote activities that consider writing an interactive process, with the definition of communicative patterns (who, for whom, and with what objectives)? Include a representative set of different speaking communities of the foreign language? Contain activities that promote the re-writing of students' own texts?"
- "In reference to linguistic elements, does the collection: propose the systematization of knowledge based on contextualized situations of foreign language use? Present concepts and information that are correct, contextualized and up-to-date?"

(p. 15)

Whatever is meant by writing production, contextual aspects and social practices are to be taken into account. Re-writing is a crucial activity to be promoted; thus, we infer that writing activities should be compelling components of each and every material.

Context is also a key element considered under the linguistic elements. We assume that context and genres are closely related when we consider meaningful tasks in different levels. This implies social practices that may change from place to place, from background to background, and from age to age.

The PNLD guidelines provide some key information about what school textbooks should include in terms of writing production and expectations for linguistic elements that should be a focus of attention, though these are very general. Next, we propose an assessment framework for writing. Even though this macroskill and its assessment are overlooked in official documents, they are both implied in official discourses. We believe that assessment is not on the radar of scholars putting these documents together. A clear articulation of issues related to writing assessment would be extremely beneficial to consider in future educational policies.

Because the document emphasizes citizenship at its core and connects citizenship development with access to multiple literacies, genres, and being critical readers, we see knowledge about genres as key to becoming citizens. The next section explores these ideas in more detail.

Framework for Inclusion of Foreign Language Writing Assessment

The framework we propose does not include full coverage of the content of the Curricular Frameworks and just focuses on key aspects for writing assessment. The standards within the framework contain statements in a chosen genre that will depend upon teachers' choices according to different social and educational contexts. To demonstrate that students have met a standard within this framework, teachers will need to have evidence based on students' writing assignments and tasks.

The framework is divided into three major sections: Genres and Purposes, Linguistic Elements, and Writing Production. Genres and Purposes includes the genres that we propose be part of Years 1–3 based on the Curricular Frameworks document and the PNDL expectations for school textbooks. Linguistic Elements provides language expectations for high school. Writing Production incorporates the components of drafting and revision as well as issues of time frames.

TABLE 4.1 Writing Assessment Framework for High School

	Year 1	Year 2	Year 3
	Genres and Purposes		
Expectations	Write for a range of purposes and audiences in various genres. Understand why different genres are used for different purposes and audiences. Be aware of social and linguistic demands and restrictions every genre poses and how these influence relationships in social contexts.		
Genre Family	**Recount**	**Explanation**	**Argument**
Genres	Personal Recount Autobiographical Recount	Sequential Explanation	Exposition
Format	Biography diary	Email Curriculum Vitae Cover Letter	Letter of Intention
Expectations	Write personal recount to establish commitment and understanding with others in the same level of study and age. Write autobiographical recount that describes likes, dislikes, and hobbies clearly.	Write emails to convey different kinds of information, ask questions, and explain situations in an appropriate manner. Write a discussion to explain past experiences in order to inform a specific audience. Write a curriculum vitae that presents relevant education and experiences organized according to expectations. Write a cover letter that explains one's objectives and goals.	Write an exposition that argues for a specific point of view with a thesis, arguments, and reiteration of thesis.

(Continued)

TABLE 4.1 (Continued)

	Year 1	Year 2	Year 3
		Linguistic Elements	
Expectations	Use language that is clear and coherent to express ideas and information. Shift between levels of formality through selecting vocabulary precisely and by manipulating grammatical structures. Employ appropriate conventions to the genres they are writing (e.g., capital letters, full stops, question marks, exclamation marks, commas for lists, and apostrophes for contraction). Develop paragraphs to organize ideas and information. Use cohesive devices (e.g., pronouns, demonstratives, substitutes) within and across sentences and paragraphs. Utilize conjunctions and transitions to connect sentences and paragraphs. Use verb forms related to specific genres accurately and appropriately.		
		Writing Production	
Expectations	Plan, write, revise, and re-write to strengthen their writing. Write as possible in and out of the classroom, in shorter or longer time frames.		

The expectations highlighted in the framework can be used to develop rubrics specific to the genres taught. Next, we provide the principles of foreign language writing assessment that should guide implementation of the framework in high school classrooms.

Principles of Foreign Language Writing Assessment

The principles presented here are based on work by Crusan (2010) and adapted to the foreign language context.

Foreign Language Writing Assessment Should Be Ongoing

This principle relates to writing assessment as an integral part of writing instruction and an ongoing process of teaching and learning a foreign language. This can be achieved by designed activities that involve writing on a weekly basis, given the constraints of teaching a foreign language in Brazil.

Foreign Language Writing Assessment Should Be Authentic

This principle involves the idea that everything a student does in the classroom relates to what they may do in real life contexts, so the writing tasks and their assessment relate to authentic uses of language. The genre families and genres we identified above are examples of authentic writing tasks that students may encounter in the future.

Foreign Language Writing Assessment Should Be Transparent

This principle relates to making foreign language writing assessment clear to students by providing them with assessment criteria and rubrics as assignments are presented to students. It also involves having students participate in the assessment process by doing peer reviews and providing feedback to their colleagues so they learn more about writing and writing assessment. A sample peer feedback form can be found in Appendix 4.1.

Foreign Language Writing Assessment Should Be an Essential Part of Instruction

This principle relates to the indivisible nature of assessment and instruction. Writing assessment and instruction should be inseparable components of the process of foreign language teaching and learning. Instruction guides assessment and assessment guides instruction.

Foreign Language Writing Assessment Should Describe Student Progress over Time

This principle involves the connection between writing assessment and student progress. Students should be assessed over the course of a semester (as schools are organized in semesters) so writing assessment can better describe student progress.

The principles of foreign language writing assessment presented here will likely be viewed as an important addition to the foreign language education curriculum.

Conclusion

This chapter reviewed the Curricular Frameworks for High School Teaching (Orientações Curriculares para o Ensino Médio) document as it pertained to the teaching of foreign languages and the National Program of School Textbooks (Programa Nacional do Livro Didático—PNLD) guidelines to select school textbooks. Based on those reviews, we proposed a framework for the inclusion of foreign writing assessment for the Brazilian educational context. Finally, we discussed principles of foreign language writing assessment that should guide assessment and instruction in high school classrooms.

As this macroskill and its assessment are neglected in the Brazilian official documents examined in this chapter, we proposed an assessment framework for writing based on genres. According to what we have discussed, teaching writing through genres implies that knowledge about genre characteristics and constraints is central to enhance citizenship, a key point in the Brazilian educational policy, as stated in the official documents. Then the principles of foreign language writing assessment presented above could connect and develop the so-called notion of being a citizen founded on discourse genres. While the National Basis for Common Curriculum (Base Nacional Comum Curricular—BNCC) is being developed, this framework may be an alternative to help high school foreign language teachers, given the constraints of teaching a foreign language in Brazil. We propose relevant use of genres that are useful for students during and after high school in their daily lives. It is important to mention that many will continue their studies while others will start working and not be able to go to college, so meeting various needs is crucial.

Notes

1 All references to the Curricular Frameworks for High School Teaching were translated from Portuguese by the authors.
2 All references to the PNLD guidelines were translated from Portuguese by the authors.

References

Aranha, S. (2009). The development of a genre-based writing course for graduate students in two fields. In C. Bazerman, A. Bonini, & D. Figueiredo (Eds.), *Genre in a changing world* (pp. 465–482). West Lafayette, IN: The WAC Clearinghouse and Parlor Press.

Aranha, S. (2015). Conscientizar para produzir: um relato sobre a implantação de um curso de redação acadêmica em língua inglesa [Consciousness-raising to produce: A discussion of the implementation of an academic writing course in English]. In R. de Castro Guerra Ramos, S. Matravolgyi Damião, & S. T. Ricardo de Castro (Eds.), *Experiências didáticas no ensino-aprendizagem de língua inglesa em contextos diversos [Didactic experiences in English language teaching-learning in diverse contexts]* (pp. 167–186). Campinas: Mercado de Letras.

Brasil. (1996). *Lei de diretrizes e bases da educação [National law for education in Brazil]*. Brasília: Planalto. Retrieved from www.planalto.gov.br/ccivil_03/Leis/L9394compilado.htm

Brasil. (1997). *Parâmetros curriculares nacionais: Introdução aos parâmetros curriculares nacionais [National curriculum parameters: Introduction to the national curriculum parameters]*. Brasília: Ministry of Education of Brazil. Retrieved from http://portal.mec.gov.br/seb/arquivos/pdf/livro01.pdf

Brasil. (2006). *Orientações curriculares para o ensino médio: Linguagens, códigos e suas tecnologias [The curricular frameworks for high school teaching: Languages, codes and their technologies]*. Brasília: Ministry of Education of Brazil. Retrieved from http://portal.mec.gov.br/seb/arquivos/pdf/book_volume_01_internet.pdf

Brasil. (2015). *Guia de livros didáticos: PNLD—Programa nacional do livro didático 2015: Língua estrangeira moderna [Guide for textbooks: National program of school textbooks 2015: Modern foreign language]*. Brasília: Ministry of Education of Brazil. Retrieved from www.fnde.gov.br/index.php/pnld-consultas

Brasil. (2016). *Base nacional comum curricular (BNCC) [National basis for common curriculum]*. Brasília: Ministry of Education of Brazil. Retrieved from http://basenacionalcomum.mec.gov.br/images/BNCC_publicacao.pdf

Britto, L. P. L. (2007). Escola, ensino de língua, letramento, e conhecimento [School, language teaching, literacy, and knowledge]. *Calidoscópio, 5*(1), 24–30.

Crusan, D. (2010). *Assessment in the second language writing classroom.* Ann Arbor: University of Michigan Press.

de Oliveira, L. C., & Avalos, M. (2018). Critical SFL praxis among teacher candidates: Using systemic functional linguistics in K–12 teacher education. In R. Harman (Ed.), *Bilingual learners and social equity: Critical approaches to systemic functional linguistics* (pp. 109–123). New York: Springer.

Gee, J. (2002). Literacies, identities and discourses. In M. J. Schleppegrell & M. C. Colombi (Eds.), *Developing advanced literacy in first and second languages: Meaning with power* (pp. 159–175). Mahwah, NJ: Erlbaum.

Haught, J., & Crusan, D. (2016). Filling the gaps: L2 grammar and assessment preparation for ELA teachers. In L. C. de Oliveira & M. Shoffner (Eds.), *Teaching English language arts to English language learners: Preparing pre-service and in-service teachers* (pp. 171–192). New York: Palgrave Macmillan.

MacDonald, R., & Molle, D. (2015). Creating meaning through key practices in English language arts: Integrating practice, content, language. In L. C. de Oliveira, M. Klassen, & M. Maune (Eds.), *The common core state standards in English language arts for English language learners* (pp. 39–52). Alexandria, VA: TESOL Press.

Martin, J. R., & Rose, D. (2008). *Genre relations: Mapping culture.* London: Equinox.

Mertler, C. (2009). Teachers' assessment knowledge and their perceptions of the impact of classroom assessment professional development. *Improving Schools, 12*(1), 101–113. https://doi.org/10.1177/1365480209105575

Meurer, J. L., Bonini, A., & Motta-Roth, D. (Eds). (2005). *Generos: teorias, metodos e debates [Genres: Theories, methods, and debates].* Sao Paulo: Parabola Editorial.

Meurer, J. L., & Motta-Roth, D. (Eds.). (2002). *Generos textuais: Subsidios para o ensino da linguagem [Textual genres: Subsidies for the teaching of language].* Bauru: EDUSC-Editora da Universidade do Sagrado Coração.

Motta-Roth, D. (2008). Análise crítica de gêneros: Contribuições para o ensino e a pesquisa de linguagem [Critical genre analysis: Contributions to language teaching and research]. *Documentação de Estudo em Linguística Teórica e Aplicada (DELTA), 24*(2), 341–383.

Motta-Roth, D., & Hendges, G. R. (2010). *Produção textual na universidade [Textual production at the university].* São Paulo: Parábola Editorial.

Stiggins, R. J. (1995). Assessment literacy for the 21st century. *Phi Delta Kappan, 77*(3), 238–245.

Tardy, C. M. (2011). The future of genre in second language writing: A North American perspective. *Journal of Second Language Writing, 20*(1), 1–5. https://doi.org/10.1016/j.jslw.2010.12.004

APPENDIX 4.1

Peer Review Form

Name of Student Reviewer:
Name of Student Writer:
Date of Review:

Read your colleague's writing and answer the following questions. Choose Yes, No, or Maybe. If you answer No or Maybe, provide one suggestion to the student writer.

PEER REVIEW

		Yes	No	Maybe	Suggestions

Genres and Purposes
1. Are the author's purpose and audience clear?
2. Does this text use the correct elements of the [genre]?

Linguistic Elements
3. Does the text use language that is clear and coherent?
4. Does the text use precise vocabulary and grammatical structures?
5. Does the text use appropriate conventions?
6. Do the paragraphs organize ideas and information well?
7. Does the text use cohesive devices within and across sentences and paragraphs?
8. Does the text use conjunctions and transitions to connect sentences and paragraphs?
9. Does the text use appropriate verb forms for the kind of text it is?

Make any other recommendations here:

5

SOCIOPOLITICAL CONTEXTS OF EFL WRITING ASSESSMENT IN VIETNAM

Impact of a National Project

Xuan Minh Ngo

Introduction

Vietnam's EFL Scene

Vietnam is a multi-ethnic country with the Kinh or Viet group accounting for approximately 87% of the population. Although Vietnamese is its official language, other minority groups reserve the constitutional right to use their mother tongues (Phan, Vu, & Bao, 2014). Once a stagnant economy, the nation has been developing rapidly since it adopted the 1986 Doi Moi (Renewal) policy that endorsed socialist market-oriented economic development. In recent years, Vietnam has actively integrated itself into the global market by joining the Association of Southeast Asian Nations (ASEAN) in 1995 and the World Trade Organization (WTO) in 2007, which has led to a boom in the teaching and learning of English, the lingua franca of trade and business, across its borders.

Interestingly, English used to be considered the devil's tongue since it was first introduced as a by-product of the Vietnam war (Pham, 2014); however, it has now become the language of international integration (Phan et al., 2014). Already by far the most popular foreign language in Vietnam, English is predicted to be even more prominent when it is officially taught to all students nationwide from primary school in 2019–2020 (Vietnamese Government, 2008) and becomes a medium of instruction for science subjects in selected secondary schools and for advanced courses at university (Bui & Nguyen, 2016). Generally, English in Vietnam is not an indicator of social class but acts as a gatekeeper when it comes to employment and education (Hoang, 2010).

Despite remarkable attention and resources, the quality of English teaching and learning in the country remains low by international standards (Hoang, 2010; Pham, 2014; Phan et al., 2014). This is seen by the government as an obstacle to Vietnam's economic development, especially when the ASEAN, of which Vietnam is a member, plans to adopt a free labor movement scheme, putting the country's workforce, equivalent to 60% of the entire population, in direct competition with citizens of high English proficiency countries like Singapore, Malaysia, and the Philippines (Koty, 2016). To remedy the situation, the Vietnamese government launched Project 2020 in 2008 by issuing Decision 1400, which highlights the major strategies and goals of the foreign language education system in Vietnam from 2008 to 2020.

Project 2020

The project's overarching goal is to produce systemic changes in how foreign languages are taught, learned, and assessed in Vietnam (Vietnamese Government, 2008). With a budget of about $5 billion, the National Foreign Languages Project 2020 (henceforth Project 2020) is generally regarded as the most significant and ambitious foreign language reform in modern Vietnam (Bui & Nguyen, 2016; Ngo, 2017; Pham, 2014).

Central to Project 2020 is the development of a six-level framework for "developing foreign language curricula, textbooks, teaching plans, and assessment criteria at all levels of education to ensure continuity" (Vietnamese Government, 2008, p. 2) in line with international standards. Interestingly, this framework was not published until 2014, when many critical activities had finished or were well under way (Nguyen & Hamid, 2015). However, a close scrutiny reveals the approved Vietnamese framework to be a near translation of the Common European Framework of Reference (CEFR) can-do statements (Ngo, 2014). Probably due to this, the framework is often known as CEFR-VN among local language specialists, whose perception of it was rather mixed (Ngo, 2017; Nguyen & Hamid, 2015). Despite the absence of a formalized framework, Decision 1400 (Vietnamese Government, 2008) specifies the foreign language graduation standard for each education level as in Table 5.1.

Assessment plays a central role in this project and is listed among seven major tasks in Decision 1400, which calls for radical reforms in language testing and assessment practices and the construction of a national test bank. A recent document (Project 2020 Management Board, 2016) places assessment as the third focal task and specifically demands that the resources of participating institutions be channeled towards (1) finalizing the exam format for each level in the CEFR-VN, establishing a national item bank, training item writers, and examiners, (2) training secondary English teachers about assessment to prepare for the four-skill English graduation test, (3) experimenting with continuous assessment aligned with CEFR-VN, and (4) finalizing regulations about testing and assessment, granting foreign language certificates, and establishing high-quality assessment centers. Although there has been no specific reference to writing assessment in such policy documents, it can be assumed that the project recommends assessing all four skills.

TABLE 5.1 Graduation Foreign Language Standard by Level of Education

Education level	Target level (CEFR-VN)	Target level (CEFR)
Primary	1	A1
Lower Secondary	2	A2
Upper Secondary	3	B1
Vocational Training	2	A2
Vocational Training (Advanced)	3	B1
University (Non-Major)	3	B1
University (Major)	5	C1
Community College (Major)	4	B2

Rationale

At the time of writing, the project has entered its final phase, but the results so far have been disappointing (Tue, 2016; Quynh, 2016; Yen, 2016). As the ministry is evaluating the project's implementation and possible extension, its impact on the actual teaching and learning of English skills, including writing, needs to be closely scrutinized. Unfortunately, few academic publications on this topic currently exist. It is this serious gap that the current chapter will attempt to bridge.

Research Methods

Overall Design

The study described in this chapter adopts narrative inquiry defined by Connelly and Clandinin as "a way of characterizing the phenomenon of human experience" (1990, p. 2). This method was chosen since it is among the most effective means of investigating teachers' professional practice (Tsui, 2007) due to its ability to provide an in-depth, holistic, and longitudinal account of human experience (Bell, 2002, 2011). Besides, narrative research focuses its lens on the research context at multiple levels, both micro and macro (Barkhuizen, 2007), responding to the call for the contextualization of teaching (Bax, 2003). Furthermore, this approach is transformative as it offers participants the chance to reflect on and gain a deeper understanding of their experiences (Johnson & Golombek, 2011) as well as the opportunity to raise their voice and exercise their agency (Pavlenko, 2007). Finally, Simon-Maeda (2004) stresses the role of teacher stories in revealing the field's "political and ideological underpinnings and rework[ing] them toward more progressive ends" (p. 431).

Data Collection

The data were derived from an unstructured interview followed by a series of semi-structured interviews with each participant over five months. An unstructured interview was first used because it is like "a natural conversation" (McDonough & McDonough, 1997, p. 184), making participants feel more willing to open up. This was succeeded by semi-structured interviews whose predefined questions ensure critical information can be obtained within the time constraint, while their flexible nature allows the chance to clarify and explore emerging themes (Dörnyei, 2007). The interview language was Vietnamese, the participants' mother tongue, due to their preference; nevertheless, they were encouraged to code-switch between L1 and L2 (English) whenever necessary.

Additionally, course guides, textbooks, teacher's books, handouts, exam papers, and all the other relevant policy documents were consulted to validate interview information. As the depth of narrative research is possible thanks to a privileged access to the otherwise secretive world of the researched (Pavlenko, 2007), considerable attempt was made to establish close rapport between the researcher and the participants, but the reminder of Clandinin and Connelly (2000) to balance between the coolness and closeness in this special relationship was also heeded.

Data Analysis

The data was prepared and analyzed as recommended in Murray (2009). First, all the interviews were transcribed in full as a precaution against "premature judgments" (Seidman, 2006, p. 115) stemming from selective transcription. Subsequently, the transcripts were sent back to participants for feedback, and upon their approval of the scripts, categorical content analysis (Lieblich, Tuval-Mashiach, & Zilber, 1998) and the constant comparative method (Glaser & Strauss, 1967) were employed to detect patterns in the professional life of each participant. This laid the foundation for the composition of individual narratives, which included the three dimensions of narrative space (Clandinin & Connelly, 2000). These life stories were then sent back to the participants for their comments, and finally "cross-story analysis" (Murray, 2009, p. 53) was conducted to uncover the common emerging themes from both stories.

Because narrative research depends heavily on the researcher's subjective interpretation (Canagarajah, 1996), various measures were taken to prevent fabrication or misinterpretation of data and a Hollywood-style happy ending in which all built-up tensions are decisively resolved (Connelly & Clandinin, 1990). These ranged from constant reference to related documents to regular consultation with both participants.

Participants

Because it is impossible to report the two participants' full professional life stories due to this chapter's scope, only key biographical details will be presented in this section. This is a common constraint facing narrative researchers (Bell, 2011; Murray, 2009), with Bell (2002) observing that few narrative studies enjoy the luxury of being published in the narrative format.

Jara

Jara (pseudonym) was an EFL lecturer with over six years' teaching experience at a foreign language-specializing university in northern Vietnam, henceforth called Lingua. She worked mainly with sophomores and had taught writing every semester since graduating with a bachelor's degree in TEFL from Lingua's fast-track program, an advanced stream reserved for the top 10%. Before she attended an MA course in Australia, Jara taught two writing courses (Writing III and IV) that focused on different types of paragraphs. However, upon her return to Vietnam, she found that Lingua's English curriculum had changed substantially and was divided into three streams (social, academic, and exam preparation), with integrated instead of discrete skill lessons. After teaching an academic English course (3A) for one semester, Jara was promoted to coordinator of two exam preparation courses (3E and 4E), taking charge of their syllabi, textbooks, and exam papers.

Natalie

Natalie attended Lingua for a BA in TEFL between 2008 and 2012, during which time she also tutored students at various levels. After graduation, she worked at a language center for around three months before joining an applied linguistics master's program in England from 2013 to 2014. Back in Vietnam, Natalie applied for a teaching position at Aquaria University (pseudonym) following advice of a relative, who was a faculty member there. Her application was accepted and Natalie became a full-time TEFL lecturer in the English Division, a unit of 20 staff members offering English courses to over 4,000 non-major students. Besides this official position, she took a teaching position at Aliana, a tertiary public institution that trained students majoring in international politics, laws, languages, and cultures.

Findings & Discussion—Impact of Project 2020

Little Change

Jara and Natalie's narratives disclose several aspects of writing assessment that seemed unaffected by Project 2020. First, summative tests remained virtually the exclusive option when English was not a major; even in Aliana and Lingua's specializing classes, they were prioritized over continuous assessment. In fact, portfolios used to be featured in Lingua's old writing courses (Writing III and IV) and received quite substantial weighting (about 30–40% of the total score). However, for the new exam courses 3E and 4E, they were discarded because they did not directly contribute to building students' test-taking strategies. Meanwhile, Natalie took the initiative of introducing an online blogging activity for a group of Aliana's English majors, but due to technical problems and students' lukewarm response, she soon discontinued it. This finding resonates with Ellis (1996) and Tran's (2007) observation that writing is predominantly considered a product rather than a process in Vietnam; hence, its assessment is largely based on fixed point exams.

Another prominent feature is the continued prevalence of indirect testing methods in non-specializing contexts. At Aquaria, TOEFL's structure and written expression items were a feature of most writing tests for both the standard and advanced program. Natalie even applauded the use of such questions, believing that it could help offset the lack of reliability in teachers' subjective assessment of writing scripts. In some extreme cases like the A2 undergraduate graduation test, multiple choice grammar and vocabulary items even replaced the letter and sentence writing tasks. In Vietnam, such practice is widely viewed as the grammar-translation approach's legacy (Pham, 2000; Tran, 2007; Trinh & Nguyen, 2014). Despite fierce criticism, the approach is popular at all education levels due to high-stakes tests' emphasis on grammatical and lexical knowledge (Hoang, 2010).

Likewise, the role of feedback remained relatively unchanged. At Aquaria, Natalie hardly offered feedback because her students were unwilling to write. For Aliana's English majors, she could focus on only one aspect of students' writing at a time due to practical constraints. Meanwhile, Jara admitted offering more comments in old courses (Writing III and IV) because these involved portfolios that required both peer and teacher feedback. However, the exam courses 3E and 4E included summative assessment only, and there was no clear policy on feedback. Hence, she did not request her students to obtain peer feedback and merely provided comments to those completing their writing in class under time pressure. This lack of attention to feedback was disappointing given the overwhelming evidence for its efficacy (Bitchener & Knoch, 2009; Chandler, 2003; Ellis, Sheen, Murakami, & Takashima, 2008). This is, nevertheless, unsurprising as both teachers faced time constraints and exam pressure as well as limited institutional advocacy, which are issues indicated elsewhere (Farrell & Lim, 2005; Lee, 2009). Notably, Natalie's narrative reveals how her Aquarian students' low motivation was further worsened by the university leadership's insistence on teacher accountability.

> So the pressure from the university management board is that teachers have to figure out a way so that students can graduate. And the pressure

from students is that [Natalie imitating a student's voice] . . . We're not going to learn, so you must figure out a way to help us graduate on your own. So the pressure is from both sides . . . students refuse to cooperate, whereas the leaders interfere too much with our business, not just the writing exam question.

Natalie's students were, nonetheless, not alone in their attitude towards writing, with their peers also viewing this skill as difficult, boring, and laborious (Tran, 2007; Trinh & Nguyen, 2014).

New Mandatory Graduation Standardized Tests

Arguably, the most prominent change resulting from Project 2020 has been the introduction of mandatory standardized graduation exams aligned with the CEFR-VN. Aquaria's undergraduate and postgraduate tests were set at Level 2 (A2) and 3 (B1) respectively, while those for Lingua's and Aliana's English majors were at Level 5 (C1) and for Aliana's non-majors at Level 4 (B2). Besides their questionable quality (see below), their format had undergone constant changes. For example, the writing exit test at Lingua initially resembled IELTS Academic, then TOEFL and finally IELTS General Training. Similarly, Aquaria adapted its A2 exam several times, considerably simplifying the writing section. In some cases, there was a serious lack of information about high-stakes exams, so Natalie had to use personal connections to obtain more information about Aliana's B2 exam. By contrast, Aquaria offered publicly available test banks whose small size meant that most items ended up in the real test.

Both teachers seriously doubted the quality of test items and rating at their universities. Regarding the first issue, Jara was concerned about writing topics unfairly disadvantaging candidates from mountainous and rural areas, whereas Natalie was dissatisfied with the oversimplification of the A2 writing section where the original letter writing task was replaced by first sentence re-writing and finally multiple-choice questions. In language testing literature, the former clearly exemplifies test bias (McNamara & Roever, 2006) and the latter is a case of construct underrepresentation since writing involves more than lexical and grammatical knowledge (Bachman & Palmer, 2010).

Meanwhile, rating was entirely at the teachers' discretion. Natalie avidly supported holistic scoring; even when analytic rating was required, she (and her colleagues) would mark papers holistically first and allocate component scores to fit the overall score later. One reason, she claimed, was the writing section's low weighting, which did not justify the intensive labor associated with analytic scoring. Also, each session involved marking over a hundred scripts, which made this time-consuming grading approach impractical. Another contributing factor was the low quality of marking rubrics, which Natalie sometimes considered "ludicrous and ambiguous." Last, little monitoring and guidance existed to ensure inter-rater reliability, even in high-stake exams where teachers had already been calibrated before the scoring process. In contrast to Natalie, Jara was a strong advocate of analytic rating, presumably due to her extensive experience in teaching IELTS writing. As a course coordinator, she required all teachers to award component scores based on the IELTS public writing descriptors, arguing that these were well designed and familiar, so teachers did not need much training to use them effectively. Clearly, the two critical facets in performance assessment, namely the rating scale and rater behavior, (McNamara, 1996; Weir, 2005) did not conform with usual standards in this case, which means writing score validity is clearly questionable.

Most worryingly, there was little attempt to validate these critical graduation tests. Even at Lingua, the country's leading institution in foreign language education, the in-house test's validity evidence was limited to a couple of internal reports. As Jara commented, this was probably due to the project's "hasty execution." In other words, conditions such as the development of all stakeholders' assessment literacy, a fully-fledged framework, and a suite of standardized tests should have been met before large-scale testing programs were launched.

Lastly, there was increased presence of international tests like IELTS, TOEFL, and Cambridge Main Suite exams as teachers and students grappled with the project's large-scale testing requirements. Preparation books for these exams became the backbone of the English curriculum at all the focal institutions (see below), and both teachers admitted creating institutional tests by copying items from such sources. Furthermore, Jara's use of the IELTS rating scales exemplifies local teachers' preference for and reliance on international testing behemoths. Nguyen and Hamid (2015) uncovered a similar situation where teachers acknowledged unethicality but still persisted in borrowing items from published materials due to their inability to write CEFR-aligned tests.

Powerful Washback

Project 2020's use of testing to implement education reforms as detailed above proves very popular with policy makers, who consider it a low-cost and quick recipe for improving learning outcomes (Linn, 2000; Shohamy, 2001). However, this approach may not always produce the intended results (Brindley, 2008; Wall, 2000) and potentially may lead to negative washback (Wall, 2014).

Evidence can be first seen in the curricular design. Aquaria's English II and III textbooks were part of a Cambridge exam preparation series at Level A2; likewise, Aliana utilized an IELTS book for its bachelor's writing course. Lingua even designed two courses to sharpen its students' test-taking skills, using materials from commercial exam preparation books.

Teachers' practice had also become more test-oriented due to their managers' demand for students' high exam success rates. For Jara, this was expected because developing exam strategies was her courses' foremost aim, a sharp contrast to

Writing III and IV, where test tips were neither offered by teachers nor expected by students. Similarly, Natalie concentrated her writing instruction in two or three sessions near the semester's end. In place of the textbook's different writing tasks, she would devote each session to an exam section, introducing the format and tips and providing some practice with sample or past papers. Aware of her students' low proficiency, she even showed them several tricks to maximize their scores.

The employment of testing as a cost-effective policy instrument is also problematic because students' increased exam results may not indicate their enhanced proficiency, but rather the effect of score polluting practices, both ethical and unethical (Haladyna, Nolen, & Haas, 1991). In Natalie and Jara's accounts, the former includes introducing exam strategies, whereas the latter involves adapting the curriculum to fit the test and supplying exam items.

Recommendations and Conclusions

The chapter has painted a rather disappointing picture of the most expensive foreign language reform in Vietnam's modern history, a depiction that is in line with media reports (Tue, 2016; Quynh, 2016) and academic papers (Bui, 2009; Nguyen, 2012). With an explicit focus on EFL writing assessment, the chapter reveals the continuing dominance of summative and indirect assessment as well as the rather limited use of feedback as formative assessment and students' low motivation towards writing. It also casts doubt on the validity of mandatory graduation English tests, whose items are often borrowed from commercial test preparation materials and whose rating scale and rater behavior still leave much to be desired, and reveals institutions' score polluting practices in their attempt to achieve the prescribed goals.

Given these findings, Vietnamese policy makers should discard their simplistic notion that imposing standardized English tests will guarantee improved proficiency, as test washback is highly unpredictable and uncontrollable (Wall, 2014). Instead, they should be wary of the enabling factors that involve teachers, resources, practical conditions, and test attributes (Spratt, 2005). As teachers ultimately determine educational reform outcomes, they should receive extensive training in language assessment both pre- and in-service, and most importantly, such training must directly serve their needs instead of following trainers' and policy makers' beliefs (Mai, 2014). Attention should be paid to highlighting writing as a process and the role of feedback in helping students improve their writing skill. Once teachers have been adequately trained, they should be offered a chance to exercise their agency and apply their knowledge via classroom formative assessment tasks such as those in Rea-Dickins and Gardner (2000) and Rea-Dickins (2001, 2002). However, this assessment alternative may give teachers an unwelcome burden, so their workload must be reduced for this recommendation to work.

Regarding graduation exams, as mounting pressure may contaminate test scores, project leadership should replace current goals, which are widely considered impractical (Bui & Nguyen, 2016), with those more realistic. What is more, substantial validity evidence must be presented before high-stake tests can be approved for use. For writing, critical aspects such as rating scales, rater training, and monitoring simply cannot be overlooked.

Admittedly, this study has several shortcomings. It focuses on only two participants and their three affiliated universities, so their accounts may not reflect the situations at all Vietnamese institutions. However, its results are largely consistent with past studies. Additionally, due to the narrative nature, it does not include a baseline study as recommended in Wall (2014); therefore, a simple causal link should not be assumed for its findings. Nevertheless, as the participants' professional activities spanned across different phases of Project 2020, their narratives arguably reflected the project's impact to a certain extent.

Overall, the chapter serves as constructive criticism of Project 2020, alerting policy makers to revise their action plan to reach the goal of boosting the Vietnamese workforce's foreign language proficiency, including writing. Hopefully, it will offer some food for thought to international readers whose countries are implementing similar educational reforms.

References

Bachman, L. F., & Palmer, A. S. (2010). *Language assessment in practice: Developing language assessments and justifying their use in the real world.* Oxford: Oxford University Press.

Barkhuizen, G. (2007). A narrative approach to exploring context in language teaching. *ELT Journal, 62*(3), 231–239. https://doi.org/10.1093/elt/ccm043

Bax, S. (2003). CALL-past, present, and future. *System, 31*(1), 13–28. https://doi.org/10.1016/S0346-251X(02)00071-4

Bell, J. S. (2002). Narrative inquiry: More than just telling stories. *TESOL Quarterly, 36*(2), 207–213. https://doi.org/10.2307/3588331

Bell, J. S. (2011). Reporting and publishing narrative inquiry in TESOL: Challenges and rewards. *TESOL Quarterly, 45*(3), 575–584. https://doi.org/10.5054/tq.2011.256792

Bitchener, J., & Knoch, U. (2009). The contribution of written corrective feedback to language development: A ten month investigation. *Applied Linguistics, 31*(2), 193–214. https://doi.org/10.1093/applin/amp016

Brindley, G. (2008). Educational reform and language testing. In E. Shohamy & N. H. Hornberger (Eds.), *Encyclopedia of language and education* (2nd ed., Vol. 7, pp. 365–378). New York: Springer.

Bui, T. T. N. (2009). *Challenges of English language learning for Thai minority students in Vietnam.* Unpublished master's thesis. University of Hawaii, USA.

Bui, T. T. N., & Nguyen, H. T. M. (2016). Standardizing English for educational and socio-economic betterment: A critical analysis of English language policy reforms in Vietnam. In R. Kirkpatrick (Ed.), *English language education policy in Asia* (Vol. 11). Cham, Switzerland: Springer.

Canagarajah, A. S. (1996). From critical research practice to critical research reporting. *TESOL Quarterly, 30*(2), 321–330. https://doi.org/10.2307/3588146

Chandler, J. (2003). The efficacy of various kinds of error feedback for improvement in the accuracy and fluency of L2 student writing. *Journal of Second Language Writing, 12*(3), 267–296. https://doi.org/10.1016/S1060-3743(03)00038-9

Clandinin, D. J., & Connelly, F. M. (2000). *Narrative inquiry: Experience and story in qualitative research.* San Francisco, CA: Jossey-Bass Inc.

Connelly, F. M., & Clandinin, D. J. (1990). Stories of experience and narrative inquiry. *Educational Researcher, 19*(5), 2–14. https://doi.org/10.3102/0013189X019005002

Connelly, F. M., & Clandinin, D. J. (2006). Narrative inquiry. In J. L. Green, G. Camilli, & P. B. Elmore (Eds.), *Handbook of complementary methods in education research* (3rd ed.). Mahwah, NJ: Lawrence Erlbaum Associates.

Dörnyei, Z. (2007). *Research methods in applied linguistics: Quantitative, qualitative, and mixed methodologies.* Oxford: Oxford University Press.

Ellis, G. (1996). How culturally appropriate is the communicative approach? *ELT Journal, 50*(3), 213–218. https://doi.org/10.1093/elt/50.3.213

Ellis, R., Sheen, Y., Murakami, M., & Takashima, H. (2008). The effects of focused and unfocused written corrective feedback in an English as a foreign language context. *System, 36*(3), 353–371. https://doi.org/10.1016/j.system.2008.02.001

Farrell, T.S.C., & Lim, P. C. P. (2005). Conceptions of grammar teaching: A case study of teachers' beliefs and classroom practices. *TESL-EJ, 9*(2), 1–12.

Glaser, B., & Strauss, A. (1967). *The discovery of grounded theory.* Chicago, IL: Aldine.

Haladyna, T. M., Nolen, S. B., & Haas, N. S. (1991). Raising standardized achievement test scores and the origins of test score pollution. *Educational Researcher, 20*(5), 2–7. https://doi.org/10.3102/0013189X020005002

Hoang, V. V. (2010). The current situation and issues of the teaching of English in Vietnam. *Ritsumeikan Studies in Language and Culture, 22*(1), 7–18.

Johnson, K. E., & Golombek, P. R. (2011). *Research on second language teacher education: A sociocultural perspective on professional development.* New York: Routledge.

Koty, A. C. (2016). Labor mobility in ASEAN: Current commitments and future limitations. Retrieved from www.aseanbriefing.com/news/2016/05/13/asean-labor-mobility.html

Lee, I. (2009). Ten mismatches between teachers' beliefs and written feedback practice. *ELT Journal, 63*(1), 13–22. https://doi.org/10.1093/elt/ccn010

Lieblich, A., Tuval-Mashiach, R., & Zilber, T. (1998). *Narrative research: Reading, analysis, and interpretation.* Thousand Oaks, CA: Sage.

Linn, R. L. (2000). Assessments and accountability. *Educational Researcher, 29*(2), 4–16. https://doi.org/10.3102/0013189X029002004

Mai, N. K. (2014). Towards a holistic approach to developing the language proficiency of Vietnamese primary teachers of English. *Electronic Journal of Foreign Language Teaching, 11*(2), 341–357.

McDonough, J., & McDonough, S. H. (1997). *Research methods for English language teachers.* New York: Arnold.

McNamara, T. F. (1996). *Measuring second language performance.* London: Longman.

McNamara, T. F., & Roever, C. (2006). *Language testing: The social dimension.* Malden, MA: Blackwell Publishing.

Murray, G. (2009). Narrative inquiry. In J. Heigham & R. A. Croker (Eds.), *Qualitative research in applied linguistics: A practical introduction.* Basingstoke: Palgrave Macmillan.

Ngo, X. M. (2014). *Diffusion of the CEFR among Vietnamese teachers: A mixed methods investigation.* Unpublished MA thesis. University of Queensland, Australia.

Ngo, X. M. (2017). Diffusion of the CEFR among Vietnamese teachers: A mixed methods investigation. *Asian EFL Journal, 19*(1), 7–32.

Nguyen, H.T.M. (2012). Primary English language education policy in Vietnam: Insights from implementation. In B. Baldauf, R. B. Kaplan, N. M. Kamwangamalu, & P. Bryant (Eds.), *Language planning in primary schools in Asia.* Abingdon: Routledge.

Nguyen, V. H., & Hamid, O. M. (2015). Educational policy borrowing in a globalized world: A case study of Common European Framework of Reference for languages in a Vietnamese University. *English Teaching: Practice & Critique, 14*(1), 60–74. https://doi.org/10.1108/etpc-02-2015-0014

Pavlenko, A. (2007). Autobiographic narratives as data in applied linguistics. *Applied Linguistics, 28*(2), 163–188. https://doi.org/10.1093/applin/amm008

Pham, H. (2000). Traditional versus modern methods. *Teacher's Edition, 2,* 20–24.

Pham, T. N. (2014). Foreign language policy. In L. T. Tran, S. Marginson, H. M. Do, Q.T.N. Do, T.T.T. Le, N. T. Nguyen, T.T.P. Vu, T. N. Pham, & H.T.L. Nguyen (Eds.), *Higher education in Vietnam: Flexibility, mobility and practicality in the global knowledge economy.* Basingstoke: Palgrave Macmillan.

Phan, L. H., Vu, H. H., & Bao, D. (2014). Language policies in modern-day Vietnam: Changes, challenges and complexities. In P. Sercombe & R. Tupas (Eds.), *Language, education and nation-building: Assimilation and shift in Southeast Asia.* Basingstoke: Palgrave Macmillan.

Project 2020 Management Board. (2016). *Focal tasks in 2016 of the National Foreign Languages Project 2020 (No 45—CV/DANN).* Hanoi: Office of the Project 2020.

Quynh, T. (2016). *The ministry of education and training: Some goals of the Project 2020 are too high!* Retrieved from http://vnexpress.net/tin-tuc/giao-duc/bo-giao-duc-mot-so-muc-tieu-cua-de-an-ngoai-ngu-qua-cao-3491191.html

Rea-Dickins, P. (2001). Mirror, mirror on the wall: Identifying processes of classroom assessment. *Language Testing, 18*(4), 429–462. https://doi.org/10.1177/026553220101800407

Rea-Dickins, P. (2002). Exploring the educational potential of assessment with reference to learners with English as an additional language. In C. Leung (Ed.), *Language and additional/second language issues for school education: A reader for teachers* (pp. 81–93). York: York Publishing Services.

Rea-Dickins, P., & Gardner, S. (2000). Snares and silver bullets: Disentangling the construct of formative assessment. *Language Testing, 17*(2), 215–241. https://doi.org/10.1177/026553220001700206

Seidman, I. E. (2006). *Interviewing as qualitative research: A guide for researchers in education and the social sciences.* New York: Teachers College Press.

Shohamy, E. (2001). *The power of tests: A critical perspective on the uses of language tests.* New York: Longman.

Simon-Maeda, A. (2004). The complex construction of professional identities: Female EFL educators in Japan speak out. *TESOL Quarterly, 38*(3), 405–436. https://doi.org/10.2307/3588347

Spratt, M. (2005). Washback and the classroom: The implications for teaching and learning of studies of washback from exams. *Language Teaching Research, 9*(1), 5–29. https://doi.org/10.1191/1362168805lr152oa

Tran, L. T. (2007). Learners' motivation and identity in the Vietnamese EFL writing classroom. *English Teaching: Practice and Critique, 6*(1), 151–163.

Trinh, Q. L., & Nguyen, T. T. (2014). Enhancing Vietnamese learners' ability in writing argumentative essays. *The Journal of Asia TEFL, 11*(2), 63–91.

Tsui, A.B.M. (2007). Complexities of identity formation: A narrative inquiry of an EFL teacher. *TESOL Quarterly, 41*(4), 657–680. https://doi.org/10.2307/40264401

Tue, A. (2016). *The ministry of education and training adjusts the goals of the National Foreign Languages Project.* Retrieved from http://news.zing.vn/bo-giao-duc-dieu-chinh-muc-tieu-de-an-ngoai-ngu-den-nam-2020-post682403.html

Vietnamese Government. (2008). *Teaching and learning foreign languages in the national education system 2008–2020 (Decision 1400/QĐTTg).* Hanoi: Office of the Vietnamese Government.

Wall, D. (2000). The impact of high-stakes testing on teaching and learning: Can this be predicted or controlled? *System, 28*(4), 499–509. https://doi.org/10.1016/S0346-251X(00)00035-X

Wall, D. (2014). Washback. In G. Fulcher & F. Davidson (Eds.), *The Routledge handbook of language testing.* Abingdon: Routledge.

Weir, C. J. (2005). *Language testing and validation: An evidence-based approach.* New York: Palgrave Macmillan.

Yen, A. (2016, August 11). 2020 National Foreign Languages Project: Does it work? *Laborer Newspaper.*Retrieved from http://nld.com.vn/giao-duc-khoa-hoc/de-an-ngoai-ngu-2020-hieu-qua-o-dau-20160811230105864.htm

6

VIGNETTE

Policy Makers, Assessment Practices, and Ethical Dilution

Hadi Banat

Assessment remains a delicate and complicated dimension in education because it determines students' success, programmatic sustainability, and institutional accreditation. Despite the prevalence of assessment in institutions, it is not always based on fair, transparent, and valid foundations. Various factors influence the validity of assessment measures adopted in writing classrooms: class size, the suitability of instruments used, and the top-down management style of institutions. Thus, poor assessment practices are not necessarily the result of gaps in the instructor's knowledge or education. Institutional politics and understudied policies can force writing teachers to use inappropriate measures to evaluate students' learning.

Huot (2002) believes that the way writing teachers evaluate students reflects their theoretical stance about assessment, and White, Lutz, and Kamusikri (1996) emphasize that assessment defines goals and conveys values. Crusan (2010) questions if all students are aware of the criteria teachers use to assess writing, and whether our assessments are valid, transparent, fair, and appropriate in connection to the context and purposes for which they are designed. A question worth considering is: Do assessment practices always convey the values of writing teachers? In contexts where curricular downgrading of writing programs accompanied by huge enrollment of students in writing classes intertwine to pose pressure and challenges, writing teachers gradually lose their autonomy and ethical stance in designing and implementing fair and valid assessment practices.

There are two types of academic institutions in the Middle East: local and foreign universities. Most foreign universities follow the U.S. model of education due to the recognition the American University of Beirut has gained since its establishment in 1866. In the United Arab Emirates (UAE), the local universities are either governmental or semi-governmental. A governmental university is tuition-free, non-profit, funded by the government, and admits Emirati citizens only, while a semi-governmental university is owned and partially funded by one of the ruling families. In the latter, admission is not restricted to Emirati citizens, and students pay tuition depending on the program they are enrolled in. Foreign U.S. universities in the United Arab Emirates are private institutions that enforce more rigorous admission requirements and higher tuition than local institutions.

Having worked at two different universities in the UAE, a semi-governmental local institution and a private foreign U.S. institution, made me realize that the type of institution, educational standards, and the policies made by stakeholders have a significant impact on assessment practices. It took me a while to comprehend how forces on top of the pyramid could control both the mundane and substantial practices of writing instructors. The chancellor and college dean make decisions regarding classroom enrollment cap that influence how instructors operate the teaching and assessment of writing. Assessment theories are grounded in research conducted in ideal classroom settings, but the conditions of writing classes are not uniform across institutions, which threatens the universality of research implications. The latter highlights a discrepancy between what writing teachers learn and aspire to accomplish and what they can realistically achieve due to a gap between theory and the realism of practice. My failure to maintain equitable standards of assessment in my writing classes at the two institutions I worked for was due to how each institution valued writing. Housed in the same university city and located a mile apart, these two institutions with their different introductory writing programs, divergent inner institutional politics, and dissimilar writing classroom settings determined the role I played as a composition instructor and the affordances at my disposal.

Institutions, Writing Programs, and Politics of Assessment

Semi-Governmental Institution in the UAE

In 2008, I was hired by a growing semi-governmental university with a student population of approximately 14,000. Two years after my arrival, the university underwent major downsizing of the writing program due to an accreditation review report prepared by the Ministry of Higher Education, which presented recommendations for increasing content courses in the disciplines. Adhering to the same number of credits in bachelors' programs while increasing content courses was a dilemma for college deans. They were under pressure because they had to respond to the ministry's recommendations, which made their decisions for change abrupt and detrimental to teachers, students, and several programs. The decision to decrease humanities coursework in the study plan and increase coursework in each respective specialization led to a reduction from two required writing classes to one. This policy shifted the population of L2 writers dramatically, lumping together students with wildly varying language proficiencies. Our frustration increased due to our belief that the curriculum used did not help students write better. We were dealing with multiple challenges that we could not solve: unfair placement procedures, different levels of student language proficiency, and highly populated writing classes, which influenced our standards in teaching and assessing writing.

Aspiring to create a bilingual community of graduates who compete for jobs with their counterparts from similar institutions and more prestigious U.S. universities in the region, the chancellor and college deans were preoccupied with pestering faculty to produce research, but their efforts to enhance the quality and conditions of teaching were minimal. The huge enrollment of students in introductory communicative English classes (Basic English, English for Academic Purposes, and Speech Communication) and English for Specific Purposes (ESP) (English for Medical Sciences, Technical Writing, English for Humanities, and English for Media) was an institutional policy that fiddled with the quality of instruction and ethical assessment. A cap of 40 to 70 students became standard practice because stakeholders treated all courses in the humanities the same. For example, if an introductory history class had an enrollment of 70 students, the chancellor and college deans enforced the same policy in an English class. Despite constant complaints about the poor writing abilities of students in the institution and the graduates who encountered constant challenges in a job market full of proficient bilinguals, the number of communication and writing courses did not increase nor did the enrollment cap decrease.

In English departmental meetings, teachers constantly discussed problems encountered in big classes of students: inadequate chances for communication, inability to do group activities, the overwhelming amount of papers to grade, feedback on multiple drafts, lack of interactive activities facilitative of learning, and unfair assessment measures. The head of the department empathized with communal concerns because he shared mutual values and beliefs about the characteristics defining an effective learning environment; however, his support did not convince the college dean, the vice-chancellor for academic affairs, and the chancellor. As long as students were not complaining, there were more essential concerns that required urgent action, such as building research centers, training hospitals, and laboratories. The buzz of Science, Technology, Engineering, and Math Education (STEM) depreciated the role writing plays in documenting and sustaining research. Effective instruction and assessment techniques were jeopardized because instructors were burnt out and had to become creative in managing their workload (a teaching load of five courses a semester) while meeting other administrative demands. Writing instructors had the knowledge and tools needed to develop and improve L2 writers' abilities; however, they were crippled in face of the difficulties and tensions posed by uninformed policies.

In order to manage their workload in highly populated classrooms, instructors came up with creative modifications. Some stopped the multiple draft process, while others decided to implement collaborative writing projects. With the former group of instructors, students produced one draft that was evaluated. The latter group of instructors was unable to give up on the value drafting and dialogic feedback offer second language writers, so they arranged their students in groups of four to produce one writing assignment, which made responding to multiple drafts less demanding. In either case, instructors made compromises in regard to their principles and beliefs about what enhances L2 writing. The critical questions teachers asked themselves upon reflection and self-evaluation in meetings with the coordinator were: What is being evaluated in writing classes? How are students getting evaluated? What kind of measures are created to encompass smoother assessment procedures in big classes? Are the assessment procedures the most suitable, most ethical, most transparent, and most valid, or are they the most convenient?

My colleagues and I realized that our assessment practices were unfair and invalid. There were problems with the curriculum and the writing process, and we did not adjust our assessment practices in ways to cope with the changing conditions of our writing classes. The modifications we implemented were unethical to students because our teaching and evaluation practices were discordant. Ignorant and impulsive institutional policies overlooked the welfare of students and shed light on how universities operate like businesses, prioritizing profit over education. The students were victims in this view of education, which encourages high tuition and quick turnover. In addition, instructors became more invested in surviving the demands of their tiresome jobs and less devoted to maintaining standards in instruction and assessment practices. The chancellor and board of trustees were satisfied with the outcomes because numbers and figures reflected the continuing prosperity of the institution. An increase in graduation and enrollment rate, university facilities, and research publications contributed to a higher ranking and status.

Private Foreign U.S. Institution in the UAE

In the 2011–2012 academic year, I accepted an adjunct faculty position in the Department of Writing Studies at a private foreign U.S. institution. I was teaching two sections of composition, while full-time MA holders were teaching four. The student population was 6,000, and the admission requirements were more rigorous than at local institutions. A minimum score of 6.5 on the IELTS was mandatory for admission. The Writing Studies Department at this institution has a curriculum of four writing courses that students take over the course of two years, depending on placement results. A cap of 20 students with no exceptions is a strict university policy; this allowed for focus on process, feedback, and teacher and writing center intervention. There was compatibility between the learning outcomes and assessment measures because products of student work were evaluated in light of the program's learning outcomes.

In the writing classroom, teachers presented each assignment sheet and discussed its requirements, success criteria, and outcomes. My colleagues and I focused on how we planned to assess student writing, and teacher-designed rubrics were transparently discussed with students. When students received feedback on a draft, they reevaluated their performance by comparing the instructor's comments in alignment with the rubric. When they visited the Writing Center for consultation, the rubric provided transparency and clarity about how teachers in the program evaluated student assignments, which facilitated intervention in constructive ways.

In meetings, the Writing Studies Department director was confident about the policies and promises she made. She was subjected to the pressure of raising capacity in writing classrooms, but her refusal was supported by the college dean and chancellor, who were realistic about the goals and vision of the institution. This university has been accredited in the United States by the Middle States Commission on Higher Education, so adherence to U.S. standards was vital to pursue accreditation in all states. As a teaching university, more emphasis was placed on the quality of teaching than on research production; thus, maintaining a logical faculty to student ratio in classrooms was crucial.

The Writing Studies Department was invested in professional development sessions, curricular revisions, and illuminative evaluation, i.e., periodic assessment of instruction techniques, curriculum, and learning. The purpose of illuminative evaluation was to provide insights about the compatibility between the pedagogies used and their effectiveness in promoting students' writing skills. Instructors' reflections on activity design, lesson planning, student-teacher interaction patterns, students' reading and writing strategies, student participation in the classroom, and assessment were shared for learning purposes and exchange of ideas and experiences.

These reflection sessions resulted in redesigning syllabi to meet curricular outcomes and cater to student needs. The writing program administrator, for example, designed a six-credit accelerated writing course that students can take in one semester to replace two consecutive writing courses. Students qualified for the accelerated course after finishing the second writing course (WRI 101) in the sequence through an application that included a portfolio of outstanding writing assignments. Applicants included a recommendation letter prepared by their instructor, which focused on the student's development throughout WRI 101 with a detailed assessment of the student's performance and potentials. Such initiatives reflected the department's continuous efforts in self-reflection, evaluation, and enhancement of its writing program. It also revealed how the department was creating opportunities for different student populations in the institution while keeping up with the writing demands of the disciplines.

The constant interaction among faculty and regular illuminative assessment sessions were successful and plausible due to a manageable workload and small classrooms where students' progress and learning were prioritized and carefully monitored. I could remember all my students' names, and I was well informed about their strengths and weaknesses. Such writing classroom environments presented sufficient opportunities for dialogic interaction, student-centered instruction, drafting, and feedback, in addition to maintaining fair and valid assessment tools to measure students' writing development.

Conclusion

Assessment cannot be detached from a well-designed writing curriculum, proper and fair placement measures, a reasonable workload for writing instructors, and reduced enrollment in classes including second language writers (Silva, 2001). Local and foreign U.S. institutions in the UAE have different ideologies about preparing their population of students for the writing expectations of the academy. English for Academic Purposes differs from First Year Writing because it shifts the concentration from the writer to the academic discourse community; i.e., writing instruction focuses on writing genres and tasks needed to succeed in an English-medium institution of higher learning (Silva & Leki, 2004). Writing assessment practices cannot be generalized to every classroom context because EAP and ESP are different contexts from First Year Writing in terms of learning outcomes and expectations, purpose, curriculum, and process. When planning valid, fair, and accountable assessment measures, they have to fit the context and purposes for which they are designed (Crusan, 2010). The reliability and validity of our methods suffer at the expense of practicality in overcrowded writing classrooms. Conducting assessment research should be extended to international contexts where writing classes have different conditions and dynamics due to a focus on EAP and ESP. Research in such contexts can produce new epistemologies whose implications can inform practitioners on designing accountable assessment measures compatible with the learning outcomes and nature of the writing classroom.

Amid the chaos of institutional politics and policies of stakeholders perceiving the humanities as the weakest link, teacher education can help writing instructors customize assessment techniques in conducive ways to the learning process and learners. Crusan (2010) compared her interest in the adequate preparation of writing teachers for effective assessment of their students' development in writing to Weigle (2007), who saw a necessity in constructing, administering, scoring, and communicating the results of valid and reliable tests and paying attention to the uses and misuses of large-scale assessments. Sufficient education and training of writing instructors is crucial to withstand the strong winds of change in institutions that give more prominence to producing graduates with specialized degrees than informed global citizens able to solve problems in a world shaped by oral and written communication.

References

Crusan, D. (2010). *Assessment in the second language writing classroom.* Ann Arbor: The University of Michigan Press. http://dx.doi.org/10.3998/mpub.770334

Huot, B. (2002). *(Re) Articulating writing assessment for teaching and learning.* Logan: Utah State University Press.

Silva, T. (2001). CCCC statement on second language writing and writers. *Journal of Second Language Writing, 10,* 229–233.

Silva, T., & Leki, I. (2004). Family matters: The influence of applied linguistics and composition studies on second language writing studies: Past, present, and future. *Modern Language Journal, 88*(1), 1–13. http://dx.doi.org/10.1111/j.0026-7902.2004.00215.x

Weigle, S. C. (2007). Teaching writing teachers about assessment. *Journal of Second Language Writing, 16*(3), 194–209. http://dx.doi.org/10.1016/j.jslw.2007.07.004

White, E. M., Lutz, W. D., & Kamusikri, S. (1996). *Assessment of writing: Politics, policies, practices.* New York: Modern Language Association of America.

7

ENGLISH WRITING ASSESSMENT IN THE CONTEXT OF IRAN

The Double Life of Iranian Test-Takers

Fahimeh Marefat and Mojtaba Heydari

Like many other countries, Iran has been affected by the ever-increasing influences of English globalization. Along with their mother tongue, children born in Iran sooner or later get familiar with the English alphabet when they see and hear the English names of their favorite cartoon characters, toys, computer games, or even snacks. Some parents enroll their kids in kindergartens or private English schools where they can learn to sing songs or write simple words in English. Even if some are deprived of private education, all children are expected to start learning English officially in the state-run schools in their seventh school year. Then, all through their high school, undergraduate, graduate, and postgraduate studies, learning English will be an inseparable element of their curriculum. At higher levels, students should improve their English to be able to find better educational or professional opportunities. In addition, sitting high-stakes English proficiency tests is inevitable for those who decide to migrate to other countries, continue their studies, or promote their careers.

The ever-increasing need for improving English proficiency (especially writing) and the diversity of international and national high-stakes proficiency tests, especially in recent years, have posed new challenges to Iranian students, teachers, and educational policy makers. In this chapter, we aim to identify such challenges by introducing and analyzing the Iranian high-stakes tests (Konkour, master's entrance exam, TOLIMO, MSRT, EPT, and MHLE[1]), and comparing them with the two most common high-stakes international English tests (TOEFL, IELTS) in the way they tap test-takers' writing abilities. The comparison between tests in this chapter will guide us through identifying the (mis)matches, both in theory and practice, in English writing assessment in Iran and around the world. For a better clarification, we will also rely on voices from Iranian experienced teachers to delve into the main concerns related to education and assessment of EFL writing in Iran. Finally, we intend to discern the implications of such (mis)matches for international and Iranian educational policy makers.

Changing Needs

Political and social factors have played a major role in shaping the current assessment practice in Iran. After the 1979 Islamic Revolution in Iran, the top political and cultural decision-makers united around a consensus to guard the country against Western cultural hegemony and the spread of secularism (Borjian, 2013). Therefore, the Iranian official education program has continued to resist the impact of English globalization. For example, Iran's Ministry of Education has designed a localized English curriculum to recognize the cultural and religious values of the country. To guarantee maximum compatibility with the cultural values, this curriculum has preferred crafted or translated texts of known content (including cultural, moral, and religious values) over authentic materials.

Reading comprehension and controlled grammar practices have long been emphasized, since the ultimate goal of learning English is assumed to be understanding the academic texts and conveying the knowledge to the country. Therefore, English curricula designed for public schools and universities in Iran have emphasized the role of written over spoken language (e.g., Borjian, 2013; Naghdipour, 2016; Riazi, 2005). The education system in Iran is centralized and assigns the same textbooks, teaching methods, and testing procedures to all parts of the country (Riazi, 2005). Also, with roots in the grammar-translation method, the official English syllabi in Iran mainly constitute reading passages, translating sentences and texts, memorizing long lists of words, and lots of grammar exercises.

Nevertheless, changes in the social, political, economic, and educational aspects of the country, especially in the last decade, have reshaped the actual needs of Iranian EFL students. Iran is now a developing country with a very young population, mostly consisting of students, with 31.5% aged between 15 to 29 in 2013 (Statistical Center of Iran, 2017). An official report published in 2013 indicates that there are more than 4.6 million undergraduate university students and about 0.6 million graduate and postgraduate university students in Iran (Iran's Ministry of Science, Research and Technology, 2017). The existence of such a big population and limited academic opportunities available for students has created a *competitive environment* for students in Iranian universities.

In this situation, as mentioned earlier, students should take high-stakes tests to prove their English proficiency and get the highest scores possible to win the competition. Furthermore, in recent years, writing in English and publishing scientific articles in well-indexed English journals has turned into a gold standard for universities. Students who want to get doctoral admission, or PhD students who are arranging for their defense session, are required to publish articles in international quality journals (ISI/ISC indexed), preferably English. Accordingly, based on SCImago Journal & Country Rank (2017), the number of indexed international documents published by Iranian students in 2015 was 39,727, which ranked Iran as the 16th research publishing country worldwide.

A Brief History of Writing Assessment

In order to shape a clearer image of the current situation of writing assessment in Iran, it is worth reviewing the world history of assessing writing. Yancey (1999) has identified three eras for writing assessment from 1950 to the present. The first era, 1950 to 1970, employs objective tests and indirect measurement. The second, 1970 through 1986, highlights holistic assessment and direct measurement. The last era, from 1986 through the present, focuses on portfolio assessment.

In the first era, indirect assessment dominated writing programs, mainly in the form of multiple-choice, cloze, and error recognition items (Hyland, 2009). During this time, the majority of high-stakes tests of writing held by U.S. institutions were standardized tests emphasizing the reliability of test scores (Yancey, 1999). Hamp-Lyons (1990) referred to the 1950s and 1960s in the United States as the "structuralist-psychometric era" where questions included in the TOEFL "Structure and Written Expression" section were, according to Kroll (1990), easy to score and allowed for instant comparison of the results. Writing instructors and their students spent much of class time coaching test-taking skills rather than writing (Hamp-Lyons, 1990).

By the end of the first era, many schools and institutes continued to complain about the inability of the students, who had successfully passed such indirect tests, to write texts at reasonable lengths and synthesize academic materials with their own critical opinions (Hamp-Lyons, 1990). In the 1970s, while researchers began to respond to such critics at the theoretical level, practitioners started to include direct tests of writing in conjunction with multiple-choice questions in some high-stake tests (Behizadeh & Engelhard, 2011). Due to serious concerns about the reliability of direct tests, direct assessment of writing could not fully replace indirect tests. Studies continued to discover ways to improve the validity of direct assessment and succeeded in reaching satisfactory reliability levels for decision-making purposes. It was in 1986 that the TOEFL introduced an optional but separate test of writing named TWE (Test of Written English), which was, as Hamp-Lyons (1990) puts it, "the final nail in the coffin of indirect measurement of ESL writing" (p. 70).

And finally, the third era is marked by the call for a shift from single drafts of writing to multiple drafts, or "portfolio assessment." This model of writing assessment was primarily set in classroom environments where students had the chance to write on different occasions and in different genres. This type of assessment is believed to be more valid and organic due to its emphasis on the process, rather than the product, of writing. While some institutes, schools, and universities have used portfolio assessment for placement purposes (Behizadeh & Engelhard, 2011), due to many practical limitations, it has never become a common type of formal assessment. In the following sections, we will use the categorization presented here to classify the types of common high-stakes tests in Iran.

Iranian High-Stakes English Tests

The Iranian assessment system is based on grades and scores, and it compares the students' achievements using the same benchmarks (Riazi, 2005). Multiple-choice and fill-in-the blank items are very common for English state-run tests, with an emphasis on knowledge of vocabulary, grammar, and reading comprehension. Classroom scores are reported on a 0–20 scale, and scores for high-stakes tests (like Konkour) are usually reported in percentages ranging from -33%[2] to 100%.

Konkour

Konkour is a nationwide entrance exam held once a year to qualify high school students for admission to universities. This is a comprehensive test comprising 200 multiple-choice questions on school subjects including Persian literature, English, Math, Physics, etc. Students answer 25 multiple-choice English questions to achieve a score ranging from -33% to 100%.

Master's Entrance Exam

Another nationwide entrance exam is held annually for university students with bachelor's degrees who aim to pursue their education through a master's degree. The test includes specific subject items based on the students' field of study plus 30 multiple-choice English questions. The scores are reported exactly as they are in Konkour.

TOLIMO

The TOLIMO (Test of Language by the Iranian Measurement Organization) is a nationwide high-stakes test held on a monthly basis to assess university students' English proficiency. The TOLIMO resembles TOEFL PBT exactly in every aspect, including task types, number of questions, timing, and scoring.

MSRT, EPT, and MHLE

The MSRT (Ministry of Science, Research and Technology), the EPT (English Proficiency Test), and the MHLE (Ministry of Health Language Exam) are all nationwide high-stakes tests; they are very similar in nature, except for some surface differences. While the tests employ multiple-choice items to assess vocabulary, grammar and sentence structure, reading comprehension, and listening (the EPT does not test listening), they do not directly assess writing. The following sample represents the two most common multiple-choice items in Iranian high-stakes tests:

I. *Identify the incorrect part of the sentence.*

   The <u>developing</u> of the submarine was hindered by <u>the</u> lack of <u>a power source</u> that <u>could propel</u> an underwater vessel.

II. *In the first few months of life, an infant learns how to lift its head, smile, and . . .*

   a) *parents to recognize . . . b) recognize its parents*
   c) *recognizing its parents . . . d) the recognizing of its parents*

TOEFL and IELTS

The TOEFL and the IELTS are so well-known that little clarification is necessary. Instead, the key information summarizing the item types for the six high-stakes Iranian tests as well as the TOEFL and the IELTS is presented in Table 7.1.

TABLE 7.1 Iranian and International High-Stakes Test Item Type and Number

	Konkour	Master's entrance exam	MSRT	MHLE	EPT	TOLIMO	TOEFL IBT	IELTS
multiple-choice fill-in-the-blank on grammar	4	No	15	15	15	15	No	No
multiple-choice fill-in-the-blank on vocabulary	8	10	No	No	25	No	No*	No*
multiple-choice error recognition	0	0	15	25	25	25	No	No
essay writing	No	No	No	No	No	1 task	2 tasks	2 tasks
multiple-choice cloze	5	5	No	No	15	No	No	No
reading comprehension	8	15	40	30	20	50	36–56*	40*
listening comprehension	No	No	30	30	No	50	34–51*	40 *
score range	-33 to 100 (%)	-33 to 100 (%)	0 to 100	0 to 100	0 to 100	310 to 677 + writing: score 1 to 6	0–120	0–9

Note: Vocabulary is not directly tested through multiple-choice items; it is integrated into other sections. IELTS and TOEFL include different types of items, such as matching, labeling, completion, etc.

The Study

In this section, we will first start with analyzing the common Iranian high-stakes tests and compare and contrast them with the way the TOEFL and the IELTS assess students' writing skills. We will then embark on our findings from interviews with teachers to shed light on the challenges facing the students preparing for such tests.

Test Analysis

We collected the recent Iranian high-stakes tests administered from 2013 to 2016. Ten versions of each test, 4,000 items overall, were examined. By analyzing the items in Iranian tests, we can categorize the tests into two classes:

1. *Konkour, master's entrance exam, MSRT, MHLE,* and *EPT*: These tests assess writing indirectly through multiple-choice fill-in-the-blank items on grammar and vocabulary, multiple-choice items of error recognition, and cloze tests. While some reading comprehension items (e.g., items related to discourse markers or passage organization) can be considered as indirect measures of a test-taker's writing ability, except for a few items on organization and rhetoric, most of the items analyzed were set out to measure the test-takers' inferencing abilities and vocabulary knowledge. Therefore, we decided not to consider them as indirect measures of writing.

    Two points regarding these tests are worth noting: first, all the items were *receptive* rather than *productive*; that is, they all involved choosing the correct item from among the provided alternatives rather than writing the appropriate answer from their own active knowledge. Second, the items in these tests lacked appropriate contextualization, preventing the test-taker from dealing with longer discourses.

    Evidently, all the tests are instances of indirect proficiency tests, which isolate different language components and consider writing as a subskill of vocabulary and grammar. With respect to the categorization presented for the history of writing assessment, all the tests listed in this class belong to the first era of writing assessment (the structuralist-psychometric era), which assumes that test-takers' performance in such sections underlies their ability to write.

2. The TOLIMO combines multiple-choice questions, similar to the first class of tests, with direct assessment of writing. Therefore, it resembles the tests popular in the late 1970s and 1980s when the field of writing assessment was striving to relocate its emphasis from reliability toward validity. The TOLIMO, as previously mentioned, takes after the TOEFL PBT, in the sense that it combines a separate test of writing, like the TWE, with typical multiple-choice questions, and the writing score is reported separately from the total score.

For the TOLIMO writing section, unlike the TWE, no rubric or criterion is publicly available for further educational uses. Besides, the current survey on admission requirements of top 20 Iranian universities indicated that none of them require students to report their scores on the writing section. Instead, the total score is considered as the ultimate criterion for making admission decisions. Therefore, it seems that while the TOLIMO includes a direct writing assessment task, the students' performance in this section is not of high importance, and the score on discrete-point items alone determines the proficiency of the test-takers.

Interview

Employing convenience sampling, the researchers selected a total of 19 Iranian EFL instructors and four private language institute supervisors (11 females and 12 males, overall) from four major institutes in Tehran. They had an average teaching experience of seven years. The participants were categorized, based on their work experience, into two groups: (1) full-time EFL exam (IELTS, TOEFL, TOLIMO, etc.) instructors working only in private institutes (n=11), and (2) EFL instructors teaching both in public schools/universities and private institutes (n=8). The respondents individually participated in an audio-recorded semi-structured interview lasting about 25 minutes. After transcribing the interviews and conducting a thematic analysis (Gillham, 2005), the findings were coded and categorized into two sections: teachers' views about Iranian students' expectations and views about the challenges of English writing instruction in Iran.

Findings

Teachers' Views About Iranian Students' Expectations

When the teachers were asked about challenges of teaching English writing to Iranian students, they frequently complained about their students' fallacies or false expectations about learning English writing. The main themes found in teachers' responses can be listed as follows:

- Nearly all students think they will learn to write well in a short time within a few sessions and "are not aware that it has taken a long time for their writing habits to shape and it takes some time to change them."
- Many students expect their teachers to provide them with a set of words and grammar rules so that they can rehearse and employ them in the exam. According to one teacher, "some students think that learning English is like learning math or physics; to memorize a list of formulas and use them to solve problems in the exam."

- Most students do not want their class time to be devoted to correction or feedback provision. As one teacher puts it: "they think they've paid much money and it's a waste of time to simply talk about their writings in the class."
- Students usually have problems handling writing longer than one or two sentences because, as one teacher complains, "they have rarely been asked to write more than one sentence, neither in the class nor for Konkour."
- A majority of students are more inclined toward surface features than the content of their writing. "My students usually try to make their writings overcomplicated in order to gain higher scores but their essays are usually difficult to understand," notes an experienced IELTS teacher.

Similar views were held by other experienced teachers, who believed that most students, regardless of their proficiency level, strive to use difficult words and complicated grammatical structures, but they hardly ever care about the opinion they propose in the text or the comprehensibility of the essay. Interestingly enough, one teacher stated, "Sometimes I think a student just wants to use a word or grammatical structure at any cost, and, to do so, they even change their opinion to put the word in the text."

Teachers' Views About the Challenges of English Writing Instruction in Iran

In addition to their views about students' expectations, teachers mentioned that the differences between mainstream second language writing instruction and national high-stakes tests have made teaching English writing challenging in some ways. A majority of the teachers (84%) stated that they cannot comply with a pure process-oriented approach to writing instruction; they are forced, instead, to employ traditional product-based instruction by giving students templates and tricks to get an acceptable score. The reasons for their decision are twofold. First, they believe that the students are not familiar with the writing process because, as one teacher stated, "they've never been taught, neither in school nor in university, how to plan for writing." Similarly, some teachers acknowledged that a good share of students have problems in brainstorming and arguing over an issue. Actually, another teacher criticized the educational system, saying that "the students are not educated to think critically and creatively in school." Blaming the assessment system, still another teacher added, "They are, unfortunately, used to rote-learning and memorization rather than analysis and I think it is mainly because of Konkour."

The cultural background and first language practices, which some teachers emphasized, made writing instruction really demanding. For example, one teacher believed that "the students usually talk *around* the topic (not *on* the topic) which leads to the inclusion of irrelevant topics." In the same way, the teachers noted that the students usually need a great deal of instruction to be explicit and focused because, in their view, in the Iranian culture "we tend to be indirect in stating our opinions."

The very fact that the students do not have enough time, or are reluctant to spend much time to learn writing from scratch, is the second reason why the instructors opt for product-oriented approaches to teaching writing. "What can we do for a student who has never written a text longer than 20 words and is preparing for a test within two months?" one teacher inquired. Similarly, another teacher also remarked,

> Students come to us very late. It is very rare that a student comes to us a year or even six months prior to the exam. Most of them get shocked when they find out how much time and work is required to do the test.

All in all, most teachers unanimously agreed that employing a process approach in their instruction involves greater effort than providing students with a set of writing templates, grammatical structures, and phrases to be memorized. They all admitted that they sometimes provide writing templates so that their students can easily copy them in the writing exam. When the students are not proficient or motivated enough, or do not have enough time to learn the process of writing, these teachers claim, the only solution left is to provide them with prefabricated writing chunks and templates.

In the same vein, most teachers are unwilling to spend their after-class time to review student writing because, as one of the teachers mentions, "they are not well-paid and . . . are under a heavy work load." Therefore, teachers admitted that in most university/school classes, if they have time to assign a writing task to the students, they will not have enough time, realistically speaking, to provide feedback on their students' writing. Some teachers, however, were willing to spend some of their after-class time to provide feedback on student writing.

Discussion

Our examination of the Iranian high-stakes tests indicated a mismatch between such tests and international tests like the TOEFL and the IELTS. Mainly, the Iranian tests do not acknowledge writing as a skill that can be directly assessed via students' performance. Instead, they include multiple-choice tests of vocabulary, grammar and sentence structure, and error recognition as factors contributing to writing. In this situation, Iranian students might find writing English articles or preparing for international examinations such a daunting task. As the official Iranian EFL curriculum strives for receptive rather than productive skills, students would find it demanding to switch from "knowing" to "performing." Indeed, such a transition necessitates a great deal of practice accompanied by quality education, which is neither cheap nor instantly available.

Writing instruction in Iran has gone largely unnoticed; public schools, private institutes, and universities have discarded teaching writing in their proposed syllabi. The mainstream official EFL instruction in Iran, as previously introduced, has traditionally emphasized translation, reading comprehension, and mastery of vocabulary and grammar. As a remedial reaction against the lack of practice on oral communicative skills in the curricula of schools and universities, private language schools have chosen to emphasize the spoken language (Naghdipour, 2016). Thus, writing instruction has been neglected by both public and private mainstream EFL instruction.

Similar problems exist with regard to writing assessment. The differences between curricular priorities of public schools/universities and private institutions, plus the differences between the nature of national and international English tests, have created a twofold gap for Iranian students. The first gap is between the common practices of local and international assessment. In national high-stakes tests, writing is reflected as a controlled, decontextualized subskill with no real-world manifestation, as the findings of the current study suggest. The only Iranian test that directly assesses writing, as noted, is the TOLIMO, which resembles an older version of the TOEFL and the TWE in that it combines multiple-choice tests with performance assessment. However, since universities do not endorse the writing score of this test, which is reported separately, candidates and instructors do not invest in practicing writing. Instead, both candidates and instructors prefer to work on memorizing grammar rules and long lists of vocabulary to achieve a higher score on the tests. When it comes to preparing for international exams, on the other hand, students have to practice performance writing and be able to write an essay in a limited time. This entails learning the micro and macroskills that have been discarded throughout their educational life from their EFL curriculum.

The substantial differences between the objectives of international tests and the real-life needs of Iranian students combine to form the second gap. While international tests such as the TOEFL and the IELTS have been modified since their early days to respond to the theoretical and practical needs of the twenty-first century, timed impromptu writing tests, such as the writing sections of the IELTS and the TOEFL, are under ever-increasing critiques from theorists in the field (e.g., Crusan, 2010; Huot, 2002; Hyland, 2009; Weigle, 2002; Weir, 2005) who have repeatedly warned against the inadequacies and limitations of such tests.

While this gap is not exclusive to Iranian students, its challenges can be intensified for Iranian students due to the problems created by the first gap. In other words, Iranian students should first prepare themselves to tackle the new requirements as they move from national to international tests and thence to real-life requirements. Given the current situation, even when the students get acceptable scores in their writing tests, they may still face problems in their future real-life writing tasks due to the impact of the first gap and the inadequacy of the high-stakes tests to assess students' real-life writing abilities.

The analysis of the interviews suggests that these two gaps have produced drastic negative washback greatly affecting educational micro policies, in general, and students' lives and teachers' practice, in particular. In this regard, one of the negative consequences is narrowing down the focus of instruction from writing skills to test-taking strategies, which, in some cases, are absolutely unrelated to real-life writing tasks. As an example, the interview data analysis suggested that macro and microskills like critical thinking, planning, receiving feedback, and reviewing are almost ignored in writing programs.

Most exam instructors, as revealed in this study, employ a product-based approach and a self-tailored curriculum to prepare students to get a higher score on the test, irrespective of the real-life needs of the students. In addition, many test-takers memorize some writing templates prepared by their instructors and use them in their exam essay. Writing these templates from memory, students should then tailor the text with words and ideas related to the writing prompt. This is reminiscent of the findings of Pennycook's (1996) study, conducted in the context of China. He reports that, to his chagrin, the students were encouraged to practice writing on numerous topics expected to appear in the test, or memorize texts produced by eminent scholars, and use them in their own texts when relevant. This tendency for memorization, in Iran, can be traced back to the negative effects of high school examinations, which Damankesh and Babaii (2015, p. 66) contend negatively influence learners by "directing them toward a measurement driven (learn-to-the-test) approach to learning." They further report rote memorization, practicing grammar exercises, working on previous test papers, and reviewing teachers' notes among some other habits of high school students.

In addition to such deep-rooted problems, most students usually lack enough time or motivation to learn writing skills. And for those who are willing, quality public education is not commonly accessible, and private education is usually costly. In this condition, "teaching to the test" has become the quickest and the most effective method for test-takers and instructors. That said, as Wiggins (1993) maintains, teaching to the test happens only when the tests do not match a proper theory of writing.

Referring back to the twofold gap discussed earlier, it seems that the mismatch between theory and practice of writing is even more significant in the context of Iran and has led to pedagogical problems as well as socioeconomic deficiencies. The socioeconomic consequences of these gaps are evident when test fees and test preparation costs are compared. Based on official reports, while the average test fees in 2017 for the IELTS, the TOEFL, and the GRE are around $210 (British Council, 2017; Educational Testing Service, 2017), the fees for national high-stakes tests like the TOLIMO and the MSRT are always less than $20 (Iran's National Organization of Educational Testing, 2017). This substantial difference becomes more significant considering the average monthly salary of an Iranian family, reported to be around $500 in 2014, based on the currency exchange rate in the same year (Statistical Center of Iran, 2017). Added to registration fees, there are still charges related to test preparation programs, mainly held by private institutes, and these usually cost more than the test fee. Test fees and test preparation costs, irrespective of the time interval the examinee has to wait to sit the test again, make such high-stakes tests even more "high-stakes" when the chances to retry the test are not high for most students and one failure to achieve the desired score can hold the examinee back from their goals. Therefore, in developing countries, as Nunan (2003) states, "a key question is the extent to which access to English is a mechanism for determining who has access to economic advancement and who does not" (p. 611).

Similarly, as interviews indicated, many test-takers do not have enough time to be prepared for international tests because they usually have incorrect assumptions about the required time for their preparation, overestimate their English proficiency, or are under external forces to get the required score as quickly as possible. Such external forces may include changes in admission requirements of universities and immigration policies.[3]

While the socioeconomic problems and preparation time limitations apply to all four basic skills involved in the tests (i.e., reading, listening, speaking, and writing), the problem is more severe for the writing skill. Due to the multiple-choice nature of the items in reading and listening sections, access to instant feedback on performance to improve test scores is easily available. However, receiving feedback on writing, and speaking, necessitates a skilled teacher who is aware of the rating criteria. Our survey showed that most students are not cognizant of the rating criteria, so they fail to judge their own performance autonomously.

Having discussed the socioeconomic challenges of international high-stakes tests of writing, it can be stated that the students' and teachers' inclination toward teaching to the test seems justifiable. The twofold gap existing between mainstream instruction and assessment of writing in Iranian and international high-stakes tests would make students vulnerable in acting as independent individuals in their future academic needs.

Conclusion and Future Directions

While the current trend warns us against future problems, taking immediate actions to bridge, or at least minimize, the current gaps are deemed urgent. At the national level, it seems necessary for policy makers to revisit educational policies, as Riazi (2005) proposes, to respond to students' needs for learning English in a communicative way. Initially, performance writing should be incorporated into Iranian official EFL curricula by considering the real needs of current and future generations of students. This way, students would become familiar with the basic steps of process writing earlier in schools and universities. This, in turn, will help less privileged students to be more prepared for their future challenges by giving them access to free education.

Also, due to its decisive effect on teaching, the current practice of assessing English writing, as well as other skills, needs to be thoroughly revised. Assessing writing in Iran is bound to practical and financial restrictions; multiple-choice testing is traditionally considered as a cost-effective and reliable method of assessment, quick to administer and easy to score. Additionally, due to the government's investment in preparing books, training teachers, and implementing tests, a strong will on the policy makers' side is vital to prepare for a major shift. To revolutionize the current practice, decision-makers should first acknowledge the existing gaps and their harmful consequences on the education system, and next attempt to implement the required changes. If this happens, policy makers should also be ready to face the upcoming challenges to implementing such modifications. Large classes in which teaching and assessing writing with a process-based syllabus is tough, inadequate teacher preparation, resistant teachers and students' negative attitudes (Casanave, 2009), rater training, and the differences between English native and Iranian raters (Marefat & Heydari, 2016) are but some of the hurdles to be tackled. Teacher training should be developed to improve teachers' agency and enable them to act as agents of change in the field of writing instruction. Given proper education and agency, in EFL contexts Iran teachers can offer innovative alternatives and suggest modifications based on local necessities (Ruecker, Shapiro, Johnson, & Tardy, 2014).

A solution to fill the existing gaps is to establish writing centers to overcome the problem of populated classes in schools and universities, where promoting process-based writing is next to impossible. While numerous writing centers now exist in universities over the world, to date, no writing center has been initiated in Iran (Marefat et al., 2015). Writing centers can be of great help by tutoring students, providing resources, directing events, and developing alternative education (e.g., computer-assisted instruction, online tutorials, and online instructions).

Finally, at the international level, major educational testing organizations are recommended to look for more effective ways to provide affordable and quality services for less affluent countries and students, to minimize the insecurity related to the costs of high-stakes tests and, therefore, encourage test-takers to engage in sustained learning. Moreover, such organizations may consider providing additional free tools and services for test-takers worldwide to promote better writing skills.

Notes

1 TOLIMO: The Test of Language by the Iranian Measurement Organization; MSRT: Ministry of Science, Research and Technology; EPT: English Proficiency Test; and MHLE: Ministry of Health Language Exam.
2 To discourage applicants from guessing, with 4-choice items, the total raw score is obtained by subtracting one-third of the number of wrong responses from the number of correct responses divided by the total number of items. Thus, choosing all the wrong options will result in -33.

3 At the moment of conducting the interviews (late 2016), it was not clear who would win the upcoming U.S. presidential election, and some interviewees worried about the future president of the U.S. and immigration policies. Later on, such concerns proved viable after Trump's Immigration Ban executive order, which prohibited entry to the USA from seven countries, including Iran.

References

Behizadeh, N., & Engelhard, G. (2011). Historical view of the influences of measurement and writing theories on the practice of writing assessment in the United States. *Assessing Writing*, *16*, 189–211. https://doi.org/10.1016/j.asw.2011.03.001

Borjian, M. (2013). *English in post-revolutionary Iran: From indigenization to internationalization*. Bristol: Multilingual Matters.

British Council. (2017). Retrieved from www.britishcouncil.gr/en/exam/ielts/dates-costs-locations

Casanave, C. (2009). Training for writing or training for reality? Challenges facing EFL writing teachers and students in language teacher education programs. In R. Manchón (Ed.), *Writing in foreign language contexts: Learning, teaching, and research* (pp. 256–277). Buffalo, NY: Multilingual Matters.

Crusan, D. (2010). *Assessment in the second language writing classroom*. Ann Arbor: University of Michigan Press. https://doi.org/10.3998/mpub.770334

Damankesh, M., & Babaii, E. (2015). The washback effect of Iranian high school final examinations on students' test-taking and test-preparation strategies. *Studies in Educational Evaluation*, *45*, 62–69. https://doi.org/10.1016/j.stueduc.2015.03.009

Educational Testing Service. (2017). Retrieved from www.britishcouncil.gr/en/exam/ielts/dates-costs-locations

Gillham, B. (2005). *Research interviewing: The range of techniques*. Maidenhead: Open University Press/McGraw-Hill Education.

Hamp-Lyons, L. (1990). Second language writing: Assessment issues. In B. Kroll (Ed.), *Second language writing: Research insights for the classroom* (pp. 69–87). New York: Cambridge University Press. https://doi.org/10.1017/CBO9781139524551.009

Huot, B. (2002). *(Re) Articulating writing assessment for teaching and learning*. Logan, UT: Utah State University Press. https://doi.org/10.2307/j.ctt46nx5z.6

Hyland, K. (2009). *Teaching and researching writing* (2nd ed.). London: Longman. https://doi.org/10.4324/9781315833729

Iran's Ministry of Science, Research and Technology. (2017). Retrieved from www.msrt.ir/

Iran's National Organization of Educational Testing. (2017). Retrieved from tolimo.sanjesh.org

Kroll, B. (1990). *Second language writing: Research insights for the classroom*. New York: Cambridge University Press. https://doi.org/10.1017/CBO9781139524551

Marefat, F., & Heydari, M. (2016). Native and Iranian teachers' perceptions and evaluation of Iranian students' English essays. *Assessing Writing*, *27*, 24–36. https://doi.org/10.1016/j.asw.2015.10.001

Marefat, F., Heydari, M., Qarachollo, M., Vaezi, M., Panahzadeh, V., Moladoust, E., & Mahdavi, M. (2015). *A review on the importance of writing centers: A global trend and a local necessity in Iranian context*. Paper presented in the 3rd ELT Conference: Novel Trends and Perspectives. October 21, at Allameh Tabataba'I University, Tehran, Iran.

Naghdipour, B. (2016). English writing instruction in Iran: Implications for second language writing curriculum and pedagogy. *Journal of Second Language Writing, 32*, 81–87. https://doi.org/10.1016/j.jslw.2016.05.001

Nunan, D. (2003). The impact of English as a global language on educational policies and practices in the Asia-Pacific region. *TESOL Quarterly, 37*(4), 589–613. https://doi.org/10.2307/3588214

Pennycook, A. (1996). Borrowing others' words: Text, ownership, memory and plagiarism. *TESOL Quarterly, 30*(2), 201–230. https://doi.org/10.2307/3588141

Riazi, A. (2005). The four language stages in the history of Iran. In A. Lin & P. Martin (Eds.), *Decolonization, globalisation: Language-in-education policy and practice* (pp. 98–115). Clevendon: Multilingual Matters.

Ruecker, T., Shapiro, S., Johnson, E. N., & Tardy, C. M. (2014). Exploring the linguistic and institutional contexts of writing instruction in TESOL. *TESOL Quarterly, 48*(2), 401–412. https://doi.org/10.1002/tesq.165

SCImago Journal & Country Rank. (2017). Retrieved from www.scimagojr.com/countryrank.php

Statistical Center of Iran. (2017). Retrieved from www.amar.org.ir/english/Statistics-by-Topic/Population

Weigle, S. C. (2002). *Assessing writing.* Cambridge: Cambridge University Press. https://doi.org/10.1017/CBO9780511732997

Weir, C. J. (2005). *Language testing and validation: An evidence-based approach.* New York: Palgrave MacMillan. https://doi.org/10.1057/9780230514577

Wiggins, G. (1993). Assessment: Authenticity, context, and validity. *Phi Delta Kappan, 75*(3), 200–214.

Yancey, K. B. (1999). Looking back as we look forward: Historicizing writing assessment. *College Composition and Communication, 50*(3), 483–503. https://doi.org/10.2307/358862

PART II

High-Stakes Assessment

8

HIGH-STAKES ENGLISH WRITING ASSESSMENT IN EGYPTIAN SECONDARY SCHOOLS

Historical Testing Orientations and Current Instructional Practices

Muhammad M. Abdel Latif and Abdelbaset Haridy

Egypt (in Arabic *Misr*) has one of the longest histories of any country in the modern world. It is a country that been continuously inhabited since the tenth millennium BC. Foreign language learning in Egypt dates back to many centuries due to its long history (see Wheeler, 2013). Of all the foreign languages currently taught in Egypt, English is the main one, and it has been officially taught in Egyptian schools for about 150 years (Abdel Latif, 2017; Haridy, 2012).

The place of English in Egyptian schools has been influenced by the political and social changes Egypt witnessed. Likewise, the English curricula taught in these schools have undergone some changes and reforms (see Abdel Latif, 2017; Haridy, 2012). Among the most remarkable and frequent changes were the ones introduced by the Egyptian Ministry of Education (MOE) into the general secondary (high) school English curricula. Since the early 1970s, the Ministry has made some curricular reforms in general secondary school English. Several factors accounted for these curricular reforms, including bringing about a methodological or cultural change in the curriculum and adopting a specific educational orientation.

Working towards these goals, the Egyptian MOE has given much attention to the general secondary school examination system, known in Egypt as *Thanaweya Amma*. At the final year of this educational stage, students sit for comprehensive exams of the core subjects—one of which is English—and their scores on these exams are used as indicators for university major admission. According to Hargreaves (2001), since the results of *Thanaweya Amma* exams are used as the basis of the selection for higher education and employment, they are the driving force behind secondary schools in Egypt, and thus Egyptian secondary school students' over-dependence on private tutoring stems from the enormous importance placed on their exam results.

Due to such importance, the General Secondary Education Certificate (GSEC) has a centralized examination system: all third-year students in the country take the same exam version of each core subject. With regard to the GSEC English exam, the MOE assigns an expert teacher to write it, following particular guidelines developed and updated annually by its examination committees. The writing part of the GSEC English exam is no exception. In other words, its structure and questions are to be consistent with the guidelines set by the MOE. Meanwhile, the guidelines of the GSEC English exam are developed in light of some determinants such as subject examination policy and curricular changes.

The question yet to be answered is: How have consecutive curricular reforms of Egyptian secondary school English influenced the high-stakes assessment and instructional practices of writing? Previous related evaluative reports were of a general nature because they focused on reviewing the changes made to English curricula in Egyptian schools and/or the English education policy in Egypt (e.g., Abdel Latif, 2017; Abouelhassan & Meyer, 2016; Haridy, 2012), or describing the status quo of English language teaching and learning in the country (e.g., McIlwraith & Fortune, 2016). Moreover, the scarce empirical studies on Egyptian secondary school EFL teachers' general classroom practices and beliefs (e.g., Abdel Latif, 2012) did not focus specifically on their writing instruction. Therefore, the study reported in the present chapter tried to answer the above question by tracing the developments of high-stakes writing assessment in Egyptian secondary schools and exploring teachers' writing instructional practices. Before presenting the study, the authors provide a description of the place of English writing in Egyptian secondary school curricula in the next section.

The Place of English Writing in Egyptian Secondary School Curricula: A Brief Historical Overview

To understand the historical place of English writing in Egyptian secondary school curricula, we need to shed light on the last four textbook series taught to students and their language teaching methodological perspectives. The four English textbook series taught to secondary school students in Egypt since the early 1970s are: *Practice and Progress* (Alexandar, 1967), *Excel in English* (Alexandar, 1986), *Hello!* (the first series) (Haines & Dallas, 1999), and *Hello!* (the second series) (Haines & Dallas, 2008). Regarding the English language teaching methodology adopted in each textbook series, both *Practice and Progress* and *Excel in English* mainly utilized the audiolingual method, but the former used a weak version of the method whereas the latter adopted a strong version of it. Likewise, the first series of *Hello!* used a weak version of the communicative language teaching approach while its subsequent series depended on a strong version.

In his (2012) study, Haridy provided a description of the English writing materials and activities included in three of these textbook series. According to him, the writing activities given in *Practice and Progress* include: practice writing simple, compound, and complex sentences; practice connecting ideas from the notes given; comprehension and précis (i.e., summary writing); short paragraphs writing; and letter writing. The *Excel in English* textbook series, by contrast, has some controlled writing activities given in the second lesson of each unit (Grammar Study and Practice). At the end of such lessons, there is a writing activity that normally provides students with some sentences and asks them to practice re-writing or joining them using the target grammatical rule. Additionally, a wide range of writing activities is given in the last page of each unit (Writing and Reading), which includes one or more of these activities: guided summary writing, dictation, guided composition, and letter writing. The writing sections in the two textbook series (*Practice and Progress* and *Excel in English*) do not include any process writing activities (e.g., brainstorming or group/pair feedback), and therefore they depend mainly on the product approach to teaching writing.

A much wider range of writing tasks is given in the two *Hello!* series, and many of these activities are dependent upon the process approach to teaching writing (indicated by textbook suggestions for sharing one's writing or discussing it with peers). Two main reasons account for this change in writing activities: (1) the two textbook series are of a communicative nature and respond to everyday communicative writing needs—especially those dictated by the communication revolution; and (2) they were designed for higher proficiency level students who received primary school English instruction, unlike their peers who previously studied *Practice and Progress* and *Excel in English*. The wider range of writing tasks can be easily noted in the second *Hello!* series currently taught to Egyptian secondary school students. In the Year 1 textbook, students practice writing short biographies, letters, two-paragraph narrative, descriptive and argumentative genres, information for a poster, and job descriptions and applications. In the Year 2 textbook, they practice writing short reports, narratives, reports based on surveys, descriptions of rules, short book reviews, poster text, formal and informal emails, and formal business letters. Finally, Year 3 students practice writing persuasive texts and letters, summaries, short factual reports and articles, instructions, and emails.

As noted, there has been a varied difference in the writing tasks included in the two English textbook types taught in the last four decades to Egyptian secondary school students: those based on the audiolingual method (*Practice and Progress* and *Excel in English*) versus the communicative ones (the two *Hello!* series). An issue not tackled yet by previous studies is how such changes have influenced writing assessment in the GSEC English exam, on the one hand, and teachers' instructional practices of writing, on the other. Though Abdel Latif (2012) examined how the latest communicative curricular reform has influenced

Egyptian secondary EFL teachers' classroom practices, his study mainly dealt with teachers' instructional time and effort allocated to the different language areas and did not focus specifically on writing assessment and instruction. Addressing this gap, the study reported in this chapter tries to provide a much more detailed account of how writing has been assessed in such a high-stakes examination system, and the impact of such assessment practices on writing instruction.

The Present Study: Research Questions, Data Sources, and Procedures

As implied above, the present study attempts to answer the following two research questions related to writing assessment in the GSEC English exam in Egypt:

1. To what extent has writing assessment been developed in the GSEC English exams since 1980?
2. How do teachers in their English writing instruction respond to the current GSEC English exam and the latest above-mentioned curricular reform?

To answer the two questions, the study depended on the following two data sources:

1. **A corpus of GSEC exams:** The corpus analyzed by the authors is composed of the GSEC exams taken by Egyptian students between 1980 and 2016. The authors were able to access this corpus through Internet searches. The exams included in the corpus are based on the tasks and activities given in the four textbook series (i.e., *Practice and Progress*, *Excel in English*, and the first and second *Hello!* series). All these were GSEC first round or session English exams taken by third year graders. In addition, all the exams are paper-delivered rather than computer-assisted.
2. **Teacher open-ended questionnaire:** This questionnaire was used to explore how Egyptian EFL teachers' writing instructional practices respond to both the latest textbook series used (i.e., the second *Hello!* series) and the GSEC English exams. The authors chose to use the questionnaire as a data source in order to access a larger number of participants. The questionnaire was developed in light of the purpose of the study. The authors developed two drafts of the questionnaire, and the final draft includes a total of nine open-ended questions that focused on asking teachers about: (1) the way they teach writing to students and the areas focused on in their writing instruction, (2) their own opinions on the writing activities and tasks given in the textbook and on the writing tasks students have to complete in high-stakes exams, and (3) their suggestions for developing the textbook writing activities and assessment in the English exams (see the questionnaire questions in Appendix 8.1). The questionnaire was sent by email to a group of

EFL teachers instructing third year secondary school graders in two school districts: Cairo and Sohag (Upper Egypt). Forty-one teachers working in nine schools returned their completed questionnaires: 23 from Cairo and 18 from Sohag.

The data analysis process was undertaken in two stages. First, the main features of writing tasks in the 37 GSEC English exams taken between 1980 and 2016 were analyzed. The two authors worked collaboratively on analyzing the 37 GSEC exams by focusing on identifying the word count required, the structure of writing tasks (i.e., task type and prompt format), and the number of tasks. Second, the respondents' answers to the questionnaire open-ended questions were analyzed using the grounded-theory approach. The authors co-worked on identifying emerging themes in the participants' responses so as to profile their English writing instructional practices and beliefs and what may influence them. They first identified the emerging themes independently, and then collaboratively reached a set of common themes in their questionnaire data analyses.

Results

The results of the data analysis are presented below in accordance with the two research questions.

The Changing Orientations in Assessing Writing in the GSEC English Exams

As mentioned above, the analysis of the 37 GSEC exams was concerned with three issues: the word count required, the structure of writing tasks, and the number of tasks. All these issues were compared across the GSEC English exams in light of the textbook series used in each period. It is noteworthy that each of the last three textbook series was introduced to Year 3 students two academic years later than the dates given above.

With regard to the word count needed and the structure of the tasks, this analysis shows that these two aspects do not vary much in the 37 GSEC exams collected; the difference was in the number of tasks included and the prompt format. As is evident in Table 8.1, the word count required is almost the same in the writing tasks across the 37 GSEC exams. The writing task instructions in all these exams differ only in their wording; indeed, there is no difference among the exams used in the four periods in terms of the word count needed, as ten sentences or lines (or even the two paragraphs of five sentences each) are expected to be of 100 words.

Another case of similarity is also noted in the writing task type used in the four periods. The exams taken in the four periods focused mainly on paragraph

TABLE 8.1 A Comparison of the Writing Task Aspects in the 37 GSEC English Exams Developed Based on the Four Textbook Series

Textbook & exam dates	Word count	Task type	Task number	Prompt format
Practice and Progress 1980–1988 (n = 9)	• no less than ten lines • about ten lines • ten sentences	Paragraph writing (eight exams) Letter writing (one exam)	Two obligatory tasks	Guided Non-guided (n = 1) Expository paragraphs Only one narrative
Excel in English 1989–2001 (n = 13)	• no less than ten lines	Paragraph writing (11 exams) Replying to a letter (two exams)	Two optional tasks (Write . . . on ONE ONLY of the following)	Non-guided Expository paragraphs Only one narrative
Hello! (first series) 2002–2010 (n = 9)	• two paragraphs of five sentences each	Paragraph writing	Obligatory task	Guided Expository paragraphs
Hello! (second series) 2011–2016 (n = 6)	• about 100 words	Paragraph writing	Obligatory task	Non-guided Expository paragraphs

writing. In fact, while limiting the task type to paragraph writing generally matches the writing task types in both the *Practice and Progress* and *Excel in English* textbooks, it contradicts the variety of the writing tasks given in the two *Hello!* series (particularly the second one and its currently used Year 3 textbook). Noted also is the variance in the number of the writing tasks given in the exams of the four periods. In the *Practice and Progress* period, students were to perform two obligatory tasks, but in the *Excel in English* era they were given two optional tasks. With the two *Hello!* series, students were asked to perform one task: paragraph writing.

The information given in Table 8.1 about the word count needed, task type, and the number of tasks in the 37 GSEC exams used in the four periods can be further illustrated by the following sample writing tasks:

Practice and Progress **Period**

> **1982:** *Write a paragraph of 10 sentences at least on:*
> a) The best friend one can have is a book.
> b) Going camping.

1987: *Write a paragraph of 10 sentences at least on:*
   a) The ideal family.
   b) Introducing technology into the system of education and into schools helps in promoting students' creativity.

Excel in English Period

1989: *Write a paragraph of no less than 10 lines on ONE ONLY of the following:*
   a) The number of tourists in Egypt has been growing in recent years. Tell how Egypt could be a big center for tourism.
   b) The recent changes that have taken place in Egypt.

First *Hello!* Period

2010: *Write two paragraphs of five sentences each about:*

Why is physical activity important for you?
   • types of physical activity—where you can practice it
   • health improvement—psychological effects
   • modern lifestyles

Second *Hello!* Period

2015: *Write a paragraph of about 100 words on:*
   • Has reading become an old-fashioned habit?

With regard to the task prompt format, all the writing tasks given to students in the *Practice and Progress* and *Excel in English* exams were non-guided, with the exception of those in the 1980 and 1993 exams. Below is the 1980 guided task:

Discomforts of living in a big city.
You can make use of the following points:

   • too much noise
   • crowded streets
   • traffic jam
   • pollution

As noted in the above task prompt, students are guided to include some ideas in the paragraph to be written. On the other hand, the second *Hello!* period exams do not include any guided prompt, whereas all the first *Hello!* period tasks are guided ones. Specifically, students were provided with some clues for ideas to write about the target topic in all the 2002–2010 exams. Due to the continuous inclusion of these guiding points, it can be argued that the writing tasks included in the first *Hello!* period exams are the easiest compared to those given in the other three periods. Noted also is the relatively increasing focus on addressing local issues in writing tasks. This can be explained by the following two exemplary task prompts:

2002: *Write two paragraphs of five sentences each about:*

The advantages of buying local products labeled "Made in Egypt."
Guiding points:

- Great variety
- Egyptian taste
- Cheaper prices
- Help local industries
- Work opportunities
- National income

2007: *Write two paragraphs of five sentences each about:*

Social work is a means through which Egyptian youth can help the society. You may use the following words and phrases:

- share
- neighborhood
- educate the illiterate
- job opportunity
- better life
- care for orphans
- bring happiness

A final issue that is worth highlighting about the format of the prompt is the type of the paragraphs students were asked to write about in the four-period GSEC exams. It was found that the paragraph tasks in both *Hello!* series exams are all of the expository type. For example:

2004: The continuous rise in prices has become a national problem for most Egyptian families.
2005: Computers in society.
2009: How has the Internet affected our lives?
2011: How to share in the progress of our country.
2012: Do today's young people show enough respect towards older people?
2014: The different ways people can keep fit and avoid diseases.
2016: Different ways to help the poor.

Similar to the paragraph prompts included in the *Hello!* series exams, those given in the *Practice and Progress* and *Excel in English* exams were expository, with the exception of three exams, which asked students to write narrative paragraphs:

> **1983:** Recently, you attended a party which you enjoyed very much. Describe the people you met, what you did there, when and how you went home.
>
> **1998:** You have just come back from a school trip. Write a paragraph how you spend time there. A story beginning with: "Last month, on my way home, I saw . . . ."
>
> **2000:** You have just come back from a school trip. Write a paragraph how you spent time there.

Accordingly, it can be concluded that expository paragraph prompts have been the main prompts used in the 37 GSEC exams with the exception of very rare cases in the *Practice and Progress* and *Excel in English* periods.

Some conclusions can be drawn from the above analysis and overview of the writing tasks given in the 37 GSEC English exams. First, hardly any concrete changes have been made in assessing students' writing performance in these high-stakes exams over a period of about 40 years. The nature and type of writing tasks as well as the level of task difficulty have almost remained unchanged. Second, the reforms made to the English curricula taught to those students have hardly influenced the process of assessing their writing in the GSEC exams. Third, the current GSEC examination system—with the writing tasks it has been using since 2011—does not mirror the variety of the tasks brought by the latest English curriculum reform with the more communicative-oriented *Hello!* series. Accordingly, we still need a concrete reform to assess students' writing in this context.

An important issue that has not been addressed by previous research is how Egyptian teachers in their English writing instruction respond to the current GSEC English exam and to the latest curricular reform. The authors expected that those teachers would be much more concerned with helping their students meet the GSEC exam writing assessment requirements, rather than trying to meet those of curricular reform via teaching all the writing task types in the currently used textbook. The authors drew this hypothesis from Abdel Latif's (2012) study, which found Egyptian secondary school EFL teachers allocate only 1.47% of their classroom instructional time to teaching writing. The data analysis in the next section will show whether this hypothesis has been confirmed or rejected.

Secondary School EFL Teachers' Writing Instructional Practices

Analyzing the teachers' responses to the questionnaire showed very important issues about their writing instruction practices and beliefs, and views on the GSEC exam writing tasks. While the Year 3 textbook includes many different types of writing tasks, the teachers' responses to the questionnaire indicate that they mainly conceptualize English writing instruction as solely limited to helping students compose paragraphs and letters/emails. The vast majority (92.6%) of the questionnaire respondents (n=38) reported that they focus primarily on teaching paragraph writing and peripherally on teaching email or letter writing. As can be noted in the following answers, the teachers justified such writing instructional practices by saying they focus only on the tasks students are tested in the GSEC English exam (i.e., washback):

- What matters more in the Communication Part in each textbook unit is paragraph writing. Students won't be very interested in doing any other writing activity in the class because they don't have a question on it in the final exam. So, what I do in this case is to teach them paragraph writing only.
- In my classes, I try to narrow or close the gap between the textbook writing activities and the final exam part of writing by focusing primarily on what they are tested in. I get students to write a paragraph related to each unit. I have to make my teaching of writing exam-focused.

Although Year 3 textbook writing activities are based on the process approach through which students are supposed to work in pairs or groups, the teachers' responses to the questionnaire indicate they rely on the product approach to teaching writing. Most of the teachers reported that in their writing instruction, they focus primarily on four aspects: grammatical accuracy, word choice, and correct spelling and punctuation. Below are examples from the teachers' answers to the question "What do you usually focus on when teaching writing to Year 3 students?":

- The basic steps and rules for writing, and using good grammar and sound spelling.
- Writing correct sentences and correcting spelling and punctuation.
- Forming correcting sentences, writing using correct tense, and improving spelling and punctuation.
- I always focus on grammar and punctuation. Grammar affects the meaning of the sentence, while punctuation helps readers understand what you want to say.

In their responses to the questionnaire, nine teachers said that they incorporate translation in their writing instruction. Not only does the inclusion of a translation part in the GSEC English exam contradict the communicative language teaching nature of the second *Hello!* series, but it seems to have also influenced classroom writing instruction practices. As the following answers show, those nine teachers depend on translation in teaching students how to form sentences, and they sometimes mix the instruction of writing with that of translation by focusing on word-for-word translation and topic-related words and phrases:

- I teach writing by explaining to students how to write English paragraph[s] and emails. I explain this to them using English and Arabic. I compare writing paragraphs in English and Arabic. With this way, I can help students come up with good ideas about the topic.
- The textbook doesn't include many paragraph writing activities. Contrarily, in the commercial textbook-related study materials, there is a vocabulary list at the beginning of each writing activity.

The teachers' responses also show that even when trying to use some of the process approach features, they do this superficially by using teacher-led oral discussion to help students find ideas about the target writing topic. Likewise, most of the teachers reported using oral corrective feedback as their main technique for assessing students' writing:

- When teaching a particular writing activity, I always ask my students to think of the ideas related to it, and discuss these ideas with them.
- I introduce the topic, and discuss it orally. This discussion helps in identifying some ideas on the topic. The next step is to get the students to write the topic, and to comment orally on their writing.

The teachers' answers to the questions about the textbook writing activities show they have varied opinions on them. While many teachers view these activities as interesting and good, other teachers reported their dissatisfaction with them. The teachers' main reported reason for such dissatisfaction is their irrelevance to the exam specifications:

- The writing question in the GSEC exam should be related to what I teach in the class. It does not cover the textbook writing activities.
- I suggest deleting the activities irrelevant to the exam from the textbook; this will make the writing activities more focused and students will pay more attention to them.

Despite their varied views on textbook writing activities, all the teachers agreed that much more time was needed for implementing them. All the teachers showed a general satisfaction with including paragraph writing tasks in the GSEC exams, but they criticized two issues: not allowing students to write on optional topics that could meet their varied interests and individual differences, and not using a clear rubric for marking students' writing (i.e., they depend on their overall impression instead). Finally, the teachers reported some suggestions for enriching textbook writing activities. Among these suggestions: allocating more time or complete classes for teaching writing, adding more real-life writing topics, and including more samples of written pieces of all genres. The last suggestion has been frequently found in the teachers' completed questionnaires (n=7), and this indicates they guide students to model sample paragraphs when preparing them for the final year exam. In fact, it is well-known that many secondary school students in Egypt depend on the commercial exam preparation materials to provide them with sample writing pieces unavailable in school textbooks.

Obviously, the nature of the writing task given annually in the GSEC English exam has greatly influenced teachers' practices. In their writing instruction, the teachers focus only on what their students are tested in. A washback effect is also clear in the teachers' reported dependence on the product approach to teaching writing and in their perceptions of the textbook writing activities. The implications of these findings are given in the next sections.

Implications and Recommendations

In this chapter, the authors reviewed the changing orientations of assessing writing in the GSEC English exam, and explored the extent to which teachers' writing instructional practices respond to its current format and to the latest English curricular reform. The description given about the place of English writing in Egyptian secondary school curricula shows that there has been a varied difference in the writing tasks included in the four English textbook series taught to Egypt secondary school students since the early 1970s. It was found, however, that these curricula reforms and the changes they brought in writing instruction activities were not accompanied by real and significant changes in assessing writing in the 37 GSEC English exams students sat for between 1980 and 2016. Thus, a clear contradiction can be easily noted, as the writing part in the currently used format of this exam does not mirror the varied writing activities and tasks brought by the latest curriculum reform. As for writing instructional practices, the study found a washback effect in which teachers do not consider the curriculum reform and prioritize tailoring their instruction to match students' writing assessment expectations. Specifically, the teachers reported limiting their instruction to paragraph and letter/email writing, depending mainly on the product approach to teaching writing, and—in some cases—resorting to using grammar-translation techniques in teaching these two written genres. Such results about teachers' reported writing instructional practices confirm the hypothesis given earlier. They also concur with Abdel Latif's (2012) study in emphasizing the little attention given to English writing instruction in Egyptian secondary school classes.

The above discussion clearly indicates a lack of curriculum alignment (Richards & Schmidt, 2010), where writing instruction and assessment do not reflect textbook activities. Such lack of curriculum alignment is a barrier to meeting the varied English writing needs of Egyptian secondary school graduates. Accordingly, the key solution to overcoming this curriculum alignment problem is to bring about a concrete change in the writing assessment policies of the GSEC English exam. As Menken (2008) stated, when assessment is used as a vehicle for driving instructional practices, teaching and testing become essentially synonymous.

Given this, the Egyptian MOE has to make a number of writing assessment policy reforms in the GSEC English examination system. It is of essential importance to bring about a concrete change in the range, structure, and types of the writing tasks included in the GSEC English exam; this will definitely result in changing teachers' instructional practices. Important also is changing the score weight of the writing part in the GSEC English exam. Currently, the writing part is given 12% of the total exam score (6 out of 50), and it is weighted less heavily than the other exam parts related to vocabulary, grammar, reading comprehension, and language functions. One way for increasing the score weight of the writing part is to delete the translation part and add its score to the writing one. This will concur with the communicative nature of the textbook used. Another important change that should later be made to the GSEC English exam as a whole is changing its format from paper-delivered to a computer-assisted. This will enrich the process of assessing writing in the target context, and will be also more relevant to students' everyday writing experiences, given that they communicate with each other using computer-mediated tools. The work of the GSEC examination committees in the MOE will definitely play a crucial role in making these desired reforms in writing assessment policies.

The study reported in this chapter was limited in focusing only on writing assessment in Egyptian public secondary schools. It is worth noting that 8% of students in Egypt attend private schools (ElMeshad, 2012) where they receive more intensive English instruction. Therefore, future researchers interested in this area may trace the features of writing assessment in these schools. Future studies may also deal with writing assessment in other educational stages in Egypt.

References

Abdel Latif, M. M. (2012). Teaching a standard-based communicative English textbook series to secondary school students in Egypt: Investigating teachers' practices and beliefs. *English Teaching: Practice and Critique, 11*(3), 78–97.

Abdel Latif, M. M. (2017). English education policy at the pre-university stages in Egypt: Past, present and future directions. In R. Kirkpatrick (Ed.), *English language policy in the Middle East and North Africa* (pp. 33–45). Berlin: Springer. http://dx.doi.org/10.1007/978-3-319-46778-8_3

Abouelhassan, R., & Meyer, L. (2016). Economy, modernity, Islam, and English in Egypt. *World Englishes*, *35*(1), 147–159. https://doi.org/10.1111/weng.12171

Alexandar, L. G. (1967). *New concept English: Practice and progress for secondary level.* London: Longman.

Alexandar, L. G. (1986). *Excel in English.* Cairo: The Egyptian International Publishing Company-Longman.

ElMeshad, S. (2012, October 5). Egypt's school system: Taking a look at schools, their curricula, and accreditation. *Egypt Independent Newspaper.* Retrieved from www.egypt-independent.com/news/egypt-s-school-system-taking-look-schools-their-curricula-and-accreditation

Haines, S., & Dallas, D. (1999). *Hello! English for secondary schools.* Cairo: The Egyptian International Publishing Company-Longman.

Haines, S., & Dallas, D. (2008). *Hello! English for secondary schools.* Cairo: The Egyptian International Publishing Company-Longman.

Haridy, A. S. (2012). *Investigating the developments of the methodologies used in English textbooks in the Egyptian public schools: A descriptive study.* MA thesis. Cairo University, Egypt.

Hargreaves, E. (2001). Assessment in Egypt. *Assessment in Education: Principles, Policy & Practice*, *8*(2), 247–260. https://doi.org/10.1080/09695940124261

McIlwraith, H., & Fortune, A. (2016). *English language teaching and learning in Egypt: An insight.* London: British Council.

Menken, K. (2008). *English learners left behind: Standardized testing as language policy.* Clevedon: Multilingual Matters Ltd. http://dx.doi.org/10.1080/13670050802499662

Richards, J. C., & Schmidt, R. (2010). *Longman dictionary of language teaching and applied linguistics* (4th ed.). London: Longman (Pearson Education). https://doi.org/10.1108/09504121111114171

Wheeler, G. (2013). *Language teaching through the ages.* New York: Routledge. https://doi.org/10.4324/9780203076453

APPENDIX 8.1

Teachers' Open-Ended Questionnaire

1. Could you please tell us about how you teach writing to Year 3 students?
2. What particular techniques(s) do you use when teaching them writing? And why?
3. Please list the activities you use when teaching them writing.
4. What do you usually focus on when teaching writing to Year 3 students? And why?
5. What is your opinion on the textbook writing activities? Please explain in detail.
6. What techniques/activities do you use in assessing your students' writing?
7. What is your opinion on the writing tasks used in Year 3 final exam? Please explain in detail.
8. Do you have any suggestions for developing the writing part in the Year 3 textbook? Please list these suggestions.
9. Do you have any suggestions for developing the writing part in the Year 3 final exam? Please list these suggestions.

9

VIGNETTE

Error Recognition: A So-Called "Writing" Assessment?

Pornpimol Sukavatee and Bee Chamcharatsri

In Thailand, English proficiency tests developed in the United States or the United Kingdom play an important role and are gatekeepers that *judge* the destinies of Thais in education and employment (Chamcharatsri, 2013). The most common tests used in Thailand are the TOEFL, IELTS, and TOEIC. All education institutions in Thailand use these proficiency test scores as one of the criteria (on top of students' GPAs, transcripts, or certifications) to accept students to academic programs. If the students do not have the minimum scores, their applications most likely will not be considered for acceptance to study at the institutions.

Because students' futures depend on these test scores, there has been a huge growth in for-profit tutoring schools. These businesses place ads everywhere, showing messages such as

> สถาบันกวดวิชายอดนิยมอันดับ 1 รับรองผลสอบ IELTS6.5+/ CU-TEP80+/ TOEIC700+ ทุกคอร์สสอนสด 100% โดยอาจารย์จากจุฬาฯ และต่าง ประเทศ พร้อม Computer Lab มาตรฐาน พิสูจน์แล้วโดยนักเรียนกว่า 10000 คนและองค์กรชั้นนำ

(One tutoring school ad in Thai)

> Our tutoring school is number 1 in popularity. We guarantee you scores of IELTS6.5+/ CU-TEP80+/ TOEIC700+. Every course is taught 100% live by Chulalongkorn University instructors and those who graduated from abroad. We also have a computer lab for our students. The course is guaranteed by over 10,000 satisfied students and leading organizations.

(Translation of the tutoring school ad)

This message is highly motivating to those who think they need help to achieve better scores on their English proficiency tests. Usually instructors who teach at these tutoring schools are either former test creators or experienced test takers. The instructors will provide exercise books that might reflect the format of those tests. Then students will be given time to do some exercises in the workbook. After that, the instructors will go over each question with strategies for eliminating incorrect answers or choosing the correct answer. In a way, students are taught strategies in how to take the test. These tutoring schools are widely available, since the cost of the tests is prohibitive. To take a TOEFL test, one must pay over 6000 Thai baht (or approximately $200) to take them. To put these costs into perspective, Bee used to work as a high school teacher, with a BA in English; he earned 8000 baht per month, which is the equivalent of $266. The average monthly income of Thai people in January 2017 was 13415.67 Thai Baht (Thailand average monthly wages, 2017), which is roughly $400 per month. It is clear, then, that the TOEFL test is very expensive for Thai students. Test takers who fail may have to repeat the test (and tutoring courses) several times to obtain a satisfactory score. This causes stress, disappointment, discouragement, and financial strain on many Thais.

Due to cost concerns, universities have developed affordable "in-house" English tests that typically cost around 900 Thai Baht (or approximately $30) to use as an alternative in assessing students' and teachers' English proficiency. The two popular standardized English tests in Thailand, CU-TEP or Chulalongkorn University Test of English Proficiency, which is designed by Chulalongkorn University (CU), and TU-GET or Thammasat University General English Test, which is designed by Thammasat University, are widely accepted in many institutions and organizations in Thailand.

Let us take a closer look at the CU-TEP, which claims to assess three language skills: Listening, Reading, and Writing. Given the focus of this collection, we will focus particularly on the Writing section of the CU-TEP. Test takers are asked to identify the error in this sentence:

Cats have a reputation <u>as</u> odd and mysterious animals. They manage <u>to appear</u> at the
　　　　　　　　　　　1　　　　　　　　　　　　　　　　　　　　　　　　　2
door when one comes home, <u>thus</u> they disappear when it is time to visit <u>the</u>
veterinarian.　　　　　　　　3　　　　　　　　　　　　　　　　　　　　　4

We once took this test and were happy because we did not have to cope with the stress of producing written essays in a limited time and were deemed proficient based on our scores. However, when we went into the real world and had to actually write reports or papers, we felt incompetent and confused because we never had sufficient practice writing in our classes or in preparing for the CU-TEP. When teachers filled our writing with questions and (grammatical) corrections in red ink, we questioned our own writing abilities because we had received high scores on the writing portion of the test. We quickly realized the limitations of the CU-TEP and other supposed tests of writing ability that rely on multiple-choice items. The CU-TEP overwhelmingly focuses on students' abilities to correct errors. Decades of research have told us that although grammar is important in the writing process, it should not be the sole focus in writing classrooms (Weigle, 2002). We are well aware that there are other features we need to consider besides grammar to be able to determine writing proficiency: audience, content, organization, voice, word choice, or mechanics. Despite this, the CU-TEP and the vast majority of in-house tests in Thailand continue to rely on this dated approach.

The CU-TEP is one of a number of high-stakes standardized tests that Thai academics rely on for different purposes, and institutions tend to accept these scores in lieu of internationally recognized TOEFL or IELTS tests. Some institutions use the test for placement, as they believe it indicates levels of English proficiency. CU uses the test results as the criteria for accepting eligible candidates to university programs at both undergraduate and graduate levels. Students are expected to score 79 or higher on the CU-TEP, a 75 or higher on the TOEFL, or a 6 or higher on the IELTS to enter the PhD in English as an international language program. At the undergraduate level, students who apply for an international program at the Faculty of Commerce and Accountancy, Faculty of Communication Arts, Faculty of Arts, or Faculty of Engineering need to show satisfactory CU-TEP test scores. Since one of the most popular assessment tools in Thailand is the multiple-choice test (Chamcharatsri, 2010), students in secondary school do not have many chances to compose essays or short writing assignments. Therefore, when these students come to university classes, it is possible that they are not familiar with academic writing tasks such as essay writing and report writing, or that they will not be able to respond to writing test tasks.

CU-TEP test scores are also required of applicants to indicate levels of English proficiency for all teaching and academic support positions at CU, as proof of English language proficiency for a prospective employer. Applicants for lecturer positions at the CU Language Institute need to have at least 79 on the TOEFL iBT, or 75 on the CU-TEP, or 6.5 on the IELTS. We question the validity of using the CU-TEP as a tool to select candidates with appropriate language proficiency to hire them for a job position.

Because Thai college students rarely write in classes, the test creators may feel that using an error recognition format is more appropriate to assess writing proficiency. However, we join others in affirming that a multiple choice error recognition test is not an appropriate tool (Bachman & Palmer, 2010; Weigle, 2002) to assess one's ability to engage in academic writing. Miller and Linn (2000) suggested that multiple-choice assessment can lead to narrower curriculum and teaching to the test. We concur with this statement since it reflects the situation in Thailand. Prospective test takers depend heavily on tutoring schools and take test preparation courses since the test content and patterns of questions do not vary much and are predictable. Moreover, it seems absurd that the Thailand education departments urge schools to implement Communicative Language Teaching (CLT) in language classrooms, but we use a multiple-choice format of assessment for students and teachers.

It is indeed time for the CU-TEP to reflect on and alter test specifications to serve real-world writing purposes and performance. Performance-based writing assessment is more appropriate and more complex in expressive language use than traditional skills or multiple-choice assessment. Furthermore, researchers have suggested that questions on grammar and syntax can only evaluate enabling skills or partial indicators of actual ability to write (Linn, Baker, & Dunbar as cited in Abedi, 2010). However, applying performance-based test tasks in large-scale assessment can have limitations, especially in terms of cost efficiency for scoring. To measure writing ability, we need robust rubrics with scoring bands and well-trained assessors (Crusan, 2010). This may make tests such as the CU-TEP more expensive to take; however, we do not see them approaching anywhere near the cost of international tests such as the TOEFL or IELTS tests.

Changing the format of the writing portion can be stressful to test takers because they may not have much practice. However, we believe that changing the CU-TEP can make a positive impact on the curriculum in school settings. Such a change will likely encourage high school English teachers to re-think their writing classes and assign more essays to their students. This may also mean that we have to re-think the curriculum in teacher education programs across Thailand. We may also need to integrate more writing assignments and/or the teaching of writing courses to our prospective English teachers in our programs. We have to change the myth that good grammar equals good writing to good writing contains meaningful content with fewer grammatical errors. We agree that this change may take time, but we think that CU-TEP should serve as a role model in creating this change and assume a leadership position in Thai English education.

References

Abedi, J. (2010). *Performance assessment for English language learners.* Stanford, CA: Stanford Center for Opportunity Policy in Education (SCOPE).

Bachman, L., & Palmer, A. (2010). *Language assessment in practice.* Oxford: Oxford University Press.

Chamcharatsri, P. B. (2010). On teaching writing in Thailand. *Writing on the Edge, 21*(1), 18–26.

Chamcharatsri, P. B. (2013). Perception of Thai English. *Journal of English as an International Language, 8*(1), 21–36.

Crusan, D. (2010). *Assessment in the second language writing classroom.* Ann Arbor: The University of Michigan Press.

Miller, M. D., & Linn, R. L. (2000). Validation of performance-based assessment. *Applied Psychological Measurement, 24*(4), 367–378. http://dx.doi.org/10.1177/0146621002 2031813

Thailand average monthly wages. (2017). Retrieved from https://tradingeconomics.com/ thailand/wages

Weigle, S. C. (2002). *Assessing writing.* Cambridge: Cambridge University Press.

10

"WRITE AN EMAIL TO YOUR FRIEND IN ENGLAND"

Assessment of the Written English Matura Exam in Poland

Aleksandra Swatek and Aleksandra Kasztalska

Little has been written about English as a foreign language (EFL) writing instruction at the secondary level in Poland (Reichelt, 2005, 2013; Siek-Piskozub, Wach, & Raulinajtys, 2008; Salski, 2016), despite the fact that there are 4.5 million EFL learners in Polish schools (Główny Urząd Statystyczny, 2016). In addition, there is a lack of peer-reviewed scholarship on the current state of foreign language writing assessment administered on a national scale in Poland. Even though EFL writing is one of the four language skills that is taught and assessed, it is the least liked by students and teachers, who find it "boring" (Salski, 2016, p. 212). Additionally, writing is not frequently taught in preparation for national exams (Lewkowicz & Zawadowska-Kittel, 2008; Reichelt, 2013). The most comprehensive and up-to-date discussion of EFL writing instruction and research in Poland was provided in Salski (2016), who found it paradoxical that a country with so many Literature Nobel Laureates does not research writing pedagogy. He attributed this in part to the belief, common among Poland's teachers, that explicit writing instruction is unnecessary because learners have the "ability to pick up writing skills by osmosis" (p. 208). This chapter is an attempt to fill the gap in scholarship by examining the sociopolitical dimensions of the EFL writing task on the Matura.

The Matura is a high school exit exam used for selecting candidates into Polish universities. It was overhauled a number of times to make national assessment more reliable and valid, as in other European countries (Eckes et al., 2005; Smolik, 2012). The latest revision, implemented in 2015, introduced a more communicative approach. However, our analysis suggests that despite substantial improvements, the writing tasks on the EFL Matura still emphasize local concerns, such as a focus on form and correctness, instead of a more global approach that values communicativeness, critical thinking, or creativity. In this way, our discussion expands on Salski's (2016) observation that not only writing instruction but also assessment is still heavily influenced by the product approach.

In this chapter, we overview and critically analyze Matura prompts, scoring rubrics, test scores, and other materials available to students and raters. As our analysis of recent scores suggests, there is great variability in how writing is taught in Poland (Salski, 2016), which leads to disparities between rural and urban examinee scores. That is, students from rural areas tend to score lower than students from urban areas on the English writing task. In light of these findings, we interpret the low pass score (30%) as an attempt to reduce the impact of differences in English teaching quality across socioeconomic backgrounds. In our interpretation, we draw on the concept of usefulness—specifically, *authenticity* and *impact*—in language testing, as presented by two language assessment scholars, Bachman and Palmer (1996). We link these concepts to critical approaches to language education as discussed by Kachru (1985), Phillipson (1992), and Jenkins (2014) to add a sociopolitical dimension to the choices made by the test designers. In particular, our analysis reveals a native speaker bias in the exam as well as in the *Common European Framework of Reference*, which informs the EFL Matura.

The Matura Exam

The current version of the Matura is based on guidelines established in 1999, the year in which the Polish education system underwent the most substantial reform yet. The reform centralized national assessment by establishing the Central Examination Board (henceforth CKE) and the Regional Administration Boards (henceforth OKE). In addition, it introduced a more competence-based focus in assessment and placed more emphasis on critical thinking skills, as well as aimed to increase transparency of national exams, improving the validity and reliability of the process (West & Crighton, 1999).

Currently, the Matura consists of three required subjects at the Standard level: Polish language and literature, mathematics, and a modern foreign language. For both the foreign language and Polish Matura, students must take a written and oral exam. The written section is a pen and paper test, with each student given some scratch paper and the examination sheet; it is usually administered to all students in a school gym and overseen by several teachers. Each student is also required to take the written Matura in at least one other subject at the Extended level. In essence, the Matura aims to measure students' knowledge of a given subject and their readiness for college (CKE, n.d.a.), and it is commonly called the "maturity exam." Although the Matura is not a mandatory exam for high school graduates, its successful completion is required for admission into Poland's tuition-free public higher education institutions. It thus has two primary functions: It is an achievement test (criterion-referenced) and a university entrance test (norm-referenced) (Smolik, 2012). Additionally, the foreign language Matura reflects the goal of Poland's Ministry of Education to prepare students for "effective communication in a foreign language, in speech and writing" (*Podstawa Programowa*, n.d., p. 61).

The foreign language Matura can be taken in English, French, Spanish, German, Russian, or Italian (CKE & OKE, 2015), but in 2016, 234, 554 examinees (about 90%) chose to take the Standard Matura exam (SME) in English, and 91% of them passed (CKE, n.d.b., n.d.c.). To pass the SME, an examinee must achieve at least 30% of all points on each required part of the exam, which is scored by CKE raters—typically, local teachers—who have completed training and passed a test, though we found conflicting information about how many individuals rate each writing response (Antoń-Jucha, 2015; Najwyższa Izba Kontroli, 2015). In addition, 49% of examinees also took the Extended Matura exam (EME) in English (CKE, n.d.b.), which does not have a cutoff score.

Written English Matura

The written portion of the English Matura consists of listening, reading comprehension, language use/grammar tasks, and a writing task. The examinee can receive up to 50 points: The writing task is worth 10 points on the SME and 13 points on the EME. Further details about the tasks and their scoring are discussed below.

Standard Writing Task and Its Scoring

The SME task requires that the examinee write an email to a friend, a blog post, or a forum post that is 80–130 words long. These genres were chosen because high school graduates should be able to write a "utility text" with elements of "description, recounting of events, justifying an opinion, including the presentation of pros and cons" (CKE & OKE, 2013, p. 17). The 2016 prompt[1] is presented below:

> **As part of an international exchange program, you and your class are traveling abroad to a sister school. In an email to a friend in England:**
>
> - **Describe a performance that you have prepared for this occasion**
> - **Describe concerns you have about the event**
> - **Explain what you bought for the trip and why**
> - **Write how you plan on spending your free time during your stay abroad.**
>
> *Extend your response in relation to the four bullet points, keeping in mind that the total length should be between 80 and 130 words (not counting words in the sentences given below). Assessed will be your ability to fully convey the information*

(4 points), coherence and logic of the response (2 points), linguistic diversity (2 points) and linguistic correctness (2 points). Sign your response XYZ.

(CKE, 2016a, p. 11)

Tasks from previous years required students to write an email to a friend in England discussing a city run (CKE, 2015) or describing the writer's preparations for prom (CKE, 2014). In responding to the prompt, the examinee must address all the so-called topical elements outlined in the four bullet points. The writer is also shown a scoring rubric. In addition, the prompt includes a visual—a mock email message box—with the first sentences of the email already provided. Technical manuals published on the CKE website explain that to assess content raters examine the degree to which the topical elements are expanded upon in the response (CKE, 2016c). Moreover, the documents also include rubrics outlining benchmarks for content, coherence and logic, linguistic diversity, and linguistic correctness. However, it is difficult to assess how many students actually read these documents.

In addition to content, raters also evaluate coherence and logic of the response, defined as clarity, intra-sentential and inter-sentential cohesion, as well as coherence at the paragraph level. Moreover, raters are instructed to consider grammar and spelling errors if these negatively affect the reader's comprehension. Next, raters examine linguistic diversity by looking at the variation of lexico-grammatical structures, avoidance of common expressions, and use of forms "typical for the given language and appropriate to the given communicative context" (CKE, 2016c, p. 14). The rater is to judge whether a phrase is common or appropriate. Finally, in assessing linguistic correctness, raters examine errors' "effect on the communicativeness of the response" (p. 15). They are also advised against calculating the score based on the number of errors in the response.

Extended Writing Task and Its Scoring

On the EME task, the examinee chooses between two topics and genres of formal letter, an article or a for and against essay. The prompt below (originally in Polish) is from the 2016 Matura:

> **Discuss one of the topics below. Your response should be between 200–250 words and should fulfill all the typical requirements for the form that is expected in the prompt. Select the topic that you chose by circling its number.**

> 1. The governments of many cities sponsor open-air celebrity concerts on New Year's Eve. Write a **for and against essay**, in which you present the good and bad sides of organizing these events to greet the New Year.

2. You recently watched a sports game, during which one of the players broke rules of fair play. Write an **article**, in which you describe this situation and justify why it is crucial to combat athletes' dishonest behavior.

(CKE, 2016b, p. 12)

Additionally, the examinee can see the grading rubric (originally written in Polish) in Table 10.1.

As is further explained in technical manuals published by CKE, prompt alignment describes specific genre expectations, divided into content and form elements. For example, a for-and-against essay must contain a "thesis related to the topic AND content of the response" (CKE, 2016d, p. 7), while an article requires writers to express their position and clearly present information on a given topic (CKE, 2016d). Moreover, a formal letter is addressed to a newspaper editor or city officials and includes a description, recount, review/recommendation, etc. In scoring form elements, raters consult a separate table that describes expectations for genre appropriateness, composition, segmentation, and length.

The technical manuals published by CKE also provide another rubric to assess coherence and logic, as well as list examples of potential errors, such as switching between verb tenses without justification (CKE, 2016d). Another rubric is used when evaluating linguistic variety, defined as the variety of lexico-grammatical expressions, and the overall "naturalness" of the structures, or a "way of expression that is characteristic for a given language" (CKE, 2016d, p. 17). "Precision" is further described as the avoidance of highly common terms, like "nice" or "interesting," while "appropriateness of style" is the usage of a style that is expected of a given text form. Finally, in assessing linguistic correctness raters evaluate "the grammatical, lexical, orthographic, and punctuation errors" (CKE, 2016d, p. 18), and may also take into consideration the "weight" of errors and their effect on "communication" (p. 18).

TABLE 10.1 Scoring Rubric on the Extended Matura (CKE, 2016b, p. 14)

Prompt alignment									Coherence and logic	Linguistic variety	Linguistic correctness	TOTAL
0–1–2–3–4–5									0–1–2	0–1–2–3	0–1–2–3	
Content elements (0–1–2)					Form elements (0–1)							
1	2	3	4	5	1	2	3	4				

Discussion and Conclusions

Over the years, CKE made a number of changes intended to increase validity and reliability of the writing task on the Matura. Among the most significant changes were using external raters instead of local teachers to score the exams, introducing procedures for increasing rater quality, standardizing prompts across the whole country, and regularly publishing comprehensive reports on exam results. Another change that has had a more direct impact on the EFL Matura is the growing emphasis on communicative competence (*Podstawa Programowa*, n.d.), defined by Savignon (1991) as the ability to use language in various sociolinguistic contexts and situations. Evidence of the communicative approach can be found in the scoring of the SME writing task, as raters must consider the overall communicative effect of the text on the reader. Despite these improvements, our analysis reveals some problematic assumptions and socioeconomic implications of the Matura.

Socioeconomic Implications

EFL Matura scores reveal differences between students' writing proficiency based on location and type of school. Using the 2016 results shared with us by CKE, we analyzed the writing task scores. Our analysis revealed that, although the SME is considered an easy exam ("Matura zdana od 51 procent?," 2017), there are persistent differences in the total Matura score (CKE, n.d.c.) and the writing task score based on school location. We analyzed the writing performance of students from rural and small towns (21.9%), mid-sized cities (37.4%) and big cities (40.7%). The mean scores for the SME writing task for these groups were, respectively, 6.5 (s=3.3, ±0.14), 7.25 (s=3.1, ±.01), and 7.86 (s=2.8, ±.009) on a 10-point scale. Our analysis also showed a stark achievement gap on the EME: The percentage of small town students who scored 0 on the writing task (23%) was much higher than students from mid-sized cities and big cities (10.6 % and 8.5%). It is unclear whether their writing was scored so low or if they did not even attempt to respond to the writing prompt. Further, Muszyński, Gajewska-Dyszkiewicz, Paczuska, and Szpotowicz (2016) claimed that students from rural areas struggle the most with writing and listening comprehension tasks, and they pointed to the lower cultural capital and lower English proficiency of rural parents as the reason. Moreover, schools in these areas often place students in mixed-level English classes and do not offer extracurricular English classes. Thus, one reason for setting a low SME cut-off score (30%) might be to reduce the impact of differences in English teaching quality across socioeconomic backgrounds. In other words, the low cutoff score allows low achieving students to pass the exam and gain access to higher education institutions in Poland.

The achievement gap between students from different locations is also important in light of the fact that currently about 40% of Polish emigrants who work and live abroad, primarily in Great Britain, Germany, and the U.S., have only a high school diploma (Hawkins & Moses, 2016; Szałtys, 2012; Wołkonowski, 2015). This means that they use EFL writing skills which they gained in high school for a variety of purposes, including formal situations, like communicating with government officials and co-workers. It is also significant that 77% of rural residents who emigrate do so to find employment abroad (Kwinta-Odrzywołek, 2014). Clearly, there is a need for rural schools to offer high-quality EFL education, as even when students remain in Poland, they are required to achieve good command of English. For example, on the most popular Polish jobsite, Pracuj.pl, 46% of current job offers require candidates to know English, while many Polish businesses want graduates to write better in English for business purposes (Walczak, 2015).

Given these socioeconomic disparities and the need for high school graduates to use English for professional purposes, it is important to draw attention to authenticity and impact of the Matura. Authenticity measures the task's correspondence to real-life situations in the target language use domain (TLU), while impact is the overall assessment of how the test influences the examinees and the larger educational context (Bachman & Palmer, 1996). Both of these concepts are useful in examining the SME writing task. First, by including informal, everyday genres like an email, the task is likely authentic and relatable to many examinees, but less authentic is the penalization of abbreviations, including "4U" or "bfr," which are common in informal emails but considered orthographic errors on the Matura (CKE, 2016c). Second, the SME emphasizes simple narrative and descriptive texts. By focusing on these skills, test designers sample from a very narrow TLU that does not fully represent the minimal communicative skills that high school graduates will have to use in the multilingual context of the EU or the increasingly international job market in Poland.

Unlike the informal SME task, the EME task includes formal academic genres that emphasize argumentation and persuasion, and are more structurally constrained. The rigidity of the EME genres and the detailed scoring instructions likely facilitate the rating of the responses, and the constrained nature of the responses is also justified because these genres have more established conventions than informal emails. As a result, what the EME examinees are really asked to demonstrate is their familiarity with "school genres." And since at least some of the examinees will use English at the university level, the genre choice may be explained as an attempt to measure their readiness for college. At the same time, university graduates are not likely to regularly use these genres outside of their classes, which puts into question the long-term usefulness and authenticity of the tasks.

Native Speaker Bias

The English Matura exhibits similar issues as commercial large-scale EFL tests, such as the TOEFL or IELTS. For example, Dryer (2016) found that while commercial tests geared towards L1 users reward writers for creativity, top test-takers on EFL exams are rewarded for sounding natural. Similarly, despite the emphasis on communicativeness, the scoring rubric for the SME writing task focuses on local concerns like linguistic correctness and grammatical-lexical diversity over global concerns, like audience needs, organization, or creativity. Thus, the Matura reflects a larger trend in global ELT and academia, where native English speakers (NESs) have the right to be creative with their English, while for non-native English speakers (NNESs) creativity is considered an error (Jenkins, 2014). As our analysis further suggests, the Matura measures the writer's communicative competence against that of a NES. The rubric for the EME writing task requires the text to sound "natural," which is defined elsewhere as a "way of expression that is characteristic for a given language" (CKE, 2016d, p. 17). The Polish government also states that the goal of EFL education is to "[approximate] the communicative competence of native users of the language" (*Podstawa programowa*, n.d.). Thus, EFL writing in Poland is understood as achieving communicative success through linguistic naturalness and approximating NES norms.

The apparent NES bias on the Matura reveals that the English valued by test designers comes from what Kachru (1985) refers to as Inner Circle countries. In particular, the prompts and other materials continuously refer to Great Britain, e.g.: "If he knew English, he'd have represented Poland at last month's conference in Great Britain" (CKE & OKE, 2013, p. 34). The SME writing prompts also ask to address a friend from England, even though in the multilingual context of the EU, Polish graduates will likely use English to communicate with its users from various linguistic backgrounds. Therefore, in using NES models, the Matura may be working against the goal, shared by Poland's Ministry of Education and the EU, of promoting linguistic and cultural "tolerance and openness" (*Podstawa programowa*, n.d., p. 32). The assumption that Polish graduates will mostly use English to communicate with people from England is challenged by global trends: Not only is the EU home to many learners of English (Special Eurobarometer, 2012), but globally NNESs have long outnumbered NESs (Crystal, 1997).

It is also insightful to examine the CEFR standards set by the European Council that informed the current Matura, as despite the EU's professed linguistic tolerance, the CEFR reveals a NES bias as well. Although the authors explicitly deny such a bias, the learning objectives for writing and other domains are repeatedly discussed in reference to NESs. For example, a B2-level language user is described as someone who "can sustain relationships with native speakers without unintentionally amusing or irritating them or requiring them to behave other than they would with a native speaker" (Council of Europe, n.d., p. 122). This suggests that NNESs should accommodate to the needs of NESs and that the learner's main goal is to simulate a NES's language—a goal difficult to achieve for many NNESs (cf. research overviewed in Birdsong, 2009).

The Council of Europe (n.d.) justifies referring to NESs in the CEFR as a matter of convenience, clarifying that the term is used only to "characterise the degree of precision, appropriateness and ease with the language which typifies the speech of those who have been highly successful learners" (p. 36). However, this choice of terminology reinforces native-speakerism, which regards NESs as ideal users and teachers of English (Holliday, 2006), an assumption that has been disputed by intelligibility studies (e.g., Smith & Nelson, 1985). Research suggests that native-speakerism underlies modern ELT (Phillipson, 1992) and academia (Saraceni, 2015). Jenkins (2014) argued that the perceived superiority of NESs and NES models leads to the devaluing of other languages in higher education, and offered additional evidence that the English valued in Polish education is overwhelmingly Inner Circle English. Jenkins' examination of two websites for Polish universities revealed "a strong link from the start, not only with English, but also with Britain" (p. 105) and a "strong focus on native English" (p. 106).

To conclude, the emphasis on NES norms in the Matura writing task and in Polish education is problematic because English is "no longer the sole property of native speakers" (Berns, Jenkins, Modiano, Seidlhofer, & Yano, 2009, p. 382). Consequently, Canagarajah (2006) argued that English language learners should be exposed to various Englishes so they can communicate with linguistically and culturally diverse interlocutors. It would therefore benefit the Matura if the writing construct were broadened to reflect findings from current EFL writing research, which emphasizes the social nature of writing (e.g., the emphasis on audience, genre studies, feedback), as well as the multiple processes involved in composing texts (e.g., importance of drafting and revision). Most importantly, it would benefit the learners if national language assessments and curriculum in Poland reflected the needs of young Poles, who increasingly live, work, and communicate in multilingual contexts across Europe and elsewhere.

Acknowledgments

The authors would like to thank Poland's Central Examination Board for making the Matura Results Data available. Additionally, we would like to thank Dr. Robert Ariel from Purdue University for assisting with statistical data analysis.

Note

1 All translations from Polish to English are done by the authors of this chapter.

References

Antoń-Jucha, A. (2015). Matura 2015: Dzisiaj zaczyna się sprawdzanie i ocenianie prac. *Dziennik Wschodni.* Retrieved from www.dziennikwschodni.pl/lublin/matura-2015-jak-beda-oceniane-prace,n,1000161745.html

Bachman, L. F., & Palmer, A. S. (1996). *Language testing in practice.* Oxford: Oxford University Press.

Berns, M., Jenkins, J., Modiano, M., Seidlhofer, B., & Yano, Y. (2009). Perspectives on English as a lingua franca. In T. Hoffmann & L. Siebers (Eds.), *World Englishes problems, properties and prospects* (pp. 369–384). Amsterdam: John Benjamins. https://doi.org/10.1075/veaw.g40

Birdsong, D. (2009). Age and the end state of second language acquisition. In W. C. Ritchie & T. K. Bhatia (Eds.), *The new handbook of second language acquisition* (pp. 401–424). Bingley: Emerald.

Canagarajah, S. (2006). Changing communicative needs, revised assessment objectives: Testing English as an international language. *Language Assessment Quarterly, 3*(3), 229–242. https://doi.org/10.1207/s15434311laq0303_1

Centralna Komisja Edukacyjna. (2014). *Egzamin maturalny z języka angielskiego: Poziom podstawowy. Przykładowy arkusz egzaminacyjny.* Retrieved from www.cke.edu.pl/images/_EGZAMIN_MATURALNY_OD_2015/egzamin_probny_2015/jez_obce_pp/angielski_pp/A1/A1J%C4%99zyk_angielski_PP_arkusz.pdf

Centralna Komisja Edukacyjna. (2015). *Egzamin maturalny z języka angielskiego: Poziom podstawowy.* Retrieved from www.cke.edu.pl/images/_EGZAMIN_MATURALNY_OD_2015/Arkusze_egzaminacyjne/2015/formula_od_2015/MJA-P1_1P-152.pdf

Centralna Komisja Edukacyjna. (2016a). *Egzamin maturalny z języka angielskiego: Poziom podstawowy.* Retrieved from www.cke.edu.pl/images/_EGZAMIN_MATURALNY_OD_2015/Arkusze_egzaminacyjne/2016/formula_od_2015/MJA-P1_1P-162.pdf

Centralna Komisja Edukacyjna. (2016b). *Egzamin maturalny z języka angielskiego: Poziom rozszerzony.* Retrieved from www.cke.edu.pl//images/_EGZAMIN_MATURALNY_OD_2015/Arkusze_egzaminacyjne/2016/formula_od_2015/MJA-R1_1P-162.pdf

Centralna Komisja Egzaminacyjna. (2016c). Egzamin Maturalny w Roku Szkolnym 2015/2016. Formuła od 2015 ("Nowa Matura"). Język Angielski: Poziom Podstawowy. Zasady Ocenienia Rozwiązań Zadań. Retrieved from www.cke.edu.pl/images/_EGZA-MIN_MATURALNY_OD_2015/Arkusze_egzaminacyjne/2016/formula_od_2015/zasady_oceniania/MJA-PP-162n_zasady_oceniania.pdf

Centralna Komisja Egzaminacyjna. (2016d). Egzamin Maturalny w Roku Szkolnym 2015/2016. Formuła od 2015 ("Nowa Matura"). Język Angielski: Poziom Rozszerzony. Zasady Ocenienia Rozwiązań Zadań. Retrieved from www.cke.edu.pl/images/_EGZA-MIN_MATURALNY_OD_2015/Arkusze_egzaminacyjne/2016/formula_od_2015/zasady_oceniania/MJA-PR-162n_zasady_oceniania.pdf

Centralna Komisja Egzaminacyjna. (n.d.a.). O egzaminie. *CKE.pl.* Retrieved from www.cke.edu.pl/egzamin-maturalny/egzamin-w-nowej-formule/o-egzaminie/

Centralna Komisja Egzaminacyjna. (n.d.b.). *Informacja o wynikach egzaminu maturalnego przeprowadzonego w maju, czerwcu i sierpniu 2016 r.* Retrieved from www.cke.edu.pl/images/_EGZAMIN_MATURALNY_OD_2015/Informacje_o_wynikach/2016/20160912%20Informacja%20o%20wynikach%20matury%20M%20Cz%20S.pdf

Centralna Komisja Egzaminacyjna. (n.d.c.). *Sprawozdanie z egzaminu maturalnego 2016. Język angielski.* Retrieved from www.cke.edu.pl/images/_EGZAMIN_MATURALNY_OD_2015/Informacje_o_wynikach/2016/sprawozdanie/sprawozdanie_matura_2016_angielski.pdf

Centralna Komisja Egzaminacyjna, & Okręgowe Komisje Egzaminacyjne. (2013). *Informator o Egzaminie Maturalnym z Języka Angielskiego od Roku Szkolnego 2014/2015.* Retrieved from www.cke.edu.pl/images/_EGZAMIN_MATURALNY_OD_2015/Informatory/2015/Jezyk-angielski_informator_od_2015.pdf

Centralna Komisja Egzaminacyjna, & Okręgowe Komisje Egzaminacyjne. (2015). Informator o egzaminie maturalnym z języka angielskiego od roku szkolnego 2014/2015. Aktualizacja w zakresie podstaw prawnych: 1 września 2015 r. Retrieved from www.

cke.edu.pl/images/_EGZAMIN_MATURALNY_OD_2015/Informatory/2015/ Informator_Cz%C4%99%C5%9B%C4%87_og%C3%B3lna_AKTUALIZACJA_1_ wrzesnia_2015.pdf

Council of Europe. (n.d.). *Common European framework of reference for languages: Learning, teaching, assessment.* Retrieved from www.coe.int/t/dg4/linguistic/source/framework_en.pdf

Crystal, D. (1997). *English as a global language.* Cambridge: Cambridge University Press.

Dryer, D. B. (2016). Appraising translingualism. *College English, 78*(3), 274. Chicago.

Eckes, T., Ellis, M., Kalnberzina, V., Piżorn, K., Springer, C., Szollás, K., & Tsagari, C. (2005). Progress and problems in reforming public language examinations in Europe: Cameos from the Baltic States, Greece, Hungary, Poland, Slovenia, France and Germany. *Language Testing, 22*(3), 355–377. https://doi.org/10.1191/0265532205lt313oa

Główny Urząd Statystyczny. (2016). *Oświata i wychowanie w roku szkolnym 2015/2016.* Retrieved from http://stat.gov.pl/download/gfx/portalinformacyjny/pl/defaultaktualnosci/5488/1/11/1/oswiata_i_wychowanie.pdf

Hawkins, O., & Moses, A. (2016). *Polish population of the United Kingdom.* Retrieved from http://researchbriefings.files.parliament.uk/documents/CBP-7660/CBP-7660.pdf

Holliday, A. (2006). Native-speakerism. *ELT Journal, 60*(4), 385–387. https://doi.org/10.1093/elt/ccl030

Jenkins, J. (2014). *English as a lingua franca in the international university: The politics of academic English language policy.* Oxon: Routledge.

Kachru, B. B. (1985). Standards, codification and sociolinguistic realism: The English language in the outer circle. In R. Quirk & H. Widdowson (Eds.), *English in the world: Teaching and learning the language and literatures* (pp. 11–30). Cambridge: Cambridge University Press.

Kwinta-Odrzywołek, J. (2014, March 18). Kierunki emigracji zawodowej. *RynekPracy.pl.* Retrieved from www.rynekpracy.pl/artykul.php/wpis.766

Lewkowicz, J., & Zawadowska-Kittel, E. (2008). Impact of the new school-leaving exam of English in Poland. *Cambridge ESOL Research Notes, 34*, 27–31.

Matura zdana od 51 procent? Zebraliśmy opinie ekspertów. (2017). *RadioZet.pl.* Retrieved from http://wiadomosci.radiozet.pl/Polska/Matura-2017-B-szef-CKE-b-szefowa-MEN-i-szef-ZNP-o-maturach

Muszyński, M., Gajewska-Dyszkiewicz, A., Paczuska, K., & Szpotowicz, M. (2016). Jak maturzyści poradzili sobie z egzaminem z języka angielskiego? Omówienie wyników matury z języka angielskiego 2015 r. *Języki Obce w Szkole, 1*, 75–85. Retrieved from http://jows.pl/artykuly/jak-maturzysci-poradzili-sobie-z-egzaminem-z-jezyka-angielskiego-omowienie-wynikow-matury-z

Najwyższa Izba Kontroli. (2015). *Informacja o Wynikach Kontroli System Egzaminów Zewnętrznych w Oświacie.* Retrieved from www.nik.gov.pl/plik/id,8629,vp,10737.pdf

Phillipson, R. (1992). *Linguistic imperialism.* Oxford: University Oxford Press.

Podstawa programowa z komentarzami. Tom 3. Języki obce w szkole podstawowej, gimnazjum i liceum. (n.d.). Retrieved from www.bc.ore.edu.pl/dlibra/docmetadata?id=233&from=pubindex&dirids=18&lp=8

Reichelt, M. (2005). English-language writing instruction in Poland. *Journal of Second Language Writing, 14*(4), 215–232. https://doi.org/10.1016/j.jslw.2005.10.005

Reichelt, M. (2013). English-language writing instruction in Poland: Adapting to the local EFL context. In O. Majchrzak (Ed.), *PLEJ_2 czyli PsychoLingwistyczne Eksploracje Językowe.* Łódź: Wydawnictwo Uniwersytetu Łódzkiego.

Salski, Ł. (2016). EFL writing in Poland: Where traditional does not mean current, but current means traditional. In T. Silva, J. Wang, C. Zhang, & J. M. Paiz (Eds.), *L2 writing in the global context: Represented, underrepresented, and underrepresented voices* (pp. 207–226). Beijing: Foreign Language Teaching and Research Press.

Saraceni, M. (2015). *World Englishes: A critical analysis.* London: Bloomsbury.

Savignon, S. J. (1991). Communicative language teaching: State of the art. *TESOL Quarterly, 25*(2), 261–278. https://doi.org/10.2307/3587463

Siek-Piskozub, T., Wach, A., & Raulinajtys, A. (2008). Research on foreign language teaching in Poland 2000–2006. *Language Teaching, 41*(1), 57. https://doi.org/10.1017/S0261444807004806

Smith, L. E., & Nelson, C. L. (1985). International intelligibility of English: Directions and resources. *World Englishes, 4*(3), 333–342. https://doi.org/10.1111/j.1467-971X.1985.tb00423.x

Smolik, M. (2012). Języki obce na egzaminach zewnętrznych: innowacje w latach 2012–2015. *Języki Obce w Szkole, 2012*(1), 22–33.

Special Eurobarometer. (2012). *Europeans and their languages.* Retrieved from http://ec.europa.eu/commfrontoffice/publicopinion/archives/ebs/ebs_386_en.pdf

Szałtys, D. (2012). *Współczesne migracje zagraniczne Polaków—w świetle badań bieżących i wyników NSP 2011.* Retrieved from http://zielonagora.stat.gov.pl/cps/rde/xbcr/zg/ASSETS_III_d_Szaltys_prezentacja.pdf

Walczak, M. (2015). Kompetencje Polaków w zakresie języków obcych i ich wpływ na działalność przedsiębiorstw. *Problemy Profesjologii, 2*, 127–137.

West, R., & Crighton, J. (1999). Examination reform in central and Eastern Europe: Issues and trends. *Assessment in Education: Principles, Policy & Practice, 6*(2), 271–289. https://doi.org/10.1080/09695949992919

Wołkonowski, J. (2015). Przyczyny i struktura emigracji obywateli Polski po akcesji do UE. *Prace Naukowe Uniwersytetu Ekonomicznego we Wrocławiu, 401*, 587–600. Retrieved from www.dbc.wroc.pl/Content/30515/Wolkonowski_Przyczyny_i_Struktura_Emigracji_Obywateli_Polski_2015.pdf

11

VIGNETTE

Assessing English Linguistic Knowledge and Writing Skills in Secondary Schools Through the State Matura Exam: The Case of Macedonia

Mira Bekar

When I started learning English as a foreign language at the age of 10, I wasn't aware of all the factors that have an impact on the process of assessing English language learners (ELLs). When I started going to elementary school in Macedonia, we learned English in public elementary schools, and we who belonged to the middle and upper class took additional classes in private language schools. Parents who thought that investing in learning English since an early age would be beneficial for their children's future education and success sent their children to private language schools. This was back in the late 1980s and 1990s. At that time, the State Matura Exam (SME), which is used for checking the progress and knowledge of secondary school students in various course subjects, didn't exist.

My interest in the topic rose from my current role as assistant professor in the English Department at a university in Macedonia, and from the fact that my colleagues and I are affected indirectly by the State Matura Exam. Specifically, students who enroll at the university are ranked on the basis of their academic success, their GPA from secondary schools, and the results from the Matura Exam. There are no entry exams at universities, aside from the final SME, as used to be the case until 2006, when I was a student. Back then, we had to take a serious entry exam checking our advanced knowledge of English grammar and vocabulary. But now, even with poor results on the SME, students get accepted at universities, which puts pressure on university professors to lower their standards.

Exploring this topic was additionally enhanced by the fact that I work with Macedonian students majoring in English, most of whom are being trained to become future teachers. I needed to understand better: (1) how the English part of the SME is designed, (2) why there are complaints from students, teachers, and parents about the suitability of the SME and if they are justified, and (3) the impact legislative and sociopolitical factors have on the process of assessing English language learners. To help you better conceptualize my efforts, I'll present information about the history of the Matura exam design, its content and the suitability of the qualitative aspect of the exam, and the skills being tested with the special focus on writing.

As someone who's been involved in test design and assessment for about 15 years, I understand that the design of graduation exams in secondary schools can be problematic, while simultaneously paying attention to the provisions to respond to students' special linguistic and cultural backgrounds. Since I had no direct contact with the whole process of the design of this test, my first step of data collection was a visit to the State Testing Center. Luckily, one of the people in charge for the State Matura Exam turned out to be my colleague from undergraduate studies, who helped me with the data collection. In countries like Macedonia, it is important to know people to get access to any data, so I should say I was lucky that a former colleague of mine is one of the people in charge of designing and distributing the English section of the Matura Exam.

My first visit to the State Testing Center was an eye-opening experience. Until then, I hadn't been aware that from 2001 to 2007, seven pilot testing procedures for the State Matura were performed—six pilot case studies and one testing pilot procedure for the whole population of 17,500 students, in which each student took two subject tests. The aim of these pilot testing procedures was to gain knowledge of the quality of measuring instruments, i.e., the tests, to check the procedures for realization of the State Matura, and to test the IT equipment used for support of the whole process.

The realization of the SME in Macedonia started in 2008. What was tested then was the knowledge of two external (electives), two internal (compulsory) subjects, and a project task. In 2009, huge efforts for inclusion of the students from art schools in the SME were made, since it was not applicable to this type of education and those secondary school students encountered problems when enrolling at universities. From 2008 until 2013, fewer external subjects were tested due to the lack of staff and the chaotic period during the establishment of the State Testing Center. Insufficient finances by the State to pay the teachers involved and to acquire the necessary equipment was another problem. From the 2013–2014 academic year, the number of external subjects increased from two to three due to better logistics. Since 2013, secondary school students have had the chance to take three types of tests: State Matura, School Matura, and Final Exam. Students, parents, and teachers got very confused due to not receiving full instructions or clarifications. What they and we as educators knew was general information, that the common feature of all these exams is the structure: a compulsory part, an optional part, and a project task. The *State* Matura was aimed at students who finished four years of secondary education and of vocational education and was a condition for selection of candidates to enroll at university. The *School* Matura is only a certificate for finished secondary education for those students who don't plan to enroll at university. The so-called Final Exam is a certificate for vocational school completion only.

Problems of various natures started to pile up. First, students, parents, and university professors started complaining because the enrollment at universities was based on the selection of best students ranked according to the results achieved at the SME. "But what if not enough students chose the option State Matura?"—university professors asked. That implies the universities won't be filled with students who satisfy the basic criteria needed to start their freshmen year. Then, parents and students rightfully have had another concern: "What if students change their mind and want to attend college later in life?" "What if they choose the School Matura instead of State Matura since they can't attend or afford university initially, but have a possibility later in life to continue with their education?" What a mess, I thought.

I needed to understand the primary goals of the Ministry of Education and Science, which should justify the whole idea of implementing this state-controlled exam and identify discrepancies with the expectations of students and parents. On the official website of the Ministry of Education and Science, I read that the goals of the State Matura exam are: (1) raising the general level of knowledge and improvement of competences among students; (2) monitoring the realization of the study programs; (3) finalizing the educational process of individuals and endorsing a diploma for completed secondary education; (4) a high-quality and fair selection for prospective university students' entrance; and (5) informing the students, parents, and educational institutions about the achievements of students measured through valid means. All these aims sounded appropriate.

So I figured out that the problem must be in the tests and analyzed two tests that assessed the English proficiency of students. As a professional teacher involved in the test design processes for private language schools and universities, as well as a test-taker of standardized tests such as TOEFL and IELTS, I expected that the same skills—reading, listening, writing, and knowledge of English grammar and vocabulary—would be tested with the SME to achieve the above-mentioned institutional aims. However, I discovered that productive skill-speaking and receptive skill-listening aren't tested. The English test consists of (1) reading comprehension—four texts; (2) writing—two tasks, which are a letter of 100–120 words and a text; and (3) "applying linguistic elements in relation to context" (fill-in-the-gap exercises and open cloze exercises testing grammar and vocabulary). When I asked some representatives in charge of designing and delivering the SME about the reasons for excluding listening and speaking, they said: "It's always logistics; improper tech-equipment, no facilities, many of us lack training."

Another concern arose from the unofficial information I gathered from colleagues and the official information from the State Testing Center about the knowledge and skills being assessed. The five skills assessed are: (1) comprehension;

(2) use of lexis, of grammar, of communicative models, and knowing the culture of the country whose language is being learned; (3) reading comprehension; (4) writing a letter and a detailed text; and (5) using linguistic elements in context. This may sound good since it is in alignment with international tests and documents such as IELTS, TOEFL, and the Common European Framework of References (CEFR). However, it's not clear that officials understand the difference between the tested skill named "comprehension" and the third and the fourth skills, "reading comprehension" and "using linguistic elements in context." To me, all are comprehension skills. And what is meant by "and knowing the culture of the country whose language is being learned"? Does it mean knowing about U.S. and British habits, traditions, and politics? Or about pop or college culture using the English-speaking world as a benchmark? Looking at the topics of the reading comprehension and writing tasks, I've confirmed that it's all about some type of "adopted" ethnocentrism: local Macedonian social, political, and cultural phenomena seem to be seen as unimportant for writing and arguing about and are seen as inferior by Macedonian English teachers in comparison to foreign standards. I believe secondary school students will benefit more from learning to write a letter of complaint that will have impact in the local culture instead of learning to write a perfect complaint letter to a U.S. company. Similarly, although it may seem universal, applying for a job in a Macedonian company differs from the whole job application process in the U.S. or UK, since domestic employers haven't been trained to follow U.S. or UK procedures for employment policies—so why would students have to follow U.S. and UK norms?

Here's an example showing why the above-mentioned issues are problematic and may affect the future success of a student. The points gained on the State Matura Exam are related to the culture specificity issue. An example of a writing that is culture-sensitive and may be difficult for students, regardless of their English language competences, is the following:

> *Your school is considering joining a job practice program during the summer. Write a text (180–220 words) for your school magazine supporting and/or discouraging the idea and give arguments for your view.*

The issue that may discourage students from developing a short essay is that the concept of "job practice program" is unknown to them. It is even unclear whether this refers to internship programs or some other professional training. The second issue that may affect students' achievement is the unclear instructions in regard to genre. What type of "text" should the students produce?

Here I think of Coombe, Folse, and Hubley's (2007) principles of designing a good test: usefulness, validity, reliability, practicality, washback, authenticity, transparency, and security. In the example I mentioned above, requiring students to argue about an issue that doesn't exist in Macedonia or using confusing terms impacts the authenticity and practicality of the test. The brief instructions affect the validity and cause negative washback in the form of complaints by parents and students.

The best thing to do to confirm the effect of negative washback is to check the beliefs and opinions of the teachers involved in the process of the Matura exam design, delivery, and assessment. Both as a concerned professor and qualitative researcher, I discussed the issues with three teachers who have been involved in the process for more than three years. Their positive energies and reflections shed a new light on the process of SME development. They praised the steady development of the exam throughout the years; the compatibility of the test content with the existing curriculum; the proper alignment with international standardized tests, which means setting and achieving higher goals by students themselves; and the clear assessment criteria used for content relevance, coherence, clear introduction and conclusion, paragraphs with topic sentences, and the criteria for proper spelling and grammar.

I learned, unfortunately, that factors related to lack of objectivity and familial factors also play huge roles in the assessment—issues such as parents overpraising their children and having great expectations from and for them, officials mobbing teachers, and cheating on exams. Higher status of parents in society means greater protection and pressure on teachers for higher scores for their children. The complaints, according to the teachers, come mainly from those students who cheated or plagiarized, got caught, and received lower grades. What increased my worries was the attitude of some of the teachers saying, "I would make the text easier, in order to make it easier for the students with low grades" because this is a discrepancy with students saying that "the test is not challenging enough."

To conclude, through this experience I've learned that the process of State Matura Exam design has been laborious and has included a significant improvement that partially satisfies teachers and test takers. Since ethical values have been seriously affected, there is a huge challenge awaiting all of us: the fight for more objective values, fair criteria, and the enhancement of ethical values among some school directors, students, and parents. We university professors need to train test designers and assessors. We need to work as a society on improving legislative and sociopolitical factors, as well as constantly strengthening our institutions involved in setting educational standards.

Reference

Coombe, C., Folse, K., & Hubley, N. (2007). *A practical guide to assessing English language learners.* Ann Arbor: University of Michigan Press.

12

RIGHTING WRITING PRACTICES?

An Exam Reform's Impact on L2 Writing Teaching and Assessment

*Benjamin Kremmel, Kathrin Eberharter,
and Michael Maurer*

It seems generally accepted that examinations, particularly ones in which stakes are high, will inevitably have an impact on learners, learning, teachers, teaching, classrooms, schools, and/or even educational or societal systems as a whole. In addition, most current validation approaches since Messick (1989) have put the notion of consequences at the heart of their framework (Bachman & Palmer, 2010; Kane, 2012; Weir, 2005). However, even if test developers do not subscribe to the idea of consequential validity, the fact that "it is widely held that examinations, particularly public examinations used for selection and accreditation purposes, have a powerful effect on what happens in education" (Wall, 2005, p. 1) means that the impact of examinations is worth monitoring, particularly if exam systems are being changed.

The impact or "effects of tests on teaching and learning" are generally referred to as washback (Wall, 1997, p. 291). Hamp-Lyons (1997) defines washback as a triangular relationship between teaching, learning, and testing, and Wall (2000) broadly describes it as the interaction of tests with "other factors in the testing situation" (p. 499). Messick (1996) states that it is the influence that tests have on teachers and learners in their process of language learning when they "do things they would not otherwise do" (p. 241). This influence may affect participants (learners, teachers, etc.), processes (learning, teaching), and products (materials, test scores) (Green, 2013). According to Spratt (2005), the washback of exams can determine different aspects of what happens in the classroom. Testing can affect the curriculum, the materials, and the teaching methods, as well as the feelings and attitudes towards learning, teaching, and assessment of all parties involved. It could be argued that the category of "materials" thereby not only subsumes textbooks but also classroom assessments.

However, it still remains unclear what and how tests exactly influence any of these components of the teaching-learning-testing interrelation. Wall and Alderson (1993) question the notion of washback, for example, and state that exams may have an impact on what teachers teach, but not on how they teach (see also Cheng, 2005, 2008). Andrews (2004), however, claims that it is testing, rather than the curriculum, that determines both what and how a language is taught and learned. In any case, "tests are held to be powerful determiners of what happens in classrooms" (Alderson & Wall, 1993, p. 115).

Elton and Laurillard argue that "the quickest way to change student learning is to change the assessment system" (1979, as cited in Andrews, 2004, p. 39). This change, however, can have positive or negative consequences. Preparing students for their exams is often a teacher's main concern, and so "teaching to the test," i.e., the narrowing of the teaching and learning to the content of the test, is a common reaction, particularly when exams are changed, and is regarded as negative washback. As such, teaching to the test as a consequence of exam reform is a constant worry of educators and test developers alike, as it is perceived as limiting when only exam-relevant content and formats are taught in the language classroom. In terms of affecting materials and classroom assessments, however, it could also be argued that a more focused orientation towards the exam could lead to better testing practices if the relevant exam is well-designed. As Green (2013) points out, "a well-designed test should encourage good teaching; a poorly designed test will tempt teachers and learners into practices that have limited value in relation to long-term learning goals" (p. 41). Therefore, a good reference test can actually improve teaching and assessment practices. Most certainly, alignment of teaching and assessment practices with the reference test, or vice versa, is a prerequisite for successful exam implementation. This chapter tracks the alignment process that Austrian language classrooms underwent after a major exam reform and investigates whether (1) the new legislation has led to observable washback effects in classroom assessment practices, and (2) whether these effects, if any were found, are viewed as beneficial or detrimental by a main stakeholder group, i.e., the language teachers.

Background

In 2004, Austria introduced a new curriculum linking foreign language teaching to the Common European Framework of Reference (CEFR). This meant that a traditionally knowledge-based curriculum, which outlined topics, grammatical structures, and literary works to be covered, was replaced by a competence-oriented, communicative curriculum that stipulated exit levels across all language skills and all modern foreign languages (see Spöttl, Kremmel, Holzknecht, and Alderson (2016) for a detailed overview). By 2007, however, the government realized that such a paradigm shift could not be achieved without reforming the school-leaving examination (Matura), which students take at ages 17–19 at the end of higher secondary schooling. Although communicative language teaching had been anchored legally in the curriculum, "traditional-minded teachers did not feel any pressure to change their methods of teaching or testing as long as the form of the final exam remained unchanged" (Spöttl et al., 2016).

In 2007, a Ministry-funded project led by language testing researchers at the University of Innsbruck, Austria, started to develop a standardized CEFR-based school-leaving exam for the modern foreign languages English and French. At that time, the exam focused on reading and writing, and often targeted recalling facts related to literary works, cultural studies, and, for vocational schools, workplace topics and text types. The reformed exam would cover all skills through communicative performance testing and therefore guarantee a closer match to principles laid out in the new national curriculum and increased validity, reliability, and fairness. Also, while the pre-reform exam was entirely in the hands of individual class teachers with little to no training or guidance on test design or marking, this new exam would be professionally developed with standardized tasks that were referenced to the CEFR level descriptors for use across all schools. While it was impossible for political reasons to attain centralized marking of the test (see Spöttl et al., 2016), the test developers tried to ensure reliable scoring throughout the country by (1) mainly using selected response formats for the receptive skills, (2) providing real-time marker support for unclear student answers by means of a hotline and helpdesk service (Eberharter & Frötscher, 2012), (3) developing and providing CEFR-based analytic rating scales for the rating of written performances, and (4) offering nationwide training sessions to instruct teachers in the application of the new rating scales.

In 2008, the new exam was administered in selected pilot schools in the politically lower-risk languages (English and French) and skills (reading and listening) (Spöttl et al., 2016). The scope of the exam soon broadened to include Spanish and Italian as well as a lexico-grammatical test component called "language in use" and a writing section (see Table 12.1). Rater training began in May 2007 and as of 2009 piloting of writing tasks for inclusion in the standardized live exam began. Additionally, new national assessment scales at two exit CEFR levels, B1 and B2, were developed in two languages, English and German (Holzknecht et al., forthcoming; Konzett, 2011). In October 2009, the government finally passed a new education bill, anchoring the exam reform legally and resulting in an "extremely controversial but audacious step" (Spöttl et al., 2016) to offer one standardized exam in the foreign languages across all school types (higher general secondary and higher vocational secondary schools).

The reform had several implications for the writing skill in particular. First, the standardized equal weighting of the skills in the exam entailed that writing

TABLE 12.1 Skills and CEFR levels of the New Exam

	Listening	Reading (6y)	Reading (4y)	Language in Use (6y)	Language in Use (4y)	Writing
English	B2	B2		B2		B2
French	B1	B2	B1	B2	B1	B1
Italian	B1	B2	B1	B2	B1	B1
Spanish	B1	B2	B1	B2	B1	B1

Note: 6y and 4y relates to the number of years students have been learning the second foreign languages French, Italian, or Spanish, which varies from school to school. English, as the first foreign language, is taught already in primary school.

could no longer be the predominant skill in classroom teaching and assessment. Second, the class teachers were no longer responsible for the writing tasks in the final exam, which meant that they had to prepare students for a range of task types and their distinctive features. The new task types included the essay, a familiar genre for most teachers and students, but also encompassed the less practiced text types report, email, article, blog, leaflet, proposal, and, for vocational schools, letter. Third, the introduction of the compulsory nationwide analytic rating scale implied that teachers could no longer score written performances according to their idiosyncratic preferences (e.g., counting grammatical errors) and methods, but had to justify their awarded marks on the basis of the four equally weighted and CEFR-informed criteria (1) Task Achievement, (2) Organization and Layout, (3) Lexical and Structural Range, and (4) Lexical and Structural Accuracy.

Such monumental changes in the school-leaving exam would be very likely to bring about changes in classroom teaching and assessment practices. Given the high-stakes nature of the exam, we hypothesized that the communicative, authentic writing tasks and newly developed scoring criteria might impact the way this skill is taught. It was also deemed necessary to investigate and monitor the impact of the exam reform following the EALTA Guidelines of Good Practice (European Association of Language Testing and Assessment, 2006). A study was designed to investigate the following research questions:

RQ1   What impact has the exam reform made on teaching and testing practices of writing in English?

RQ1.1   Did writing assessment practices change after 2007? If yes, what features of writing tasks used in progress checks have changed?

RQ1.2   Have writing teaching practices changed since 2007 and if so, in what way?

RQ1.3   Might any of these changes be due to a washback effect? If yes, is this washback effect positive or negative?

Methodology

In order to answer these research questions, we combined data from a close analysis of writing tasks designed before and after the beginning of the reform, and a teacher questionnaire. As English has by far the largest impact in the Austrian context we decided to limit sampling to teachers and students of English.

RQ1.1 was addressed by analyzing progress test writing tasks administered before and after the beginning of the exam reform. We contacted teachers through mailing lists of local school authorities and personal contacts and asked them to provide writing tasks they had designed in the last ten years for class-room progress tests.[1] We received 302 writing tasks developed and administered between 2004 and 2013. As details about the new exam were rolled out nation-wide during 2007, we defined this year as cut-off point and grouped the tasks as pre- (n=111) and post- (n=191) exam reform. Teams of two researchers each then coded the tasks according to an adapted version of the "Writing Task Analysis Grid" provided in the *Manual for Relating Language Examinations to the Common European Framework of Reference for Languages (CEFR)* (Council of Europe, 2009, p. 161). This Writing Task Analysis Grid has three parts: (1) general fea-tures of the writing component of each test (e.g., number of tasks, allocated time), (2) features of the prompt and input (e.g., prompt type, integration of skills, length of input), and (3) features of the expected response (e.g., number of words, genre, language functions). The grid allowed a detailed description of 28 task features[2] and a standardized comparison of the 302 tasks across the two chronological categories. The coded features were then entered into SPSS and analyzed by means of chi-square tests, t-tests, and Mann-Whitney U-tests respec-tively, depending on the variables' level of measurement, to determine significant changes from pre- to post-exam reform practices.

RQ1.2 and RQ1.3 were answered by means of a teacher questionnaire. We developed a survey consisting of 48 questions concerning teachers' teaching and testing practices before and after 2007. Unfortunately, there was no baseline study available for this investigation, which is why participants had to think back and judge their practices from more than six years ago. While a clear limitation of this study, this procedure seemed the best solution to deal with the lack of baseline data. The questionnaire asked teachers about the percentage devoted to teaching writing pre- and post-reform, about which text types and aspects of the writing construct they would focus on in their teaching, and about their professional development regarding assessment literacy. The survey also comprised 12 statements on teachers' attitudes towards the new exam, which teachers judged on a four-point Likert scale from strongly agree to strongly disagree and an "I don't know" option. We implemented the survey online and, after piloting (n=7), distributed a link to the survey via the same channels as the call for writing tasks. One hundred and twenty teachers responded to the survey and the data was analyzed using SPSS.

TABLE 12.2 Sample Section of Adapted Writing Task Analysis Grid

Prompt and input (task level)

Type of prompt	base prompt		framed prompt		text-based prompt
Language of prompt	English		German		
Length of prompt	no. of words:___				
Language of input text (if applicable)	English		German		
Length of input text (if applicable)	no. of words:___				
Genre of input text (if applicable)	specify: ___				
Integration of skills	none	reading (>150 words)	speaking		listening
Time permitted/ suggested for task	___ minutes		not given		
Guidance regarding content	*(1)* fully specified	*(2)*	*(3)*	*(4)*	*(5)* not specified
Pictures included	yes		no		

Results

> RQ1.1   Did writing assessment practices change after 2007? If yes, what features of writing tasks used in progress checks have changed?

Classroom Assessment Writing Tasks Become More Authentic

Based on McNamara's definition of authenticity (2000), we categorized each task according to its degree of correspondence with real-life tasks (low/medium/high). There was a significant increase in the degree of authenticity of writing tasks after 2007 (p=.000). In the pre-2007 group, 94.1% of all tasks scored low on authenticity and only 3% were judged to exhibit high authenticity. By contrast, only 51.6% of the tasks post-2007 were judged to be of low authenticity. Of the post-2007 writing tasks, 24.7% were judged to be highly authentic.

Classroom Assessment Writing Tasks Converge to Matura Writing Task Types

As mentioned above, seven different task types form the pool of task types for the standardized Austrian school-leaving exam at B2 level (essays, reports, emails/letters, articles, blogs, leaflets, and proposals). It was found that these seven task types featured considerably more frequently in the classroom writing tests after 2007. As can be seen in Figure 12.1, the amount of creative writing tasks and

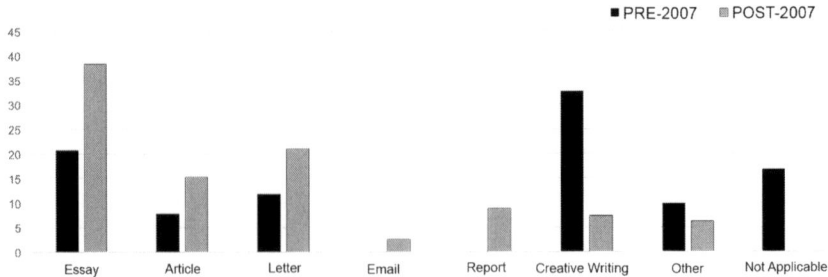

FIGURE 12.1 Writing Task Types in Classroom Progress Checks Before and After Beginning of Exam Reform

tasks that could not be classified with the analysis grid (e.g., when the instructions were simply to "write a text") decreases markedly, while the percentage of essays, articles, letters, emails, and reports increases. The latter two only appear in the classroom writing task sample after 2007.

Classroom Assessment Writing Task Prompts Become Increasingly Framed

Based on Tankó's (2005) classification of writing task prompts, we found that there was a significant trend (χ^2(2, n=289)=49.54, p=.000) for prompts after 2007 to be framed, placing the writing task into a richer context and usually describing a situation from which candidates can understand who they are, why they are writing, what they are writing about, and who will read their text. Framed prompts, compared to vague and decontextualized base prompts, are clearly more in line with communicative testing and the revised curriculum. In addition, we found that tasks after 2007 also provided more content guidance (p=.008), putting less imagination burden on the candidates and enabling more comparable and thus hopefully more reliable scoring. As a further consequence, tasks after 2007 incorporated more contextualizing pictures (χ^2(1, n=291)=6.35, p=.012), which are also a key feature of the writing tasks in the standardized reformed exam.

In terms of intended readership, the analysis showed a strong tendency to provide students with information about who will read the text (χ^2(1, n=291)= 35.23, p=.000). As the anticipated audience determines both content and style of the writing in real life (Tankó, 2005), specifying this information in the tasks makes writing tasks more authentic and gives test takers the chance to show that they can apply their sociolinguistic competence and register awareness. While before 2007 only 19.8% of all prompts contained information about the intended readership, 56.8% included this information after 2007. Accordingly, the genre of the expected response was also more clearly indicated to students in tasks developed and administered after 2007 (χ^2(1, n=291)=15.05, p=.000).

Classroom Assessment Writing Tasks Focus More on the Construct of Writing

For the sake of construct validity, integration of other skills is undesirable in the case of assessing writing alone. For instance, longer reading inputs increase the likelihood of test takers lifting language from the prompt, and test takers might be penalized for misinterpreting the text (Weigle, 2002). In 20% of all analyzed writing tasks before 2007, students had to read and comprehend at least 150 words of input text, in many cases much more, to complete the writing task. However, after 2007, the number of tasks integrating reading into the writing task went down by half, which implies a significant change from testing a mixture of skills to assessing writing only (χ^2(1, n=290)=6.23, p=.013) and a clearer understanding of the construct at hand.

Classroom Assessment Writing Tasks Change Their Focus in the Communicative Functions Required of Students in Their Performances

The new standardized writing tasks explicitly state three different communicative functions that test takers need to address. Arguably due to the shift in the task types used, the functions elicited from the test takers in writing progress tests also changed. While 'give opinion' is the most frequently used operator both before 2007 (20.7% of the writing tasks explicating functions) and after 2007 (37.1%) as it links up with the essay task type, the frequency of other operators differs quite considerably. "Narrate" (18.9%), for instance, was the second most frequently elicited function in writing tasks before 2007, but the operator seems to disappear almost completely after the beginning of the reform (6.3%). The operator "persuade" (third rank at 12.6% pre-2007), albeit arguably also highly relevant to opinion essays, is only used in 10% of writing tasks after 2007. It appears to have been replaced by the function "discuss," the usage of which increased from 2.7% before 2007 to 19.9% after 2007.

RQ1.2   Have writing teaching practices changed since 2007 and if so, in what way?

The exam reform appears not only to have had an impact on the way teachers design their classroom writing tasks, but also in terms of their teaching of writing. This is illustrated by the following results from the teacher questionnaire analysis.

We asked teachers which genres or text types they included in their writing instruction before and after 2007. As can be seen in Figure 12.2, letters and essays continue to be key components of teaching writing, but more teachers now also allocate time to text types that feature in the new standardized exam. While the amount of summary writing, writing interior monologues (often of

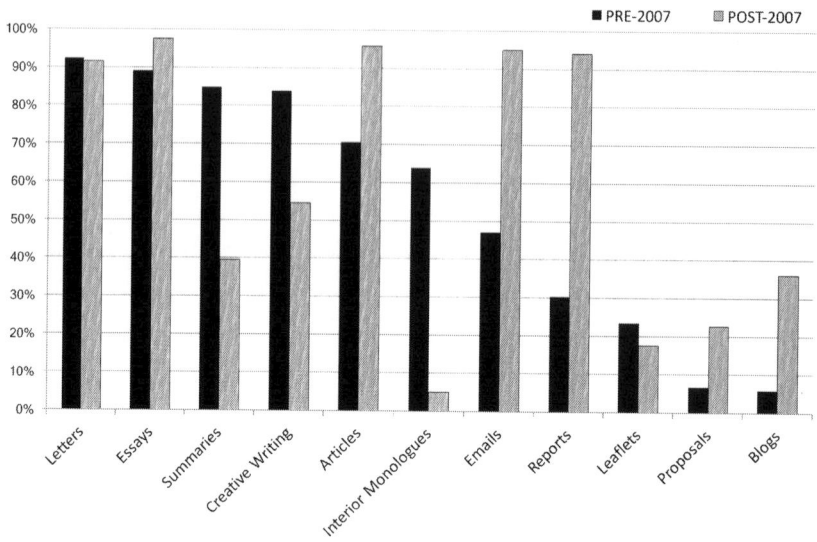

FIGURE 12.2 Text Types Taught by Teachers Before and After 2007

literary characters), and other types of creative writing decreases considerably, the number of teachers indicating teaching articles increases by 25%. Similarly, an increase in teaching emails (by 48%), reports (by 64%), proposals (by 16%), and blogs (by 30%) was observed. Interestingly, however, the number of teachers devoting time to the new task type leaflet decreased by 6%.

In the questionnaire, we asked which aspects of writing teachers focused on in their lessons, as it was hypothesized that there would be a shift towards those features that were also described in the analytic rating scales. Indeed, the most marked differences can be observed with "text organization" and "cohesion," which form a criterion in the newly developed scale (Organization and Layout), but did not feature in many of the plethora of rating scales in use before the reform. Of the teachers surveyed, 70.8% indicated that "text organization" was a feature they addressed very frequently or frequently in their teaching of writing after 2007, compared to only 50.4% before the reform. Similarly, "cohesion" was taught very frequently or frequently by 67.5% of the teachers after 2007, which equates to an increase of 21.4% compared to before 2007 (see Figure 12.3).

In general, we found that there was more explicit input on writing provided in the lessons after 2007 (14% more teachers), accompanied by an increased use of coursebooks as sources for input on how to write (34% more teachers). Figure 12.4 also illustrates that teachers saw more need for professional development in teaching and testing writing, as 33% and 42% more of them, respectively, sought training in these areas after 2007. A further substantial increase was found in

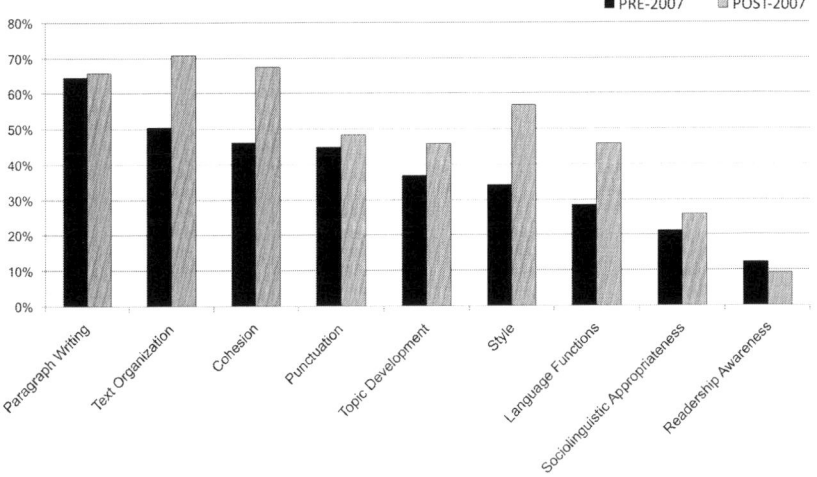

FIGURE 12.3 Aspects of Writing Taught Before and After 2007

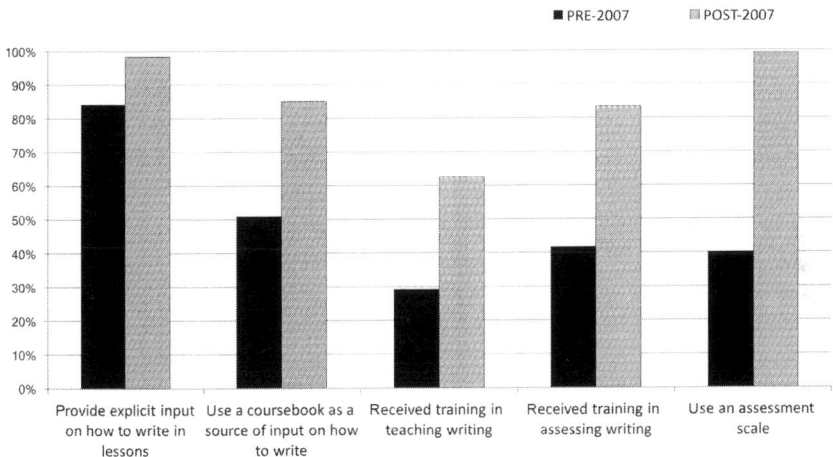

FIGURE 12.4 Teacher Professional Development Before and After 2007

respect to the use of assessment scales. While only 40% of surveyed teachers used a rating scale before 2007, almost all of them (99.2%) now score written performances according to a predefined rating rubric, in most cases the one offered by the standardized exam, even in classroom assessments.

RQ1.3   Might any of these changes be due to a washback effect? If yes, is this washback effect positive or negative?

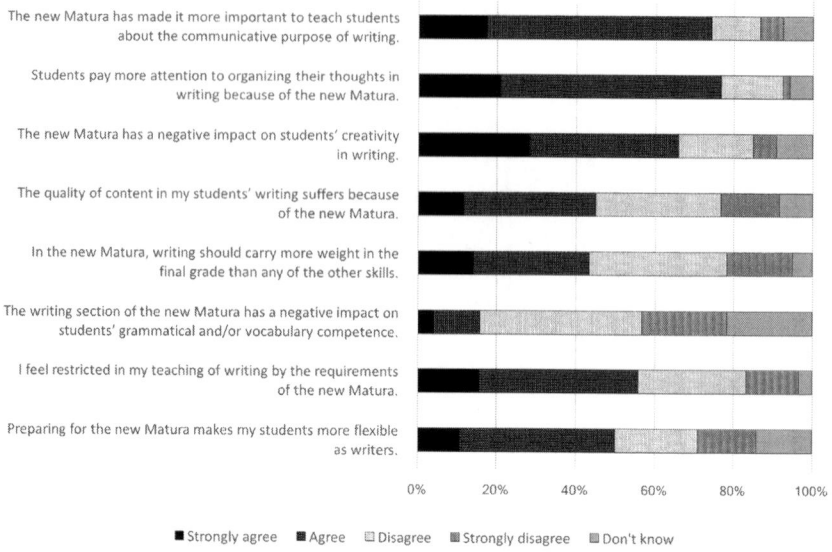

FIGURE 12.5 Attitudes of Teachers Towards the Writing Section in the New Exam

In order to confirm whether teachers do things differently in their lessons due to the introduction of the new exam, and whether they think these changes are beneficial or detrimental, one section of the teacher questionnaire concentrated on their attitudes towards the writing part of the new exam. The results of this section are presented in Figure 12.5.

The teachers appear to ascribe their change in teaching towards a more communicative approach to the introduction of the new exam. The majority of the teachers (74.2%) agreed or strongly agreed that the new exam has resulted in assigning more importance to teaching students about the communicative purposes of writing. Since the communicative curriculum was in place before the exam reform, this seems somewhat surprising, but highlights that the exam was a key component and political driving force in actually implementing the curriculum targets and principles in language classrooms. Teachers also stated that students now paid more attention to the organization of their writing (76.7% agreed or strongly agreed), which could be regarded as a positive washback effect. The sample population was split in regards to the increased flexibility of their students as writers, with only 50% agreeing or strongly agreeing with the statement, but 35.8% disagreeing or strongly disagreeing (14.2% indicated "Don't know"). Also, teachers seemed to have mixed opinions regarding the equal balance of the skills in the new exam, with 43.3% agreeing or strongly agreeing with the statement that writing should carry more weight in the final exam grade than the other skills.

Teachers did not feel that the new exam had a negative impact on the quality of their students' writing or their students' grammatical and/or lexical competence. More than half of the teachers, 45% and 15.8%, respectively, agreed or strongly agreed with these statements. Teachers did, however, feel that the new exam was restricting them in their teaching of writing (55.8% agreed or strongly agreed), and that their students' creativity in writing was suffering as a consequence of the new exam (65.8% agreed or strongly agreed). The ramifications of these findings and an evaluation of the beneficence of the washback effect found here will be discussed in the following section.

Discussion

The findings above all suggest that the exam reform in Austria has caused a traceable washback effect on the classroom teaching and testing of writing. The political decisions regarding assessment appear to have impacted classroom practice. The task analysis of 302 writing tasks showed that classroom writing tasks have become more explicit and authentic in that they focus on communicative writing purposes and functional language use and provide realistic writing contexts. By that measure, the validity of classroom writing assessment has improved. Writing tasks are not only more in line with the national curriculum, but also with principles of communicative language testing. Authenticity and increased attention on communicative purposes for writing play a crucial role here. Test takers need to be provided with test tasks that represent their target language use in the real world, and the present study has shown that the exam reform instigated a change towards more authenticity not only in the final school-leaving exam, but also in the preparatory assessments leading up to it. Test takers are now asked to compose texts they are also likely to write in the target language outside the classroom and are provided with more instructions regarding their intended readership. Teachers in Austria seem to have become more aware of the notion of authenticity and how to put it into practice in teaching as well as testing, as it was found that they are trying to implement it in their own task design. However, the results presented also show that there is still a lot of room for improvement, as 75.2% of the analyzed post-2007 tasks were not categorized as highly authentic. The findings indicate that changes are taking place, and since they are mostly in line with the requirements and design of the new exam, it can be argued that there is indeed a detectable washback effect. It further appears that there is a clearer understanding by teachers of the construct of writing after the exam reform. Before 2007, reading comprehension was consistently a part of writing sections of exams. With less integration of other skills in writing tasks, as shown in the present findings, teachers minimize construct-irrelevant variance in their classroom writing tests, and the increased contextualization and specification in writing tasks adds to higher levels of validity in terms of communicative writing assessment. This change towards more curriculum alignment and adherence to good testing practice in classroom assessment can certainly be evaluated as beneficial washback of the exam reform. As Messick (1996) argues,

> negative washback per se should be associated with the introduction and use of less valid tests and positive washback with the introduction and use of more valid tests because construct underrepresentation and construct-irrelevant variance in the test could precipitate bad educational practices while minimizing these threats to validity should facilitate good educational practices.
>
> *(p. 247)*

It seems that the Austrian exam reform has achieved beneficial washback in this respect.

A second positive washback effect emerged in that the findings suggest that teachers' focus in teaching and testing writing has shifted towards the real-world writing needs of students. While interior monologues and other types of creative writing had featured strongly in teaching before 2007, the exam reform has prompted a change towards focusing on text and task types that are more tailored to the students' future writing needs. However, this convergence of text types comes at the cost of exploring other text types and genres. Since 2007, teachers tend to stick to the school-leaving exam task types, and reject incorporation of other genres in their progress checks. This could be seen as an unintended consequence, and appears to be seen as a rather negative washback effect of teaching to the test by the language teachers.

A third detected effect that could be ascribed to the exam reform was that both teachers and students appeared to focus more on organizational aspects of writing after 2007. Since this is one criterion in the rating scale, which became compulsory for the school-leaving exams as of 2015, it seems obvious to interpret this as a consequence of the exam reform. Also, the increasing familiarity with certain text types, such as the "report," reflects changes in teaching, which are due to the exam reform. This text type was not on the agenda of teachers before the reform at all, and the teacher questionnaire data support the interpretation that, because of the inclusion of this text type in the new standardized exam, it is now increasingly taught in language classrooms.

In fact, the responses to the teacher questionnaire indicate that a number of changes in writing teaching and assessment practices might be due to a washback effect. However, they also suggest that teachers have split views on some aspects of the exam reform and the washback might not be seen as entirely beneficial. Writing is still seen as the most prominent skill or at least most important area of classroom instruction. The fact that many teachers see students' creativity endangered might hint at a willingness to teach to the test. It appears that the test developers need to further promote language assessment literacy and market the benefits of this new approach to teaching and testing writing ability.

The findings presented here, however, are somewhat limited as no baseline data was available and teachers had to remember how they taught more than six years before. In addition, sample sizes are fairly small given that this is a nationwide exam. Further insights into teachers' perspectives and their writing teaching and assessment practices would need to be gained, for instance through systematic classroom observation (Alderson & Wall, 1993), and future developments in these areas would need to be monitored, particularly since the standardized tasks and rating scales became operative in general schools in 2015 and in vocational schools in 2016. An analysis of more recent classroom assessment writing tasks would not have been useful for the purposes of this research as teachers are obliged, as of October 2013, to use the same task types in their progress checks as in the final Matura. This is also the reason why the data gathering with the two instruments was done before that point in time. The analysis of actual classroom test tasks, however, has proven highly useful in tracking washback effects, particularly in conjunction with the teacher questionnaire data.

Conclusion

Reforms of high-stakes examinations are commonly believed, among other things, to instigate change in classrooms. The present study explored the impact of the Austrian government's decision to introduce a communicative curriculum and standardized school-leaving examination on EFL classroom teaching and assessment of writing. By means of task analyses and a teacher questionnaire, the assessment practices before and after the introduction of the new, competence-based exam, as well as the teachers' attitudes towards the new standardized exam, were investigated. It was found that Austria's teachers have indeed reacted to the educational reform by changing the assessment practices for writing. Teachers' opinions about the new exam, however, are mixed, which leaves questions about the beneficence of the initiated changes, their pervasiveness and persistence, and teachers' general language assessment literacy. Harking back to the title of this paper, test developers would certainly claim that teaching and assessment practices of writing have been "righted" through positive washback and have been made more authentic, valid, and reliable. However, from the view of those primarily implementing the change, i.e., the teachers, the question of whether writing practices have been "righted" requires a more differentiated answer. As teachers' attitudes towards the reform seemed ambiguous, it remains to be seen whether these changes happened due to formal requirements or an increased level of language assessment literacy among teachers. If the former, any changes may only be short-term lip-service and teaching to the test. If the latter, positive washback effects of the exam reform may have indeed righted writing practices in Austria. Most likely, in light of the current findings, the reality will be somewhere in between these two extremes.

Notes

1 The data for this study was gathered in 2013 and was presented first at the EALTA Conference 2013 in Istanbul (Kremmel, Eberharter, Konrad, & Maurer, 2013).
2 A copy of the adapted Writing Task Analysis Grid can be obtained from the authors upon request.

References

Alderson, J. C., & Wall, D. (1993). Does washback exist? *Applied Linguistics, 14*(2), 115–129. http://doi.org/10.1093/applin/14.2.115

Andrews, S. (2004). Washback and curriculum innovation. In L. Cheng, Y. Watanabe, & A. Curtis (Eds.), *Washback in language testing: Research contexts and methods*. Mahwah, NJ: Lawrence Erlbaum.

Bachman, L. F., & Palmer, A. S. (2010). *Language assessment in practice*. Oxford: Oxford University Press.

Cheng, L. (2005). *Changing language teaching through language testing: A washback study: Studies in language testing: Volume 21*. Cambridge: Cambridge University Press.

Cheng, L. (2008). Washback, impact and consequences. In E. Shohamy & N. H. Hornberger (Eds.), *Encyclopedia of language and education, 2nd edition, volume 7: Language testing and assessment*. New York: Springer.

Council of Europe. (2001). *Common European Framework of Reference for Languages: Learning, teaching, assessment*. Cambridge: Cambridge University Press.

Council of Europe. (2009). *Manual for relating language examinations to the Common European Framework of Reference for Languages (CEFR)*. Strasbourg: Language Policy Division.

Eberharter, K., & Frötscher, D. (2012). Quality control in marking open-ended listening and reading test items: Issues and practice. In D. Tsagari, S. Papadima-Sophocleous, & S. Ioannou-Georgiou (Eds.), *International experiences in language testing and assessment*. Frankfurt am Main: Peter Lang.

Elton, L., & Laurillard, D. M. (1979). Trends in research on student learning. *Studies in Higher Education, 4*, 87–102. http://doi.org/10.1080/03075077912331377131

European Assessment of Language Testing and Assessment. (2006). Guidelines for good practice in language testing and assessment. Retrieved January 12, 2017 from www.ealta.eu.org/guidelines.htm

Green, A. (2013). Washback in language assessment. *International Journal of English Studies, 13*(2), 39–51.

Hamp-Lyons, L. (1997). Washback, impact and validity: Ethical concerns. *Language Testing, 14*, 295–303. http://doi.org/10.1177/026553229701400306

Holzknecht, F., Kremmel, B., Konzett, C., Eberharter, K., Konrad, E., & Spöttl, C. (forthcoming). Potentials and challenges of teacher involvement in rating scale design for high-stakes exams. In D. Xerri & P. Vella Briffa (Eds.), *Teacher involvement in high stakes language testing*. New York: Springer.

Kane, M. T. (2012). Validating score interpretations and uses. *Language Testing, 29*(1), 3–17. http://doi.org/10.1177/0265532211417210

Konzett, C. (2011). *Every word counts: Fine-tuning the language of assessment scales: A field report*. Presentation at the IATEFL TEASIG Conference, Innsbruck, Austria.

Kremmel, B., Eberharter, K., Konrad, E., & Maurer, M. (2013). *Righting writing practices: The impact of exam reform*. Poster presented at the 10th Annual EALTA Conference, Istanbul, Turkey.

McNamara, T. (2000). *Language testing.* Oxford: Oxford University Press.

Messick, S. (1989). Validity. In R. L. Linn (Ed.), *Educational measurement* (pp. 13–104). New York: Palgrave Macmillan.

Messick, S. (1996). Validity and washback in language testing. *Language Testing, 13,* 241–256. http://doi.org/10.1177/026553229601300302

Spöttl, C., Kremmel, B., Holzknecht, F., & Alderson, J. C. (2016). Evaluating the achievements and challenges in reforming a national language exam: The reform team's perspective. *Papers in Language Testing and Assessment, 5*(1), 1–22.

Spratt, M. (2005). Washback and the classroom: The implications for teaching and learning of studies of washback from exams. *Language Testing Research, 9*(1), 5–29. http://doi.org/10.1191/1362168805lr152oa

Tankó, G. (2005). *Into Europe: The writing handbook.* Budapest: Teleki Lazlo Foundation and the British Council Hungary.

Wall, D. (1997). Impact and washback in language testing. In C. Clapham & D. Corson (Eds.), *Encyclopedia of language and education.* New York: Springer.

Wall, D. (2000). The impact of high-stakes testing on teaching and learning: Can this be predicted or controlled? *System, 28,* 499–509.

Wall, D. (2005). *The impact of high-stakes examinations on classroom teaching: A case study using insights from testing and innovation theory, studies in language testing: Volume 22.* Cambridge: Cambridge University Press.

Wall, D., & Alderson, J. C. (1993). Examining washback: The Sri Lankan impact study. *Language Testing, 10,* 41–69. http://doi.org/10.1177/026553229301000103

Weigle, S. C. (2002). *Assessing writing.* Cambridge: Cambridge University Press.

Weir, C. J. (2005). *Language testing and validation: An evidence-based approach.* Basingstoke: Palgrave Macmillan.

13

IMPACTS AND RESPONSES TO A UNIVERSITY HIGH-STAKES WRITING TEST

Gordon Blaine West and Bala Thiruchelvam

High-stakes English language testing has become unavoidable for South Koreans. English language exams determine, at least in part, what high school and university they will attend, whether or not they will be able to graduate university, and where they will be able to work after they graduate. In this chapter, we will examine one such high-stakes writing exam at a large, private Korean university, on which students must achieve a minimum required score to graduate.

There have been numerous studies of the washback effects of standardized, high-stakes testing on education systems around the world in recent years. One recent large-scale review of the literature concluded that findings were similar around the world: when schools and educational systems engage in high-stakes testing, the curriculum becomes restricted to teaching a narrow set of skills, and teachers are limited in the pedagogies they employ and the creativity with which they teach courses (Polesel, Dulfer, & Turnbull, 2012). This has also been true in South Korea, where the focus on English language testing has led to a largely instrumental view of the language as being something you learn (or teach) in order to pass an exam, which it is believed will aid in your social advancement in society (Choi, 2008). Park (2011) warns, however, that this view of language as a neutral "skill," or of testing as neutral process, is detrimental, and leaves out vital questions about the political nature of language learning and testing that need to be asked.

We focus on one South Korean university's required, standardized English exam, the Computer-Based English Test (CBET) writing exam. To see how it impacts students and teachers, we conducted an interview study with instructors from the English Language Program department, and with students who have failed the CBET. Using grounded theory (Charmaz, 2006), we analyzed the data to find five major themes that give us a better idea of how participants viewed the test as having both positive and negative aspects, its impact on teachers' pedagogy and students' lives, and their responses to combat what they felt were harmful effects of the test. Very few studies either globally or in the Korean context have used interview data to examine questions about testing qualitatively, with most relying on quantitative survey studies (i.e., Choi, 2008). Our study attempts to add to this vital area of testing research by giving voice to the students whose lives are impacted by high-stakes testing.

Overview of the South Korean Context

Historically, Korean society and government have been largely bureaucratic in nature, and tests have traditionally been used to award positions or to secure social and professional advancement (Seth, 2002). This emphasis and focus on testing as a means of sorting the population has continued to the present day and has had a part in driving the English language testing market. English language testing exists at every stage of Korean education. English plays a large part in the Korean Scholastic Aptitude Test (KSAT) for college applications, most universities require a minimum score on one of several standardized English exams (i.e., TOEIC, TOEFL, TEPS) to graduate, and many companies require a minimum score on the TOEIC to apply for a position.

Many of the tests focus mainly on receptive skills (reading and listening) or discrete language skills (i.e., grammar forms, vocabulary items, etc.). This focus on receptive and discrete skills creates a focus on memorizing vocabulary, studying grammar points, and practicing reading for multiple choice comprehension questions at the expense of any focus on writing or speaking. The negative washback effects of this exam have been examined and critiqued in the Korean press for producing students who can take tests well, but fail to communicate in English (i.e., Ahn, 2015). This critique in popular culture has driven many attempts at reform, though with little success, given the outsized importance of performance on these exams in determining the livelihoods of test takers. Reforms are met with pushback from the public and usually result in families investing more money in private tutoring and test prep schools (Chosunilbo, 2016), despite the fact that most teachers and test takers feel deeply unsatisfied with the state of testing in Korea (Choi, 2008).

Computer-Based English Test

In this context, the CBET was developed. The CBET consists of two different exams, a speaking exam and a writing exam, but focuses entirely on productive skills, rather than receptive skills. For writing, students are expected to complete three timed tasks: writing an email response to a prompt (7 minutes), writing a description of a graph or visual data (10 minutes), and writing either an argumentative or compare and contrast essay to a prompt (30 minutes). The rubrics for rating also focus on assessment of language as holistic instead of focusing on discrete points. For instance, raters are instructed to rate "grammar" only in part on actual grammar errors, and to look instead at how easy it is to understand the point the writer is trying to communicate. In this way, the test was created to better align with the goals of communicative language teaching, and to help combat the negative washback effects of other tests.

In the late 1990s, the CBET was developed by the university in hopes of competing with the established tests TOEIC and TOEFL. Several other universities created their own tests at the time as well, with the most well-known and widely used being the Test of English Proficiency (TEPS), developed by Seoul National University. The public regard for Seoul National University as the top ranked university helped this test become widely trusted in Korea, while other tests developed at that time, including the CBET, ended up being relegated to largely intramural use.

Since the early 2000s, achieving a certain CBET score has been a graduation requirement, with different departments requiring different scores depending on the major field of study. The policy has been revised a few times, and in the early 2010s, the test was amended to create a scaled-down version of the CBET for students, with fewer test items to complete.

The test policy today requires students to take the scaled-down version of the CBET as part of the regular English Language Program (ELP) courses (reading and writing course students take the writing CBET, while speaking and listening students take the speaking CBET). They must take both the speaking and writing exam. If students fail to achieve the required score on the scaled-down version after taking their ELP courses, they have a few options: (1) pay to take the full CBET or (2) take either the TOEFL or TOEIC and use that score for the graduation requirement. If they fail to get the score they need on the full CBET or on another test, their third option is to take an alternative CBET course, at an additional cost, administered by the university. The alternative course is a 40-hour intensive course that is offered only during semester breaks and is taught mainly by part-time faculty from different departments, which serves to emphasize the marginalized position of the students in the course. Instead of taking one exam at the end of the course, the students take a total of three smaller exams and one full writing exam during the course. Their tests are rated by two raters to determine whether or not they have achieved the necessary score on their writing to graduate.

Given the goals of the exam were to foster better pedagogy, imagined as a communicative approach to teaching, and to combat negative washback effects, we wanted to examine how this test was actually affecting teachers and students. Our research questions were: (1) How does the CBET affect the way that teachers approach their ELP reading and writing classes (what kind of washback does it create), and (2) how does failing the CBET affect students? We focused on the writing exam specifically because our research began following the semester where instructors were teaching mainly writing ELP courses. We focused on students who failed the CBET because although a majority of students pass the test, around 60 students each semester enroll in the alternative course to graduate, and they often seem to be the ones whose experience is most overlooked by researchers and administration.

Methodology

Interview data from three sources form the basis for this study. Interviews were conducted with seven instructors from the English Language Program, two instructors who taught part-time in the alternative CBET course, and four students who had recently completed the alternative CBET course. Participants were recruited through email surveys sent to instructors and students at the end of the course. Respondents were then asked if they would like to participate in an interview about their experience with the course.

Participants

To protect the identities of our participants, we will offer only a general summary of their backgrounds. All instructors at the time of the study had taught in the department for between three to ten years and had an MA degree, although not always in a field related to applied linguistics. None had a background in language testing, nor did any have a particular background in teaching or researching second language writing before beginning to teach in the department. The instructors interviewed were non-native English speakers (NNESs) and native English speakers (NESs).

Two instructors from the alternative CBET course taught full time in different departments at the university, and this was a course they taught during the semester breaks. Neither had much experience in teaching the course, and the course was under redevelopment at the time of the study. The instructors for the alternative CBET courses also had their MA degrees and were from English native-speaking countries.

The students interviewed were recruited after having completed their CBET alternative course. All had their graduation dates postponed because they had failed to meet the English examination requirement. Their ages ranged from early to late 20s and all were Korean.

All names are pseudonyms. The names of the test (CBET) and university department (ELP) have also been changed.

Interviews

Both authors took turns conducting interviews with the participants, depending on time and availability. The interviews took between 30 and 90 minutes, following different interview schedules for students, ELP instructors, and CBET alternative course instructors.

Analysis

All of the data gathered was coded using a data-driven approach that follows some protocols of constructivist grounded theory (Charmaz, 2006). Grounded theory protocol offers a practical and rigorous way to synthesize findings across different sets of data (interviews with ELP department instructors, CBET students, and alternative CBET course instructors). Charmaz's (2006) constructivist version of grounded theory is more amenable to this study's critical orientation. Knowledge from a constructivist paradigm is considered to be co-constructed between participants and the researcher. In this, we view knowledge as being political in the sense that since the knowledge producers are political creatures, the knowledge produced will naturally follow from their ideological understandings of the world. Examining tensions between different understandings can lead to rich analysis and new understanding.

Findings

Five major themes were identified from the data: views of the exam (utility and disconnection), impacts of the test (on pedagogy and on students), and responses to the exam. For reasons of space and clarity, we will focus on the impacts and responses to the exam only.

Impacts on Pedagogy

Every instructor interviewed described the CBET as significantly shaping the way they designed and taught their writing courses. Technically, the courses are listed as "ELP Reading/Writing," although all instructors admitted to teaching writing almost exclusively because reading was not tested on the CBET. Several expressed an extremely high focus on test prep in their writing classes, as Ben does in Excerpt 1.

Excerpt 1. Ben: My main objectives are very much influenced by the CBET.

Bala: You kinda mentioned already you want to incorporate a little bit of culture into your classes and also showing [students] the purposes of learning English. Ah, what other main objectives do you have and how much control do you have in setting them?

Ben: Sorry in setting the um. My main objectives for writing class?

Bala: Yes.

Ben: Um. I think my main objectives are very much influenced by the CBET. Completely. I mean it's (. . .) For level 1 students, and I keep on repeating this, but for level 1 students and level 2, even level 2s, although I have seen a great increase in the abilities of students these these last years. I can see that they are getting better and better and more students are actually going abroad but a lot of them are still very scared of English. And they have this absolute hatred for English, some of them, and they are just petrified of it.

He discusses the different levels of classes. Students are separated by a placement test and put into either level 1, 2, or 3 for English Language Program courses, although all levels take the same version of the CBET at the end of the semester as a final exam. He justifies this focus on the CBET as stemming from the students' fear of English and their need to pass the test. Later in the interview he goes on to clarify just how great his focus on test prep is in his various writing courses (Excerpt 2).

Excerpt 2. Ben: Time spent on CBET prep.

Ben: And so for me, the CBET is a huge part of it [a common end goal for students to aspire to]. And if you're talking about level 1 students, I would say it's [class time spent covering CBET prep specifically] 90%. If you're talking about level 2 students, I'm saying it's 80%.

Bala: Right.

Ben: When we hit level 3 students it tends to maybe drop down to 50% because those students should already be able to pass the CBET. That's why they are in the level 3 class.

Although 90% of class time spent on test prep seems like an extreme number, others reported spending similar amounts of time on preparing students for the test. One instructor, Sally, stated that her entire writing class, 100% of the time in class for level 1 students, was dedicated to preparing them to pass the CBET. In this context, Ben was merely representative of the type of washback that instructors reported and the strong impact that the exam had on their courses.

This strong focus on the exams stood perhaps a bit in contrast to the high degree of autonomy and freedom that instructors reported feeling in designing their courses. All reported relative freedom from administrative oversight, which fostered a feeling of professionalism in the instructors. However, instructors also understood the implications of failing the CBET for their students, and so shaped their courses around it, although some felt that it went against the wishes of administrators. Beth (Excerpt 3) expressed this tension of going against administrators' wish to not "teach to the test."

Excerpt 3. Beth: They would prefer us not to teach exactly to the test.

Gordon: Do you feel like it [CBET] gives you like a good goal and structure for your class?

Beth: Yeah, to some extent, yeah. And, and we don't have to, we don't have to, in fact they [administrators] would prefer us to not teach to, exactly teach to the test. They want them [students] to be able to just react in different situations, and not just those [on the test], but they kind of I guess picked those because they're a good, you know . . .

Gordon: Good tasks?

Beth: Good selection across the board, I guess is how they picked them. I wasn't, I didn't have a part in creating it.

While Beth alludes to how much the CBET shapes her class without ever being as specific as Ben is, she gives a hint at how it shapes her class by stating both her autonomy and the fact that the administration would prefer that they not teach to the test, suggesting some tension between what administration wants and what she feels is necessary. She also expresses a feeling about the utility of the exam tasks, and her disconnection from the process with her final statement that she is not involved in the creation. Her focus on preparation and utility, though, seemingly outweigh her feelings of disconnection, which would also be consistent with a more instrumental approach to teaching, where the focus is on helping students to pass without focusing too much on the politics of the exam.

Impacts on Students

The impact of the CBET on students centered on three subthemes from our interviews: financial costs, life plan delays, and emotional costs. After the first time taking the CBET, students had to pay around $90.00 for each subsequent test they wanted to take. For comparison, the TOEIC costs roughly $40 per exam in Korea (Jung, 2016). Many had taken the test multiple times. For those who needed to enroll in the alternative course, the cost was a further $250 for each course, writing and speaking. Financial impacts of English testing are far more wide-ranging than the CBET, and impact students at almost every level in Korea (Choi, 2008).

In terms of life plan delays, all students interviewed had to delay their graduation from university because they lacked the required CBET score. For one, this resulted in her acceptance to a graduate school being rescinded. For others, job contracts depended on passing the alternative course. One described her life as being almost on hold for a few years after she failed to attain the required score on CBET and was not allowed to graduate.

One of the biggest impacts tied together with financial and delays in life plans was the emotional cost to students. One of the students, Autumn, relates how she felt as a result of both financial and life delay burdens from the exam in Excerpt 4.

Excerpt 4. Autumn: I think my life was ruined.

Bala: What was your CBET alternative class experience like?

Autumn: As I said before, um, I was very frustrated and my life was (laughing). My life was, in the first time I think my life was ruined.

Bala: Ahh.

Autumn: What should I do if the graduation [graduate] school didn't allow me again [reject her application]. I was very frustrated and

Bala: Worried

Autumn: Nervous. Yeah, and the alternative courses are very experience, very expensive. Yeah, and I worked very hard for the (in Korean: what was the word?) . . . the money.

In this excerpt, Autumn lays clear the consequences of failing the exam. She not only lost her spot at graduate school and paid a lot of money for the course, but also felt the emotional impact of all these negative consequences. While she is laughing in the excerpt, it is preceded and followed by more emotional exchanges. Here, the laughter helps her to discuss a topic that might otherwise be too painful.

This type of emotional cost was articulated by all student participants, and was one aspect of the impact on students the instructors seemed least aware of. They understood the financial costs (if a bit abstractly), and that the CBET can delay graduation. Only Doug acknowledged the emotional toll. For many students in the alternative class, Doug felt that they had lost faith in their own abilities, although an excerpt from one student, Seomin, helps to show that students also lost faith in the testing process as well.

Excerpt 5. Seomin: Actually, I can't believe CBET test.

Bala: What did it mean to you the first time failing and second time failing? What does it mean for your graduation? Does that mean . . .?

Seomin: Ah, to graduate my major, I have to

Bala: Pass

Seomin: Yeah, I have to get Advanced level. But at first time I got Intermediate level and second time also I got Intermediate. So, and also I didn't, even now, I don't know what is the criteria of evaluation actually. I don't know why I got Intermediate and there is no feedback about my writing and my speaking, so I couldn't improve myself, and I couldn't prepare next time. So I decided to take alternative courses. Because actually, I can't believe CBET test.

Seomin expresses a disconnection from the testing process because of the lack of clear feedback and not understanding what she could do to improve, or even what the test raters wanted her to improve to achieve her required score of "advanced." Throughout this exchange she is quite upset recounting her experience. This vagueness in the evaluation process leads her to question the validity of the test itself.

Responses

Among those who felt that the test had largely negative impacts, there was a higher likelihood that they were working to respond to and attempt to compensate for those negative impacts. Five out of the 13 participants talked about ways they were trying to resist, subvert, or simply respond to aspects of the exam they considered harmful. We will briefly outline three before looking more closely at two others.

One response was to spend extra time helping students to understand the exam. One instructor discussed taking extra time to meet with students he felt were in danger of failing and holding one-on-one tutoring sessions with them. One student also discussed a similar response. Autumn reported holding study groups to share notes and insights she had learned from the alternative class with several of her friends who needed to pass the CBET but lacked feedback on how to improve, or what the criteria were. Autumn shared what she had learned in the alternative course with her friends to help them pass the test. These responses were more typical of what we might expect of a dedicated teacher or friend; however, other responses were larger in scope.

Several of the participants expressed the need for a more recent exam prep book, similar to those that exist for other exams like the TOEIC or TOEFL; however, the most recent CBET book was published in 2006. One instructor shared a test prep book that she had written herself for students who were required to take only a partial CBET, and was in the process of creating one for her ELP students also. She reported using the materials in class and sharing them with students free of charge. Her stated reasons for doing this were in response to a sense of frustration with a perceived impenetrable bureaucracy functioning behind the CBET.

This sense that the test was administered by a far-off entity, which was not responsible directly to the students, drove the final two example responses also. Although they do not write the questions or administer the exam, ELP department instructors, as part of their regular duties, are required to undergo CBET rater training and rate exam responses at the end of each semester. The responses are anonymous, and they are not assigned any of their own students. One instructor, Jamie, discussed several problems she felt with the administration of the test and exam questions. In Excerpt 6, she discusses her response to poorly phrased questions as a rater by deviating from the rubric and giving the students a higher score than she might otherwise have.

Excerpt 6. Jamie: You don't ding them right down for not answering the question properly.

Gordon: In the situation where you get a question that's grammatically incorrect or something, what do you do?

Jamie: So basically what I do is, I look at the question and then I just have to turn around and say OK well if the content seems a little confused, possibly that's because the question is confusing. So then I have to kind of um, or if perhaps the student doesn't seem to have answered the question as I have interpreted it, I have to basically turn around and be like, well I'm sympathetic because . . this question is open to interpretation. It's not clear. Um, so then I still have to look at, you know, the other parts of it. So, what is the general vocabulary, the spelling, the other kind of . . . grammar etc. So even if the question is confusing, how have they dealt with the content they have produced.

Gordon: Sure.

Jamie: So even if it doesn't answer the question, that I think the question is saying, what have they done? So there's one part on the CBET where it is about answering the question and so for that um you're just a bit more lenient. You don't ding them right down for not answering the question properly. Because you can look at it and go it's a terrible question. So you might drop them a little.

She further explains how not only does she adjust how she is rating, but that ELP instructors send out faculty-wide emails when they find a question they find confusing or poorly worded (e.g., the email task should have a problem to resolve and offer possible solutions for, but the question instead asks the students to respond to a proposed solution). The email system is intended to warn other raters about the question and to work collectively to avoid giving the students lower marks on that question.

The strongest responses, though, came from Doug, who taught the alternative course. Doug discussed several of the ways he works to help students pass the CBET, and the alternative course at the time of the interview had been set up so that students' homework and attendance can also boost their test scores. If a student needed to get an intermediate score in order to pass the writing exam, s/he could attend all classes, do all the homework, score a low basic on the exam and still be able to attain the intermediate level s/he needed to graduate. Doug explains this in Excerpt 7.

Excerpt 7. Doug: We have those bulwarks in there.

Gordon: Has anyone ever failed this one [CBET Alternative Course]?

Doug: Um, it's difficult to fail.

Gordon: Ok.

Doug: Unless (. . .) they don't come. That's, cuz that's 40% out of 70 or 75 right there.

Gordon: Ah, ok.

Doug: So, that's how it's set up. Um (. . .) I did have one fail. Or, or if they skip any of the tests or definitely the final exam cuz those are drops of 5, 10%. Um, I had one fail in summer. Emm, and it wasn't through any fault of her own, but I think she needed Advanced and she was really functioning at like Low Intermediate. So she came to almost every class, and I'm sure she tried hard but according to the cri . . . She just didn't . . . yeah. She didn't make, ummm. [details omitted for identity] . . .

Gordon: Yeah, yeah.

Doug: So, but it is. It is hard to fail because we have those bulwarks in there for, I think, to account for the fact that some people are just not good at taking tests.

Doug shared feeling a strong sense of responsibility to help the students graduate. Having the agency to act in his situation, and being able to shape the course and alter to some extent the final exam they would take as a modified CBET, plus rate the exams of the students himself, gave him the opportunity to help students more than ELP instructors had. He raised concerns though about the validity of the process, which we will address further in the discussion.

Discussion and Paths Forward

While the original intent behind developing the CBET was to create a counterbalance to the negative washback effects of other standardized English tests and to focus more on communicative skills, largely, that has not been the impact. We found that almost all instructors agreed that their classes are taught to the test, but that it is a test they do not have any influence over creating. Given the high-stakes nature of the exam, instructors adopted an instrumental view of teaching their courses, contributing to the previously reported issue of language being viewed simply as a means to passing an exam (Choi, 2008). In a similar study conducted with teachers in the United States, Rex and Nelson (2004) found that the teachers, when faced with pressure to teach to the test, ended up refusing and relegating the test to a secondary consideration, based on a moral view of teaching where high-stakes testing is an invalid driver of education. The instructors in our study, however, held more neoliberal views of language teaching, in which learning English is a skill that increases one's marketability (Park, 2011).

One consideration for teachers and administrators in creating writing exams or setting testing policies for second language writers is Lynch's (2001) ethical framework for testing. In his paper, he calls for a critical view of the ethics and validity of testing, including a focus on "impact/consequential validity" (Lynch,

2001, p. 365), whereby the validity of an exam should not only be judged based on traditional psychometric measures of validity and reliability, but also in such a way that the impacts that the test has are accounted for, not only on students, but also on the ways in which teachers change their approaches to teaching because of the test. After looking carefully at the ways in which a test impacts teachers and students, all stakeholders should jointly negotiate whether these impacts are positive or negative, and if negative, then discuss ways to mediate the negative impacts.

The exam has also had severe impacts on students. They faced delays in their graduation, financial burdens, and in one case, a retraction of a graduate school acceptance, based on their inability to achieve the required score on a standardized writing exam. This would be one area to examine to determine the impact validity of the exam, but it is also important to raise questions about the political economic context of the CBET. Templer (2004) does an investigation that raises questions of who benefits and who is ill-served by the TOEFL and IELTS exams, asking questions about who profits from these tests. He finds that often those in poorer countries end up paying those in wealthier countries to learn their language, and that process is measured and mediated by exams created by the wealthy countries. Here, on a local scale, we have an exam that was created by the university, in good faith, but questions should still be raised about who is benefiting from this testing process.

Shohamy (2001/2014) gives us a set of principles to consider when we are creating and evaluating language assessments. Especially pertinent here are three of her principles: (2) we need to encourage active, critical responses from test-takers, (3) test-takers are political subjects within a political context, and (5) we need to raise questions about whose agendas the tests serve (Shohamy, 2001/2014, numbers from her original list). Following these guidelines can help us to question the political context and purpose of the exams more effectively, and can also help test-takers to have a greater voice in the process. The students are the ones with the most to lose from testing, and accordingly should have more of a voice in the process.

Following Shohamy's (2001/2014) principles in developing writing exams and Lynch's (2001) impact validity in evaluating tests can help us better orient ourselves to view second language writing not just from a neutral, instrumental perspective, but to understand that it is a political process and we are all actors in that process. Understanding our role as actors is the first step in encouraging greater agency and action, as was found in the responses from several of the participants in our study. Those responses and actions by participants to work to limit the negative impacts of the CBET are encouraging, although they would go further if the process were more open to receiving input, more transparent, and if those involved as stakeholders felt that they had more a role to play in shaping the test.

References

Ahn, S. B. (2015, November 13). What use is the English part of the college entrance exam? *The Chosunilbo*. Retrieved from http://english.chosun.com/site/data/html_dir/2015/11/13/2015111301822.html

Charmaz, K. (2006). *Constructing grounded theory*. Los Angeles: Sage.

Choi, I. (2008). The impact of EFL testing on EFL education in Korea. *Language Testing*, 25(1), 39–62. https://doi.org/10.1177/0265532207083744

Chosunilbo. (2016, February 29). Spending on private crammers hits new record. *The Chosunilbo*. Retrieved from http://english.chosun.com/site/data/html_dir/2016/02/29/2016022901342.html

Jung, G. H. (2016, June 27). The costly, complicated hurdle of TOEIC. *The Korea JoongAng Daily*. Retrieved from http://mengnews.joins.com/view.aspx?aId=3020498

Lynch, B. K. (2001). Rethinking assessment from a critical perspective. *Language Testing*, 18(4), 351–372. https://doi.org/10.1177/026553220101800403

Park, J. S. Y. (2011). The promise of English: Linguistic capital and the neoliberal worker in the South Korean job market. *International Journal of Bilingual Education and Bilingualism*, 14(4), 443–455.

Polesel, J., Dulfer, N., & Turnbull, M. (2012). *The experience of education: The impacts of high stakes testing on school students and their families*. Literature Review prepared for the Whitlam Institute, Melbourne Graduate School of Education, and the Foundation for Young Australians. Retrieved from www.whitlam.org/__data/assets/pdf_file/0008/276191/High_Stakes_Testing_Literature_Review.pdf

Rex, L. A., & Nelson, M. C. (2004). How teachers' professional identities position high-stakes test preparation in their classrooms. *Teachers College Record*, 106(6), 1288–1331. https://doi.org/10.1111/j.1467-9620.2004.00380.x

Seth, M. J. (2002). *Education fever: Society, politics, and the pursuit of schooling in South Korea*. Honolulu: University of Hawaii Press.

Shohamy, E. (2001/2014). *The power of tests: A critical perspective on the uses of language tests*. New York: Routledge.

Templer, B. (2004). High-stakes testing at high fees: Notes and queries on the international English proficiency assessment market. *Journal for Critical Education Policy Studies*, 2(1), 1–8.

PART III

Seeking Solutions

Assessing Better Locally and Internationally

14

WRITING ACADEMICALLY AND CREATIVELY

Moving Beyond Test-Driven Writing Instruction in a Chinese University

Chenchen Huang and Xiaoye You

Every April, English major college students in China prepare for two national exams, TEM-4 and TEM-8 (Test for English Majors-Band 4 and -Band 8). TEM tests have become a rite of passage for English majors in China since 1991, when they were first administered to evaluate English proficiency. Recently, both tests went through substantive changes, with emphases for different exam items rearranged. The changes immediately generated heated discussions over paradigm shifts, exam strategies, and pedagogies within academic circles. This is not at all surprising since the exam policies affect hundreds of thousands of test-takers. In China, where testing results reign over other considerations when evaluating educational excellence, how do English and writing instructors nourish students' creativity and agency, if at all?

This chapter aims to illustrate how English writing instructors at Guangdong University of Foreign Studies (hereafter GDUFS), a reputed university specializing in teaching and research in foreign languages and trade in Southeastern China, negotiated with the national assessment mandates to move beyond test-driven writing instruction. Through document analyses and interviews, we sought to understand how large-scale, high-stakes assessments impacted this local university's curricular design and teaching priorities. We discovered that faculty members had devised a variety of pedagogical initiatives to actualize the national assessment mandates. Our research intended to unravel the intricate interplay between writing standards and its local implementation in an English as a foreign language (EFL) context. Moreover, we hoped to draw upon lessons from China where writing instructors had negotiated nationwide assessment mandates within an examination-driven system to inform domestic practitioners who are committed to locally developed and decentralized assessment methods.

The Politics of Second Language Writing Assessment

Despite its widely acknowledged importance, writing assessment has been largely marginalized in the field of composition studies. It is commonly considered as "a necessary evil inextricably woven into the fabric of education in which [composition instructors] participate out of obligation or coercion" (Neal, 2010, p. 747). Fortunately, this issue has garnered an increasing amount of scholarly attention in the past two decades with the successful launch of a series of flagship journals (e.g., *Assessing Writing* and *Journal of Writing Assessment*). Writing professionals started to insert their voices into the ongoing discussion about assessment and wrested power from corporate assessment agencies. For instance, in the United States, scholars criticized the rise of large-scale, nationally normed tests brought on by the ill-fated No Child Left Behind as well as the arrival of the Common Core State Standards. Invariably, they pointed out these tests' inability to judge writing, let alone further learning and development (Applebee, 2007; Condon, 2013; Deane, Williams, Weng, & Trapani, 2013). Their distrust of commercial testing enterprises has led to a wide suspicion of nationwide standards or mandates such as the Common Core State Standards. Ruecker, Chamcharatsri, and Saengngoen (2015), for example, examined how the Common Core State Standards as well as its attendant assessments overlooked English Language Learners (ELL) student populations. Similarly, Addison (2015) examined the implementation process of the Common Core State Standards and observed that it ushered English Language Arts into skill-based instruction, whose influence should be contained and mitigated in college writing classrooms. As large-scale writing assessment expands and is further facilitated by automated essay scoring technology, how writing instructors can negotiate its overwhelming effects begs immediate investigation.

Meanwhile, scholarship on second language writing assessment, a crucial segment of writing assessment, continues to grow. Crusan (2010) published a book-length project on assessment in the second language writing classroom, in which she brought attention to biases and inconsistencies in assessment (e.g., teacher, cultural, disciplinary, and administrative biases). Similarly, others have dwelled upon inclusion and diversity (Crusan, 2006; Hamp-Lyons, 1996; White, Lutz, & Kamusikiri, 1996). Their critiques targeted the fact that assessment methods were most often not ethical or meaningful. Commenting on the adoption of "reliability" and "validity," criteria used to legitimize writing assessment, many writing specialists accused it of failing to take into account contextual factors that might have impacted and even confounded assessment results. Hamp-Lyons (1996) listed a series of challenges that writing professionals might encounter when approaching second language writers—cultural biases, prior exposure to varieties and dialects of English, professional training in second language writing, familiarity with different language groups, preferred rhetorical structure and style, etc. Moreover, Crusan (2002) laid bare the arbitrariness of writing assessment. As she pointed out, the rationale of adopting a particular assessment format is primarily determined by "cost and ease of administration" (p. 37). These investigations have helped composition specialists problematize the one-size-fits-all assumption that undergirded many large-scale assessments. Instead, they advocated that assessment should be site-based, locally controlled, context-sensitive, rhetorically based, accessible, and theoretically consistent (Crusan, 2010; O'Neill, Moore, & Huot, 2009; Weigle, 2006).

Nevertheless, extant publications on second language writing assessment have heavily emphasized a North American academic context, as Ruecker and Crusan have discussed in the introduction. In particular, most research has predominantly focused on second language writers attending universities in the United States (Crusan, 2002, 2006, 2010; Song & August, 2002), leaving second language writers elsewhere untended. For a few scholars that ventured outside academic institutions in North America, they further confirmed that scholarship on second language writing assessment developed in North America might not ring true (Lee & Coniam, 2013; Xu & Liu, 2009). Local universities faced challenges of putting pedagogical scholarship produced outside their immediate educational milieu into practice. Instead, these universities discussed the necessity of coming up with a more accessible and effective assessment that was more tailored to their respective population of service. For example, Lee and Coniam (2013) conducted a case study through which they discovered how Assessment for Learning (AFL) was implemented in an examination-driven Assessment of Learning (AOL) system in Hong Kong. According to them, local instructors found it difficult to meet some agendas outlined in an AFL system due to its conflict with their more conventional concerns, especially instructional practices arising from an EFL context. In fact, English writing instructors from different countries have experimented with innovative assessment methods that would better accommodate local English learners (Ali, 2013; Burner, 2014; Öz, 2014). With a few exceptions (e.g., Lam, 2015; Lee, 2017), assessment scholarship has yet to examine assessment policies in other parts of the world as well as their impacts on the teaching of English and English writing. If we continue to be at ease with restricting ourselves to politics and educational concerns in the United States, we may perpetuate a cultural bias and leave an important segment of composition scholarship untended. This chapter, therefore, adopts an international perspective for writing assessment. It will turn to China where large-scale language and writing assessments prevail (Sun, 2010), and examine local efforts to negotiate the influence of national assessment mandates in the service of regulating English learning and teaching. Through a case study, we intend to address the following questions:

1. What do national assessment mandates require of undergraduate English majors regarding their English writing?
2. How do local instructors negotiate the national assessment policies?
3. What has enabled or discouraged their acts of negotiation?

Methodology

Context and Subjects

The study was conducted within the Faculty of English Language and Culture at GDUFS. All the students enrolled through the Faculty were considered English majors, though they specialized in six different concentrations—British and American literature, culture and communications, international conferences and exhibitions and tourism, linguistics, information management, and translation and interpretation. For the first two years of their college experience, students received training in general English writing. In these courses, they practiced various modes of writing. They developed research skills by conducting library and field research and learned journalistic and reporting styles by writing newspaper feature stories. In the seventh semester, the students took a ten-week course of Academic Thesis Writing to familiarize themselves with the MLA writing conventions and the BA thesis requirements for English majors. Towards the end of the semester, the students contacted professors of their choice to discuss their tentative topics and proposals for their undergraduate theses. In the last semester, the students drafted their theses under the mentorship of their chosen advisers.

For our study, we recruited two participants—Nan and Jianjun from GDUFS.[1] Both were senior lecturers in the Department of Translation and Interpretation. Nan was a specialist in translation and interpretation and an experienced thesis advisor. In the year the study was conducted, she had coached ten advisees in total and four of them received recognition because of the distinguished quality of their theses. Considering her experience at GDUFS, we were particularly interested in how Nan interpreted and interacted with the assessment documents. Jianjun, likewise, has taught at GDUFS for nearly a decade and was recently put in charge of overseeing a writing exchange activity between GDUFS and the Pennsylvania State University (hereafter PSU). In our interview with him, we concentrated on his experience in fostering students' participation in extracurricular writing events. Since we both have worked closely with faculty from GDUFS, including the two colleagues we described above, we also relied on our firsthand observations of various teaching and research activities conducted at or with GDUFS.

Data Collection and Analysis

For the sake of the current study, we collected two types of documents for preliminary analyses—outcome statements and exam rubrics issued at different historical periods. Outcome statements delineate pedagogical objectives, course offerings and workload, pedagogical standards, principles, and methods that universities with English departments are expected to follow. Correspondingly, exam rubrics illustrate the assessment procedures—skills to be tested, the scope of the tests, and test formats. For the outcome statements, we collected the "College Teaching Syllabus for English Majors" ("高校英语专业教学大纲") published in 1979, "College English Syllabus for English Majors at the Foundation Stage" ("高等学校英语专业基础阶段英语教学大纲") published in 1989, "College English Syllabus for English Majors at the Advanced Stage" ("高等学校英语专业高年级阶段英语教学大纲") published in 1990, and "National College English Teaching Syllabus for English Majors" ("高等院校英语专业教学大纲") published in 2000. These policy documents shaped and determined undergraduate curriculum for English majors across Chinese universities when in use, as the 2000 Syllabus continues to do today.

In addition, we gathered exam rubrics for TEM-4 and TEM-8 in three different editions: the "Outline of Test for English Majors-Band 4" ("英语专业四级考试大纲") and "Outline of Test for English Majors-Band 8" ("英语专业八级考试大纲") released in 1997, their reissues in 2004, and the "Clarification on Changes to Test for English Majors-Band 4/Band 8" ("关于英语专业四级/八级考试题型调整的说明") in 2015. Produced by the National Advisory Commission on Foreign Language Teaching in Higher Education, the 1997 Outlines were an unprecedented endeavor to standardize and quantify teaching outcomes through high-stakes assessment.[2] In 2004, the Advisory Commission tailored the assessment outlines in accordance with the 2000 Syllabus. More recently, it updated the 2004 Outlines and adjusted exam items. When analyzing the documents, we first made comparisons between the outcome statements as well as between the exam rubrics in order to gauge the changes being made over time. We then juxtaposed both types of documents and traced the overlaps and dissonance between them. With a specific interest in assessing English writing, we highlighted the areas where English writing was addressed and color coded them against a coding scheme with identifiers such as "politics," "objectives," "speed of output," etc.

Meanwhile, we investigated how the incumbent set of assessment mandates (i.e., the 2000 Syllabus and the 2015 TEM-4 and TEM-8 exam rubrics) had been implemented in a local context. Our research data came from a multi-year collaboration between GDUFS and PSU. In 2015, we worked with Nan, from whom we secured 82 undergraduate theses as well as instructional materials and assessment rubrics. In particular, we paid attention to her involvements in her advisees' research and writing process. We collaborated with Jianjun, who helped us facilitate writing exchanges between students from GDUFS and PSU for two semesters in 2016. We also interviewed Nan and Jianjun and solicited their opinions of how the English program has been operating at GDUFS in relation to the 2000 Syllabus and its attendant testing battery. We juxtaposed our analyses of the policy documents against data procured from interviews in order to shed light on the instructors' local attempts to contend with the national assessment mandates.

Results

Analyzing Assessment Documents

After arranging the assessment documents chronologically, we observed an increasing emphasis on writing, especially practical genres, over time as well as a growing interest in adopting English to partake in global knowledge production. These two trends are indicative of English's changing role in college education in China during the past four decades. On the one hand, English was treated with caution. For example, to shield students from the baneful corruption of Western ideologies, the "College English Syllabus for English Majors at the Advanced Stage" stressed politically correct writing, which should contain "neither Western political ideas without thorough criticism nor information that misrepresents the Chinese social reality or the government policies." On the other hand, English was harnessed in service of China's national modernization project and cross-cultural exchange. In the "College English Syllabus for English Majors at the Foundation Stage," communicative English is greatly emphasized: "the objective of foreign language teaching lies in fostering abilities to communicate in foreign languages." An important component of communication as it is, writing was nonetheless restricted to practical genres such as notices, minutes, or letters. In comparison, the 2000 Syllabus manifests a heightened attention to thought development through English writing as well as to English's service value to other disciplines.

In response to the changes brought by a market economy, the 2000 Syllabus provides guidelines for preparing students to become "professionals with multiple skills" (复合型人才). Specifically, it acknowledges the importance of writing. The Syllabus mandates that writing classes will be offered for three or four consecutive semesters, with the first one offered in the first semester of the sophomore year. Furthermore, it clarifies what these writing classes should entail. It states that teachers should start English writing from vocabularies and sentence structures, then proceed to create templates, examples, and scenarios to encourage imitations, and gradually transition to paragraph-level writing techniques, arrangement, and essay writing. Moreover, instructors are encouraged to train students to master writings of different genres and rhetorical modes, such as description, narration, exposition, argumentation, etc. The Syllabus specifies a practical writing class as an elective but does not determine when it should be offered. Practical writing aims to familiarize students with the linguistic features, organizations, and conventions of practical writings such as notes, business letters, and other professional documents. Another component of composition instruction is academic writing. An Academic Thesis Writing class is required in the first semester of the senior year. Nevertheless, the 2000 Syllabus also allows for modifications of the course offerings and workload by individual universities as they see fit.

Unlike the salient differences between syllabi, the exam rubrics manifest minimal changes over time. The percentage writing accounts for remains stable.

The writing component in TEM-4 fluctuated from 20% in 1997 to 25% in 2004 and dropped back to 20% in 2015. For the 1997 and 2004 Outlines, the writing section consisted of two parts of timed essays: note taking and prompt-guided composition. However, note-taking was removed in the 2015 Clarification for TEM-4. Regardless, the 2015 Clarification increased the minimum words required in this section to 200 words in comparison to 150 words outlined in previous documents. Evaluative criteria in the assessment documents appeared the same with generic descriptors, including "relevant and robust content," "coherent and cohesive language," and "proper wording and diction."

When comparing the outcome statements with the exam rubrics, we started to notice some overlapping components. The 2000 Syllabus imported standards from the 1997 Outlines to formulate its standards for teaching and learning. Students completing the fourth semester of studies should be able to "produce an essay between 150 and 200 words that corresponds to the requirement of a given title, outline, graph, or caricature." It is expected that the essay "meets the topical requirement," "is carefully structured, logical and clear, free of grammatical errors," and "reads smoothly and uses appropriate vocabularies and expressions." The document also emphasizes the speed of writing production. It indicates that students should be able to produce a 60-word writing of a practical genre within ten minutes. When we examined the 1997 Outline for TEM-4, we observed a discernible overlap between the evaluative criteria in its outline and the 2000 Syllabus. Moreover, the instructions paraphrase what is stated in the Syllabus about the standards students completing the fourth semester are expected to achieve.

However, the timed-essay format in TEM-4 and TEM-8 and the thesis requirement in the 2000 Syllabus indicate a conceptual lacuna between the outcome statements and exam rubrics. The Syllabus asks students to independently research and draft an undergraduate thesis between 3,000 and 5,000 words upon graduation. The undergraduate thesis is an important device to gauge students' overall accomplishment and comprehensive abilities. Students are anticipated to produce a coherent and cohesive thesis that would demonstrate good judgment, clear logic, and clarity. Granted, TEM-4 and TEM-8 are not capable of effectively evaluating thesis writing due to logistical difficulties. However, they compromise what the Syllabus proclaims to achieve—students' cumulative learning and creativity—by perpetuating, however unwittingly, formulaic writing conventions as well as an attitude that prioritizes quantity over quality.

Negotiating the National Assessment Mandates

Though writing instructors were prescribed with teaching objectives, standards, and assessment rubrics, they also attempted to challenge what was already in place. We began with the questions of how the national assessment mandates had influenced the local curriculum. Nan, in response, emphasized that the undergraduate thesis was a prerequisite for any student to be conferred with the bachelor's degree. She also brought to our attention GDUFS's close compliance with the 2000 Syllabus by pinpointing the Academic Thesis Writing course offered in the seventh semester. Nevertheless, Nan was skeptical about the thesis requirement. In her view, the thesis requirement did not adequately prepare undergraduates at GDUFS for the professional duties that would be asked of them upon entering the job market. According to her, many students would benefit from carrying out a translation project more than writing a thesis. Well versed in translation theories and practices, Nan noted how the Master of Translation and Interpreting (MTI) programs in China had afforded graduates a competitive edge and wanted that for her students as well.

Whereas Nan articulated a criticism due to her school's rigid compliance, Jianjun insisted that neither the national syllabus nor the testing battery exerted a direct influence on the curriculum. He shrugged his shoulders at our question if TEM-4 and/or TEM-8 played a role in the instructional decisions of GDUFS faculty. In his words, "we take it for granted that students trained at GDUFS should pass TEM-4. TEM-8 may be a bit more difficult, but our instructors do not teach for exams." Students registered for TEM-4 and TEM-8, though neither test was treated with seriousness in classroom teaching. No additional time was spent preparing students to pass or score highly on the tests. When soliciting his opinions about the undergraduate thesis requirement, Jianjun ultimately acknowledged it as the sole influence of the Syllabus. Yet, he mentioned that the instructors were left to decide how to run the Academic Thesis Writing class and how to grade student theses since the Syllabus didn't provide any instructions.

Though Nan's and Jianjun's responses appeared contradictory at first sight, they represented the typical manner through which local instructors interacted with the national assessment mandates. Even though facets of the Syllabus were dutifully fulfilled, instructors from GDUFS took curriculum design into their own hands and adopted the Syllabus as a guiding document selectively. This way, they forestalled the over-determinism of test-driven instruction and developed alternative venues to facilitate and enhance learning in and outside of class. We further invited Nan and Jianjun to discuss their inventive approaches to mitigate the impact of high-stakes assessment.

In the Syllabus, thesis writing is described in broad strokes—it should demonstrate the student's solid language skills, lucid reasoning, convincing evidence, and scholarly insight. In keeping with these guidelines, GDUFS faculty composed a complementary writing textbook and a grading rubric to particularize assessment standards and help deliver their pedagogical agendas. The textbook was composed of ten units, including "Choosing the Topic," "Searching for and Evaluating Sources," "Quoting Skills," "Citation and Documentation," "MLA

Documentation and Format," "Thesis Statement and Outline," "Writing the Introduction and the Conclusion," "Revising the Rough Draft," "Faculty of English BA Paper: Style and Format," and "Sample BA Paper (Literature)." It prepared students with necessary knowledge about topic selection, research resources, MLA citation and formatting conventions, and research ethics before they embarked on their independent research journey. Because of its preponderant emphases on proper citation and documentation, the textbook served both as an instructional manual and a reference book. According to Nan, most of her students had never used any documentation style before thesis writing and they often had to consult the textbook for MLA style. On the other hand, the assessment rubric was designed to ensure fair grading. It entailed topic establishment ("立论"), topic reasoning ("论证"), the use of sources ("参考资料"), textual organization ("篇章结构"), and so on. The rubric did not simply espouse Greco-Roman rhetorical tradition but enriched it with elements from local prose development.

Throughout her advising, Nan often referred to the writing textbook and rubric when she reviewed her students' draft theses. When she read thesis drafts and noticed that a student had deviated from the stylistic convention, she would direct the student to a certain page in the textbook. Nan also resorted to the rubric when grading and offering content-level suggestions. Some of her comments in the margins dealt with audience, topic establishment, topic reasoning, and documentation style, such as: forge a dialogue with scholars ("与学者对话"); the argument is not clearly established ("立论不够明显"); the connections between the argument and its supporting evidence are not strong enough ("论证不够强"); provide relevant sources ("相关文献"); and search for supporting evidence ("找证据").

In our interview with Jianjun, he introduced how writing instructions at GDUFS enabled students to write with emotions and creativity, which corresponded to the school's legacy of adopting a communicative approach (i.e., Communicative English for Chinese Learners) to English acquisition. According to him, writing classes were offered from the second to the fifth semester respectively, one semester earlier than what was specified in the Syllabus. During the second and third semesters, writing instruction (Intermediate Writing One and Two) dwelled upon narrative writing, though argumentation would be approached towards the end of the third semester. Instructors would focus on argumentation in Advanced Writing One in the fourth semester. The fifth semester, when Advanced Writing Two was offered, students concentrated upon field reports. Noticeably, little to no effort would be spent on other rhetorical modes that fell under the purview of TEM-4. When asked about the predominant treatment of narration and argumentation, Jianjun explained that students would find these two modes most useful to express themselves to the fullest ("抒发真感情").

In addition, Jianjun brought up the writing exchange activities through which students opted to participate in conjunction with their two-year required writing classes. During their studies at GDUFS, students obtained a series of opportunities to interact and collaborate with university students in the U.S. and Australia. Jianjun spoke enthusiastically of these exchanges. He remarked that the activities encouraged students to value meaning and content over language forms. Many students participated in these activities in hopes of improving their "linguistic skills" or to see if they could "be understood by a native speaker." Though most of them recognized the utter impossibility of producing an error-free prose in a short span of time, they gained confidence through their direct interaction with native-English-speakers. Besides, many students became unsatisfied with language checkups and turned to global issues such as development, structure, and coherence. The writing exchanges complemented in-class lectures and exercises by supplying Chinese students with an incentive as well as a natural environment to use English for communication. Moreover, the students were reassured of and took pride in their communicative competence and meaning making practices, which might mitigate their anxiety and fear in cross-cultural scenarios where the stakes of failed communication would be much higher.

Discussion

Nan and Jianjun typified GDUFS faculty's endeavors to negotiate the national assessment mandates. As we credited their innovative efforts, we should also take note of the enabling factors that have allowed their negotiations, or even outright criticisms: the flexible nature of the assessment mandates, the paradigm shift of English Language Teaching (ELT) in China, and the institutional culture of GDUFS.

First and foremost, we discovered that the flexible manner in which the 2000 Syllabus and its attendant testing battery were carried out allowed for teacher creativity, unlike what was reported in the U.S. (Applebee, 2007; Condon, 2013). Admittedly, standards could create "lock-step curricula" to the extent that they would perpetuate a one-size-fits-all type of instruction (Crusan, 2010, p. 37). However, Crusan also commented on the positive side of standards: "Standards are useful tools to help teachers determine what to teach and the order of teaching content." Without the thesis requirement, students would not have the motivation to develop a close working relationship with their professors or participate in the knowledge production of their chosen field. In other words, the Syllabus fostered learning. Though it enforced measures for control and accountability over the teaching of English and English writing, individual instructors did not have to react to nationally normed standards with passivity. In fact, the Syllabus was deliberately broad and left open to interpretation.

Lacking specific guidelines for the thesis requirement, the Syllabus afforded Nan and others an opportunity to create classroom experiences that would be conducive to writing development and knowledge growth. Jianjun, in keeping with the Syllabus's call for engaging students, diversified his teaching methods by supplementing generic writing classes with extracurricular components.

Second, the changing landscape of ELT also lent support to Nan's and Jianjun's negotiations. Similar to the shifting trends in writing assessment in the United States (e.g., the objective writing, the holistic wave, the portfolio and program assessment wave, etc.), writing assessment in China also evolved over time. Paradigm shifts in the United States were closely related to shifts in composition history and particularly sensitive to scholarly debates over what counted as good writing. In comparison, paradigm shifts in China were contingent upon the Government's economic and political agendas. As You (2010) characterized the history of English composition in China, "English composition in China has been marked by a continuous, critical search for effective pedagogies over the years" (p. 172). As China appropriated English composition to serve its own purposes at different historical moments, aspects of English writing had been differentially championed or dismissed. In the 1990s, English composition was tasked with "prepar[ing] flexible and multifaceted students for worldwide competition and opportunities" (You, 2010, p. 144). Today, ELT in China has arrived at the stage where a positivist and objectivist approach to language is no longer adequate to address the needs of a globalizing and translingual society. As the need for training professionals to staff a growing creative industry becomes ever more acute, China is again on the lookout for a fitting assessment that will deliver its preferred social and educational values to boost its citizenry's competitiveness in the global economy. As many of the college-educated start to compose in or across multiple languages, English structures and interacts with their worldviews. They are no longer content with learning English simply for its instrumental use. As writing instructors, Nan developed inventive strategies to teach research skills and academic writing and Jianjun charted a space to nourish his students' bilingual creativity. Their pedagogical interventions exemplified an ongoing quest to tailor English in keeping with China's economic and political ambitions when the nationwide assessment mandates fell short. Moreover, they represented collective and cumulative attempts at rejuvenating the national assessment mandates so that ELT in China will advance into a brand-new paradigm.

Third, GDUFS's institutional culture must have cultivated and enabled these negotiations. According to Jianjun, GDUFS is known for its communicative approach to English learning. This approach advocates that students apply their learned skills through communicative practices under simulated scenarios or natural environments. The writing exchanges Jianjun directed have been part of a funded project at GDUFS for many years, where the communicative approach has been adopted schoolwide. Other than that, Jianjun's indifference to TEM-4 and TEM-8 is also telling of GDUFS's unique institutional culture. When many English departments still offered crash courses to underprepared students, instructors at GDUFS presumed their readiness to take and pass the exams. The high English proficiency level, though presumed, surely afforded instructors like Nan and Jianjun more latitude to grapple with the national assessment mandates more assertively. Regardless, we would be naive to think that national assessment mandates posed no limits on local agency. Nan's thwarted attempt to substitute the undergraduate thesis with a translation project sensitized us to the power that the national assessment mandates continued to exercise and their ossifying effects on local curricula.

To conclude, we have looked at how writing instructors in a Chinese university negotiated the national assessment mandates. Through interviews, we identified pedagogical practices by which the instructors moved beyond test-driven writing instruction. Despite the pressure imposed by standardized assessments, the instructors managed to reinvent the national assessment mandates as a teaching and learning practice, not a system of accountability and control. They developed a two-semester thesis writing mentorship and integrated cross-cultural writing elements with composition instruction. By illustrating how a regional program tailored the national assessment mandates to cultivate students' agency and creativity, we suggested that EFL writing instructors should actively negotiate a deterministic assessment culture. In addition, we examined the enabling factors that have contributed to their negotiations. We acknowledged the benefits the national assessment mandates have brought to writing instruction and advocated for their flexible adoption per instructors' needs. We also argued that the bottom-up negotiations were tolerated because they worked to the advantage of a burgeoning knowledge industry and creative enterprise, in which China hoped to partake in the years to come. We also speculated that institutional culture would greatly shape individual instructors' decision to act upon their agency. Future research should investigate how the nationwide assessment mandates have influenced students, which may complement or problematize the instructors' perspective presented above.

Notes

1 These are pseudonyms. Consent was obtained from research participants for reporting the data, following IRB approval.
2 Local interventions emerged in response to the publications of "College English Syllabus for English Majors at the Foundation Stage" and "College English Syllabus for English Majors at the Advanced Stage." Consequently, high-stakes assessments thrived across the nation in the 1990s. For example, Sichuan Foreign Languages College designed the Achievement Test for English Major-Level 4 in 1989. However, it was not until 2000 that the Syllabus validated TEM-4 and TEM-8 through policy initiatives.

References

Addison, J. (2015). Shifting the locus of control: Why the common core state standards and emerging standardized tests may reshape college writing classrooms. *Journal of Writing Assessment, 8*(1). Retrieved from http://journalofwritingassessment.org/article. php?article=82

Ali, H.I.H. (2013). In search for implementing learning-oriented assessment in an EFL setting. *World Journal of English Language, 3*(4), 11–18. https://doi.org/10.5430/wjel. v3n4p11

Applebee, A. (2007). Issues in large-scale writing assessments: Perspectives from the national assessment of educational progress. *Journal of Writing Assessment, 3*(2), 81–98. Retrieved from http://journalofwritingassessment.org/archives/3-2.2.pdf

Burner, T. (2014, May). *An intervention study of formative assessment in English as a foreign language writing classes in Norway.* Paper presented at the International Association for Educational Assessment: 40 Annual Conference, IAEA, Singapore.

Condon, W. (2013). Large-scale assessment, locally-developed measures, and automated scoring of essays: Fishing for red herrings? *Assessing Writing, 18*(1), 100–108. https://doi.org/10.1016/j.asw.2012.11.001

Crusan, D. (2002). An assessment of ESL writing placement assessment. *Assessing Writing, 8*(1), 17–30. https://doi.org/10.1016/S1075-2935(02)00028-4

Crusan, D. (2006). The politics of implementing online directed self-placement for second language writers. In P. K. Matsuda, C. Ortmeier-Hooper, & X. You (Eds.), *The politics of second language writing: In search of the promised land* (pp. 205–221). West Lafayette, IN: Parlor Press.

Crusan, D. (2010). *Assessment in the second language writing classroom.* Ann Arbor: The University of Michigan Press.

Deane, P., Williams, F., Weng, V., & Trapani, C. S. (2013). Automated essay scoring in innovative assessments of writing from sources. *Journal of Writing Assessment, 6*(1). Retrieved from www.journalofwritingassessment.org/article.php?article=65

Hamp-Lyons, L. (1996). Applying ethical standards to portfolio assessment of writing in English as a second language. In *Performance testing, cognition and assessment: Selected papers from the 15th language testing research colloquium* (pp. 3–151). Cambridge: Cambridge University Press.

Lam, R. (2015). Language assessment training in Hong Kong: Implications for language assessment literacy. *Language Testing, 32*(2), 169–197. http://dx.doi.org/10.1177/0265532214554321

Lee, I. (2017). *Classroom writing assessment and feedback in L2 school contexts.* Singapore: Springer Nature. http://dx.doi.org/10.1007/978-981-10-3924-9

Lee, I., & Coniam, D. (2013). Introducing assessment for learning for EFL writing in an assessment of learning examination-driven system in Hong Kong. *Journal of Second Language Writing, 22*(1), 34–50. https://doi.org/10.1016/j.jslw.2012.11.003

Neal, M. (2010). Assessment in the service of learning. *College Composition and Communication, 61*(4), 746–758.

O'Neill, P., Moore, C., & Huot, B. (2009). *Guide to college writing assessment.* Logan, UT: Utah State University Press.

Öz, H. (2014). Turkish teachers' practices of assessment for learning in the English as a foreign language classroom. *Journal of Language Teaching and Research, 5*(4), 775–785. doi: 10.4304/jltr.5.4.775-785

Ruecker, T., Chamcharatsri, B., & Saengngoen, J. (2015). Teacher perceptions of the impact of the common core assessments on linguistically diverse high school students. *Journal of Writing Assessment, 8*(1). Retrieved from http://journalofwritingassessment.org/article.php?article=87

Song, B., & August, B. (2002). Using portfolios to assess the writing of ESL students: A powerful alternative? *Journal of Second Language Writing, 11*(1), 49–72. https://doi.org/10.1016/S1060-3743(02)00053-X

Sun, C. (2010). *An introduction to Major University English Tests and English Language Teaching in China.* Master's thesis. Brigham Young University. Retrieved from http://scholarsarchive.byu.edu/cgi/viewcontent.cgi?article=3443&context=etd

Weigle, S. C. (2006). Investing in assessment: Designing tests to promote positive washback. In P. K. Matsuda, C. Ortmeier-Hooper, & X. You (Eds.), *The politics of second language writing: In search of the promised land* (pp. 222–244). West Lafayette, IN: Parlor Press.

White, E. M., Lutz, W., & Kamusikiri, S. (Eds.). (1996). *Assessment of writing: Politics, policies, practices.* New York: Modern Language Association of America.

Xu, Y., & Liu, Y. (2009). Teacher assessment knowledge and practice: A narrative inquiry of a Chinese college EFL teacher's experience. *TESOL Quarterly, 43*(3), 493–513. http://dx.doi.org/10.1002/j.1545-7249.2009.tb00246.x

You, X. (2010). *Writing in the devil's tongue: A history of English composition in China.* Carbondale, IL: Southern Illinois University Press.

15

VIGNETTE

When Are Students Ready Enough? Issues and Dilemmas Around Assessment of L2 Writers in a WAC Program

Hee-Seung Kang

It was the middle of the semester, and I had yet another meeting scheduled with a disciplinary faculty member who wanted to discuss his multilingual students. As he sat down wearily, he glanced at a group of international students passing by outside my window and began, "So . . . I'm not sure whether the two ESL students on my roster are even ready to take the class." He handed me a pile of multilingual students' writing assignments. The first page was covered with handwritten comments and edits. I started reading the first sentence, which contained several grammatical corrections. I noticed a similar pattern as my eyes moved down the page.

While I saw several comments on the student's ideas, the majority of the feedback was about sentence structure, with frequent edits on comma usage, articles, and prepositions. As I read through the last paragraph, the faculty member said, "My ESL students work extremely hard on their essays, but if I graded them like other native English-speaking students, they would probably earn a low C or D. How should I evaluate their writing assignments?"

Conversations like this one are not uncommon. I receive emails titled "ESL issues" and "ESL problems" on a regular basis, often from disciplinary faculty who are concerned, perplexed, and even frustrated by the second language (L2) writers in their classes. As an ESL Writing Program Director, I work closely with disciplinary faculty, providing consultations and workshops on how to work with L2 writers in the classroom. Among the many topics I face every semester, the issue of evaluating L2 writers' writing is particularly challenging, largely because of a wide variety of approaches to language difference in the grading process, which is often cryptic to students.

The number of international students studying in the U.S. has increased exponentially in recent years, surpassing one million in the 2015–2016 academic year (IIE, 2016). As a result, many universities and colleges in the U.S. have experienced unprecedented growth in their non-native English speaking student populations. The increased presence of L2 writers in the classroom is pushing faculty to reconsider their teaching approaches and evaluation of student work.

Because writing assignments are an essential element of any writing class (Crusan, 2010), previous studies in L2 writing have examined issues pertinent to L2 writing assessment in higher education. Studies in this area have primarily investigated how L2 writing is evaluated differently from the writing of native speakers based on factors such as students' nationality and language background (Lindsey & Crusan, 2011; Rubin & William-James, 1997). Recent studies have examined faculty concerns and expectations for L2 student writing in Writing Across the Curriculum (WAC) courses (Ives, Leahy, Leming, Pierce, & Schwartz, 2014; Zawacki & Habib, 2014), but few studies have discussed the issues and dilemmas disciplinary faculty face in L2 writing assessment. As an ESL specialist working with disciplinary faculty and ESL instructors, I hope that sharing my experiences and perspectives will stimulate further discussions about ways writing programs and teachers can design equitable and inclusive writing assessment policies for L2 writers. Although my experiences are limited to one institution, the challenges I describe in this chapter will resonate with those working in WAC courses and writing programs at other institutions.

Faculty's Varying Expectations of L2 Writers

In addition to commenting on essays, L2 reading practices is another area of concern that I have encountered in working with faculty. I recently received an email from a disciplinary faculty member in which he shared his concerns about Amy (pseudonym), an L2 writer in his WAC class. The professor first noticed that Amy's in-class diagnostic essay demonstrated reading and writing skills that did not match his standard, and her inability to respond to his questions sufficiently in class concerned him. Because his class required intensive reading and writing, he argued that any student who could not read and summarize an article rapidly should not be taking his class. Based on his in-class diagnostic essay, he questioned how a student with low reading and writing proficiency could pass the university's ESL classes, and he was doubtful that Amy ought to be taking a WAC class with other native English-speaking students.

Another faculty member in the disciplines contacted me to discuss two L2 writers in her class, describing the problems they were having with English grammar. In comments on their essays, the instructor spent most of her time correcting sentence-level issues rather than responding to student ideas. She felt frustrated as a result, believing that these students were unable to benefit from the content of her course. She doubted that her L2 students could "fully engage in intellectual conversation when they cannot even write a sentence correctly." Furthermore, she felt that these students diminished the quality of discussion and learning in her classroom. She had finally decided to stop giving comments on their "unacceptable" essays and instead required them to seek help from the writing center to re-write their essays entirely.

When disciplinary faculty come to me with concerns, many of them tell me that their L2 students are not ready to be in their classes. Instead, they claim, these students need to take ESL classes until they can read and write as well as native English-speaking students. These faculty overlook the fact that developing academic literacy in a second language is a gradual and painstakingly long process (Leki, 1992; Spack, 1997). Their expectations become particularly problematic when faculty assess students' performance in WAC classes through in-class exercises. Although summarization is one of the fundamental literacy skills in academic writing, being pressured to read new content during class in a relatively short time can be challenging for L2 writers. Summarization is a complex activity that entails cognition, metacognition, schemata, and L2 acquisition (Kirkland & Saunders, 1991). Silva (1993) characterizes L2 writing as being more "laborious, less fluent, and less productive" (p. 668) than that of native speakers. Despite the distinct characteristics of L2 writing, some faculty continue to evaluate all students based on L1 standards. When faculty assume that students should be "native English speakers of a privileged variety of English" (Matsuda, 2006, p. 638), L2 students are often branded as deficient or problematic.

Because L2 writers' texts tend to be less fluent and less accurate than their L1 counterparts (Silva, 1993), some faculty question L2 writers' devotion to class work or their ability to succeed. Disciplinary faculty who overly emphasize the importance of writing error-free sentences sometimes resist reading and evaluating the content of students' assignments when they see a level of grammatical errors that they find unacceptable. L2 writers' essays that contain many sentence-level errors can at times overwhelm disciplinary faculty. The acceptable level of error varies by faculty member, and some who are less flexible feel that correcting all perceived errors prepares students for workplace expectations and their future trajectories (Zawacki & Habib, 2014). However, syntactic and rhetorical differences in L2 students' writing should be negotiated and accommodated so that students have an opportunity to learn content even as they are acquiring English as a second language. Focusing on accuracy and grammatical errors while L2 writers are still acquiring the English language is neither productive for students nor faculty (Ferris, 2011). Instead of marking all errors, disciplinary faculty comments ought to identify several error patterns that impede comprehension and focus on engaging the students' ideas, thus equipping students to meet the learning outcomes of an assignment. Crusan (2010) reminds us that best practices in L2 writing assessment are to establish criteria for assignments. By creating rubrics, disciplinary faculty can clearly communicate the expected learning outcomes with students and focus on their growth and accomplishments. If clarity of writing is important, it can be included as one of the evaluating criteria. In evaluating for clarity, however, faculty should focus on comprehensibility rather than grammatical accuracy.

Faculty's Assessment Practices and Ideas on Fairness

During a recent ESL workshop, I spoke on the importance of designing inclusive writing assignments to accommodate L2 students' needs. One of the faculty members from the business school responded that he did not want to change any aspect of his writing assignments, arguing that making any changes to his policies or assignments was a disservice to his L2 writers. Since international students come to study at an "American university," he felt that keeping the same standards for all students was an important part of their experience. He is not the only faculty member to insist that every student in the classroom be evaluated according to the "same standards." Another instructor explained to me that while he empathizes with his L2 writers, he thinks accommodating their needs would raise other ethical questions. For example, what about first-generation college students? What about the student who has two other essays due that day and has a note from a professional psychological counselor that he has time management issues? Where does one draw the line? Given the increasing number of international students in his classrooms, this faculty member felt that it would be unfair to change the class policy and assignment deadlines to accommodate L2 writers since he does not accommodate any other population of students.

While many disciplinary faculty are open to adopting culturally and linguistically inclusive assignments and assessment practices, some faculty perceive changing writing assignment design and assessment practices as unnecessary and even detrimental to students' learning. Some assume that making any changes for L2 writers will compromise their high standards and insist that leaving their expectations intact is crucial to keep the "American university standard." This "American university standard" requires that students be familiar with U.S. history and culture, speak English fluently, and acquire Standard American English (SAE).

Although it can be tempting to equate fairness with using the same standard for L1 and L2 students, it is critical for faculty to design assignments that embrace culturally and linguistically diverse students. For example, disciplinary faculty can ask the following questions:

- Does this writing assignment require extensive knowledge of U.S. history and culture?
- Does the writing assignment provide a reasonable amount of time for L2 writers?
- Does my assessment of L2 writing focus on clarity rather than accuracy?
- Is it possible to give multiple submission opportunities so that students can better achieve course outcomes?

Faculty who change their assessment practices by asking questions like these are not treating their L1 students unfairly. On the contrary, these practices should be supported to benefit all kinds of learners.

Toward Culturally and Linguistically Inclusive Writing Assessment

With the growing number of L2 writers in U.S. higher education, it has become crucial to modify existing curricula and reconsider the ways in which we evaluate our students in the WAC program context. "How can I respond to and accurately evaluate L2 students' writing while being fair to other students?" "How can I design culturally and linguistically inclusive writing assignments?" Disciplinary faculty often express their desire to assess their students fairly and accurately, but they are not always aware of best practices.

WAC programs need to closely work with second language specialists on campus to educate disciplinary faculty about L2 students and their English language acquisition process. By learning more about the characteristics of L2 writers and the challenges they face, faculty may realize that their expectations are unrealistic or unfair to students who don't speak English as their native language. They can create effective rubrics articulating targeted learning outcomes of an assignment and focusing on comprehensibility rather than penalizing linguistic differences. Assignments should not assume extensive knowledge of U.S. culture, U.S. history, and Western philosophy and should be culturally accessible to all students. Faculty can also modify their assignments by allowing students to integrate cross-cultural and intercultural perspectives. For example, an academic essay assignment that asks students to analyze a monument in the U.S. capital, Washington, D.C., can be modified to analyzing a monument in the capitals of any country, or students could still work with a U.S. monument but look at it from their home culture's lens. If possible, faculty can consider providing opportunities for multiple drafts or do peer reviews as a homework assignment based on teacher-guided questions.

When faculty assume and demand a monolingual standard, multilingual students are often categorized as problematic or deficient. Just as college composition courses can be reimagined as a "multilingual space" in which language differences are assumed and embraced (Matsuda, 2006), so too can WAC programs value language diversity and create linguistically and culturally inclusive standards of writing assessment. Adopting linguistically and culturally sensitive assessment practices benefits all students, regardless of their native language, the culture they associate themselves with, and the kinds of learners they are.

References

Crusan, D. (2010). *Assessment in the second language writing classroom.* Ann Arbor: University of Michigan Press.

Ferris, D. (2011). *Treatment of error in second language student writing* (2nd ed.). Ann Arbor: University of Michigan Press. https://doi.org/10.3998/mpub.2173290

The Institute of International Education. (2016). *Open doors 2016: Executive summary: International students in the United States.* Retrieved from www.iie.org/en/Why-IIE/Announcements/2016-11-14-Open-Doors-Executive-Summary

Ives, L., Leahy, E., Leming, A., Pierce, T., & Schwartz, M. (2014). "I don't know if that was the right thing to do": Cross-disciplinary/Cross-institutional faculty respond to L2 writing. In T. M. Zawacki & M. Cox (Eds.), *WAC and second language writers* (pp. 211–232). Anderson, SC: Parlor Press.

Kirkland, M. R., & Saunders, M. A. (1991). Maximizing students' performance in summary writing: Managing cognitive load. *TESOL Quarterly, 25*(1), 105–121.

Leki, I. (1992). *Understanding ESL writers: A guide for teachers.* Portsmouth, NH: Boynton/Cook.

Lindsey, P., & Crusan, D. (2011). How faculty attitudes and expectations toward student nationality affect writing assessment. *Across the Disciplines, 8*(4). Retrieved from http://wac.colostate.edu/atd/ell/lindsey-crusan.cfm

Matsuda, P. K. (2006). The myth of linguistic homogeneity in U.S. college composition. *College English, 68*(6), 637–651.

Rubin, D. L., & William-James, M. (1997). The impact of writer nationality on mainstream teachers' judgments of composition quality. *Journal of Second Language Writing, 6*(2), 139–153.

Silva, T. (1993). Toward an understanding of the distinct nature of L2 writing: The ESL research and its implications. *TESOL Quarterly, 27*(4), 657–677.

Spack, R. (1997). The acquisition of academic literacy in a second language: A longitudinal case study. *Written Communication, 14*(1), 3–62.

Zawacki, T. M., & Habib, A. S. (2014). Negotiating "errors" in L2 writing: Faculty dispositions and language difference. In T. M. Zawacki & M. Cox (Eds.), *WAC and second language writers* (pp. 183–210). Anderson, SC: Parlor Press.

16

ACCOMMODATING WRITING TESTS FOR SECOND LANGUAGE LEARNERS WITH DISABILITIES

Natalie Nordby Chen and Renée Saulter

As recent as the mid-twentieth century, those with physical or cognitive disabilities were systematically excluded from public school, placed into segregated schools, institutionalized, or kept at home (Starr, 2016). This began to change in 1954 with the Supreme Court's decision in *Brown v. Board of Education*, which confirmed that education "is a right which must be made available to all on equal terms." Applying these principles, in *Wolf v. State Legislature* (1969) a Utah court ruled the exclusion of children with intellectual disabilities from public schools unconstitutional. The milestone 1975 Education for All Handicapped Children Act (amended as the Individuals with Disabilities Education Act in 1990) includes provisions that no child should be excluded from a free appropriate program of public education and related services, tailored to fit the individual student's needs (Neuhaus, Smith, & Burgdorf, 2014), thus ending the practice of mandatorily placing disabled children in segregated schools, and paving the way for the Americans with Disabilities Act.

Introduction

The Americans with Disabilities Act of 1990 (ADA) mandates that equal access and reasonable accommodation be provided to all learners within the United States; this unlocks opportunities to access both education and concomitant assessment. Since that time, almost 200 countries have passed similar disability civil rights laws (Shapiro, 2015), ranging from Australia's Disability Discrimination Act (1992) to India's Persons with Disabilities (Equal Opportunities, Protection of Rights & Full Participation) Act (Ministry of Law, Justice, and Company Affairs, 1996) to Vietnam's National Law on Persons with Disability (Nguyen, 2010). Even so, such access is neither universally applauded nor regulated. There remain regions in which disability presents as a lifelong stigma, preventing opportunities for full participation in social, educational, or professional domains. Mariga, McConkey, and Myezwa (2014) detail reasons for barriers to educational access as linked to the ignominy associated with disability that still persists in many cultures, communities, and countries; in areas that are poorly resourced, policy makers and educators alike may feel it is not worth investing in education for a disabled child. Paradoxically, for many learners in such situations, education would be the primary means to enfranchisement; further, a key to higher education and gainful employment is facility in a second language. To prove this proficiency, access must be granted to high-stakes language exams used for these purposes.

Within the language testing industry, the legal and ethical responsibility to make assessments accessible is recognized and acted upon by the major players in this field, including ETS, Cambridge Assessments, Cambridge Michigan Language Assessments, and Pearson. Khalifa and Weir (2009) noted that "over the last decade increased attention has been given to issues of fairness in testing, to the rights of test takers, to testing candidates with disabilities and to the responsibilities of producers and users of language examinations." This is manifest in establishment of guidelines such as those found in the Association of Language Testers in Europe *Code of Practice and Quality Assurance Checklist* (ALTE, 1994); the American Educational Research Association, American Psychological Association, and National Council on Measurement in Education *Standards for the Educational and Psychological Testing* (AERA, APA, & NCME, 1999); and the International Language Testing Association's *Code of Ethics* (ILTA, 2000).

When selecting accommodations for second language examinations, test developers endeavor to provide a fair assessment of the linguistic proficiency of individuals with disabilities. This chapter explores the challenges faced and practices employed when discerning how to adapt the content, format, and administration of writing assessments for second language learners with various disabilities, whilst ensuring that the construct tested remains constant and the score meaning equivalent. Valid accommodations produce scores for students with disabilities that measure the same attributes as standard assessments measured in students without disabilities (Chase, 2005).

Americans with Disabilities Act Applied to Assessment

In 1990, the Americans with Disabilities Act (ADA) became law after being signed by United States President George H. W. Bush. The ADA, as well as similar legislation in other countries, aims to provide equal opportunities for all people, ensure that they have certain protections from discrimination in its various forms, and allow those with disabilities participation in activities that the rest of the population may take for granted. It covers multiple areas of everyday life, and has had a positive impact with regard to the implementation of barrier-free building codes and transportation, non-discriminatory employment and hiring practices, inclusive education, and more (Americans with Disabilities Act, 1990).

Educational opportunities have increased for people with disabilities through the creation and implementation of barrier-free access to buildings, use of assistive technologies, and mandated reasonable accommodation in the classroom. In the United States, testing is a common part of the educational experience from a young age in the form of state-wide assessments used to monitor progress, through to university entrance exams. As such, students with disabilities are required to demonstrate their academic abilities alongside their peers. Both teachers and assessment providers have a responsibility to provide accommodations for individuals with special needs if their tests are not already universally accessible, to allow those individuals the best opportunity to demonstrate their proficiency within a subject area. In the United States, the ADA is the guiding force behind the provision of such accommodations. It

> ensures that individuals with disabilities have the opportunity to fairly compete for and pursue such opportunities by requiring testing entities to offer exams in a manner accessible to persons with disabilities. When needed testing accommodations are provided, test-takers can demonstrate their true aptitude.
>
> *(U.S. Department of Justice Civil Rights Division)*

Section 309 of the ADA requires examinations be made accessible to people with disabilities. The implication for testing companies is a matter of changing how a test is taken rather than altering the construct tested so as to appropriately assess the test taker in a manner that affords the same opportunity as other, non-accommodated test takers. Those instances where an accommodation would alter the construct of a second-language writing assessment are explored later in this chapter.

The ADA covers a variety of exams, including entrance exams for high school, college, professional programs, and graduate school, as well as high school equivalency and licensing exams (U.S. Department of Justice Civil Rights Division). Testing companies, such as ETS and Cambridge Michigan Language Assessments, which create large-scale high-stakes assessments used to measure English language proficiency, often used by North American colleges and universities as part of the admittance requirements for international students, provide accommodations in accordance with the requirements of the ADA, even though the test takers may be outside the borders of the United States, and therefore beyond the jurisdiction of the ADA.

The ADA requires that tests be administered in a manner that does not discriminate against individuals with disabilities, whether physical, cognitive, or temporary. To that end, it is the legal and ethical responsibility of testing organizations to modify their assessments in such a way as to ameliorate the effect of the individual examinee's disability, while ensuring that the accommodations do not provide an unfair advantage to those who require them (Elliot, 2013; Banerjee, Chen, & Dobson, 2013; Sireci, Scarpati, & Li, 2005).

In order to level the playing field to the extent possible, a variety—or combination—of accommodations may be necessary. In terms of high-stakes writing assessments, these accommodations will vary depending on the needs of the individual test taker. They may include presenting a writing prompt in braille or large print format, providing adjustable seating, applying speech-to-text or text-to-speech software, or engaging an amanuensis to whom the test taker will dictate a response. These are explored in more detail below.

Accommodation Practices, Considerations, Challenges

Accommodating writing assessments for second language learners with disabilities in order to meet both legal and ethical standards may pose a number of challenges for large-scale testing organizations. Determining who qualifies for accommodations, and which accommodations best meet the test taker's needs, is a multi-stepped procedure. The actual detailed processes by which such decisions are made differ little from organization to organization.

Securing Accommodations

In most cases, accommodations must be requested in advance of the test administration. This allows time for the testing organization to prepare special materials (i.e., braille test books), obtain assistive aids (software), hire specialized staff (amanuenses, extra proctors for separate room administrations), and secure adequate testing space and time.

Before accommodations are granted, assessment organizations require documentation of disability. This may take the form of a current physician's letter or a medical certificate. Note that accommodations are not determined by the physician; rather, the physician outlines the nature of the disability, for example type, degree, or configuration of hearing loss (American Speech-Language-Hearing Association, 2015). Nor is an Individualized Education Program (IEP) plan sufficient to mandate the accommodations to be employed. The IEP, as a learning-focused document created and implemented by the school, focuses on the type of accommodations available in a classroom setting, such as use of dictionaries, spell check programs, or read-aloud text. Within a standardized test administration, however, some accommodations could alter the construct tested, and would therefore be inappropriate. The actual accommodations are determined by the testing organization, often in consultation with the test taker. Shaw and

Weir (2007) explain that when testing organizations make special arrangements, the goal is to

> enable candidates to understand the questions and tasks, to express their answers and to demonstrate their English to the best of their ability. The purpose of these arrangements is to permit such candidates' level of attainment to be fairly and objectively assessed. Provisions are generally intended . . . to remove, as far as practicably possible, the effects of the disability on the candidates' ability to demonstrate their true level of attainment in relation to the assessment objectives.
>
> *(p. 20)*

To that end, it is critical that test takers be familiar with the accommodations available, especially with regard to the use of specialized assistive technologies. For this reason, details of the type of provisions that can be offered should be publicly available. Providers of English language proficiency tests such as IELTS, MELAB, and TOEFL, among others, list commonly available arrangements on their websites (British Council, 2017; Cambridge English Language Assessment, 2017; Cambridge Michigan Language Assessments, 2017; ETS, 2017).

The type of accommodation implemented during writing assessments for language learners with disabilities varies depending on the nature and degree of the disability. In certain situations, additional time may be all that is required to allow for the test taker to complete their responses. Circumstances which may warrant extra time include challenges to reading or writing, including cognitive processing concerns such as dyslexia or movement disorders such as cerebral palsy. In addition, those utilizing braille may need twice the testing time, given the slower nature of reading, proofing, and correcting one's own braille text (Banerjee et al., 2013; Shaw & Weir, 2007; Taylor & Chen, 2016).

As each learner and disability is unique, accommodations would ideally be determined on a case-by-case basis. For example, although accommodations for the deaf and hard of hearing are often similar, there is an incredible spectrum of experience, from pre-lingual to post-lingual hearing loss, and with a range of severity from mild to profound (Chase, 2005). As such, a one-size-fits-all accommodation is less than optimal. Taylor and Chen (2016) write:

> It is important to note that individuals with similar disabilities will not necessarily all benefit from the same accommodations (Taylor, 2012). Likewise, it may be necessary to make several different accommodations for test takers with multiple special needs.
>
> *(p. 309)*

With this in mind, one notes the desire to consider each learner's situation individually, implementing the best accommodations for that test taker. This, however, is often impracticable for large-scale assessment bodies serving hundreds of thousands of examinees annually. Shaw and Weir (2007) explain:

> Despite the central importance of the test taker in any assessment activity, it is often difficult for an exam provider to cater for individual variation across test takers and at the same time adhere to the requirement for test fairness. This becomes a critical issue when dealing with a large and/or highly heterogeneous test population, e.g. an international test candidature or a population of test takers with a potential age range from 17 to 70. . . . Instead, examination boards tend to adopt a largely pragmatic approach.
>
> *(p. 17)*

Even so, an exploration into the practices of international providers of high-stakes language assessments reveals an acute desire to allow learners the fairest opportunity to demonstrate their proficiency, ameliorating the impact of a disability and ensuring that the construct tested is unaltered and the scores provided are equivalent in meaning to those of other test takers.

The University of Minnesota National Center on Educational Outcomes created a taxonomy of accommodation adapted by Pearson, which includes Timing/Scheduling, Setting, Administration, Presentation Format, and Response Format (Chase, 2005). These will be discussed herein, as will considerations for the task itself and the test's score meaning.

Task Design

Universal Design

Test tasks, delivery, and specifications should be designed with all test takers, including those with disabilities, in mind. That is,

> when assessments are first conceptualized, they need to be thought of in the context of the entire population of who will be assessed (AERA et al., 1999; National Research Council, 1999). . . . [T]he target population needs to include every student. Assessments need to be responsive to growing demands—increased diversity, increased inclusion of all types of students in the general curriculum, and increased emphasis and commitment to serve and be accountable for *all* students.
>
> *(Thompson, Johnstone, & Thurlow, 2002)*

The notion of Universal Design (UD), however, is relatively new. With roots in late twentieth-century architecture, the principles have spread to domains including personal (audiobooks, Velcro), public (dropped curbs, kneeling buses), and educational, wherein the concepts of UD apply to instruction as well as assessment. The suggestions Allman (2009) and Thompson et al. (2002) make for applying UD to task development include pilot testing tasks with intended populations, including those requiring accommodation. To create a writing task true to these notions, the testing organization would need to pilot test each on a sample of every type of student expected to participate in the final assessment, including learners with a wide range of disabilities. While this is a more common practice for state-wide K–12 general education assessment providers with large populations of test takers requiring accommodation, including such populations in pilot testing poses a challenge for international high-stakes language testing organizations, as the number of such test takers is limited. For example, in a five-year period, less than 1% of the total number of Cambridge Michigan Language Assessments' test takers from all four major testing programs requested any sort of accommodation (Banerjee et al., 2013). These organizations must make decisions through smaller-scale trialing, in addition to careful study of the literature, policies, and practices employed within the industry.

Pilot testing on a range of test takers helps test developers determine whether tasks are inaccessible for certain groups of students and whether they lend themselves to accommodation in terms of presentation and response capture. This would reveal, for example, that if spelling is important to the written construct, dictation tasks are inappropriate for deaf and hard-of-hearing learners, as presenting these tasks in sign language may involve finger spelling. It would also reveal that prompts based on pictures or complex graphics do not lend themselves easily to visually impaired test takers, as presenting the information in a text-based manner may provide the test taker with vocabulary that the assessment is intended to elicit.

The goal of organizations providing these exams is to make modifications and accommodations available to ensure that test takers with disabilities are not disadvantaged, nor is the construct tested altered. Shaw and Weir (2007) note, "the touchstone of any decisions taken in respect of background variables is that no candidate should be discriminated against except in terms of their ability in the intended construct."

Construct

To ensure that the writing task measures the same skills equitably in varying populations, the construct itself must be clearly defined. Considering the scoring rubric and the competencies critical to measure, the test developer designs tasks that tap that skill for an inclusive assessment population (Allman, 2009).

Large-scale writing assessments need to measure the writing proficiency of learners with a wide range of abilities, ensuring that those with diverse learning needs receive opportunities to demonstrate competence on the same content. That is, standards should not be relaxed nor constructs measured altered based on the test taker. Rather, the same scoring guides should be applied regardless of differing presentation or response capture formats. It must be clear from the outset that in order to be equitable, writing tasks must measure the achievement of all learners on the same standards (Thompson et al., 2002).

This is another benefit of pilot testing on diverse populations: ensuring that the application of accommodations does not introduce construct-irrelevant variance, or that "test scores are affected by processes that are extraneous to its intended construct" (AERA et al., 1999).

Some debate and controversy surrounds the question of whether the use of certain accommodations affects the constructs writing tasks are intended to measure. Those with special needs may require assistance recording their written responses. In some instances, they may employ the use of speech-to-text software or dictate their responses to amanuenses. In the latter case, although the test taker must spell unfamiliar words and indicate punctuation (Cambridge Michigan Language Assessments, 2013), some are concerned about the conflagration of spoken and written proficiency. Others argue that if this is the method by which individuals create text to be read by others in non-assessment situations, then this is, indeed, "writing," and should be assessed as such.

Content

Consideration must be given to the accessibility of the task topics in an effort to avoid both bias and construct-irrelevant variance. One way to reduce bias is to investigate whether any items are more difficult for students from particular subpopulations. This can be accomplished through pilot testing, with a close review of test taker responses to determine whether any particular group was disadvantaged by unfamiliarity or inexperience with the content presented. Further, if the population is large enough, differential item functioning (DIF) analysis can be conducted. DIF occurs when students equated on relevant ability but representing different groups do not have the same probability of responding correctly to test items (Thompson et al., 2002). While DIF analyses are most traditionally used to detect different performance by race or gender, they can also be applied with regard to disability.

Chase (2005) notes that many deaf and hard of hearing students do poorly on standardized tests, not because they lack skills necessary to make correct test item responses, but because they do not understand the tasks that they are required to perform. Communicating the intent of the tasks is of paramount importance, as is ensuring that test developers are cognizant of the potential introduction of bias when selecting topics. A prompt asking one to "describe what you see when you first wake up in the morning" does not allow visually impaired test takers the same opportunity to demonstrate written descriptive ability as their sighted counterparts. Likewise, asking one to recommend one's favorite vacation spot might disadvantage those who have not had the opportunity to travel.

Accommodations

Test takers with special needs often require accommodations with regard to the presentation of the writing task, the manner in which the response is captured, and/or the physical situation of the test administration. Such accommodations are employed to increase the test taker's access to a needed assessment by ensuring

> all examinees be given a comparable opportunity to demonstrate their standing on the construct(s) the test is intended to measure. Just treatment also includes such factors as appropriate testing conditions and equal opportunity to become familiar with the test format, practice materials, and so forth . . . [and] that all examinees be afforded appropriate testing conditions.
>
> *(AERA, 1999)*

Task Presentation

One way to limit bias in test items with regard to learner experience is to provide test takers with a choice of prompts. Often the practice for standard test administrations, it is important to provide the same choice to those taking accommodated tests. Given a desire to elicit the best sample of a learner's writing performance, Cambridge English attempts to make test events as positive as possible by providing the test takers with choices regarding the prompt upon which they write. By doing so, test takers are able to select the one that allows them the most comfort (Shaw & Weir, 2007). Even so, Cambridge notes that it is crucial that these prompts be equivalent in difficulty and the constructs and abilities measured are comparable.

In terms of assistive materials, test takers with challenges such as scotopic sensitivity syndrome, which is related to the ability of the brain to process visual information, may benefit from the use of colored plastic overlays for paper-based assessments. If the test is computer delivered, the test taker may be allowed to select reverse-contrast or other screen background and foreground colors to ease eye strain (ETS, 2017).

To respond to oral prompts, learners who are deaf or hard-of-hearing may require the use of a sign-language interpreter. For text-based tasks, those with limited vision may be able to respond if it is presented orally (either employing a reader or screen-reading technology), as large print, or in braille, although the last of the three is becoming a less common option. Until the early 1960s many blind people were routinely taught to read and write braille as part of early education. However, by the 1960s the braille literacy rate had declined to near 10% (National Federation of the Blind, 2017). That is not to say that those with visual impairments do not engage with written text. Rather, this waning is due to a number of factors, including a shortage of educators qualified to teach braille, a dearth of braille material, and advances in assistive technologies. Even so, 89% of teachers of blind students recommend that such technology be used as a supplement to braille rather than as a replacement (Jernigan Institute, 2009).

As previously discussed, writing prompts based on graphic images can be challenging for this population. Test developers should avoid the use of construct-irrelevant graphs or pictures, vertical or diagonal text, and prompts that depend on reading of graphic representations (blueprints, floor plans) that do not also have verbal/textual descriptions that can be translated into braille (Thompson et al., 2002). Such highly graphic and technical content does not translate to braille easily and with the type of accuracy necessary for testing materials (Allman, 2009).

Response Capture

The manner in which a test taker's written response is recorded will vary based on both the nature and type of disability, as well as familiarity with and availability of assistive technologies. This may include the use of an amanuensis; speech-to-text or text-to-speech software; a Perkins brailler, akin to a braille typewriter; allowing a test taker the option of keying or handwriting; providing larger, graphed, or colored paper; use of specialized pencil grips, rulers, or magnifying glasses; or engaging a transcriber if the presentation of a candidate's answers causes difficulty for raters. For example, where a disability such as multiple sclerosis results in poor quality handwriting and largely illegible text, Cambridge English makes provision for the production of a transcript. The purpose of the transcript—which is produced immediately after the writing examination and usually in the presence of the candidates—is to aid raters in focusing on the content of the response rather than its presentation (Shaw & Weir, 2007).

Whatever tools are employed, ensuring test taker familiarity and facility with their use prior to the exam is of critical import. In addition, providing sample tasks and scoring guides help to warrant full awareness of the test's demands.

Administration

Accommodations may also take the form of changes to the physical testing location or the amount of time provided for the test administration. With regard to the testing location, wheelchair accessibility is critical, as are accessible tables. Those reading braille or large print materials may need a larger table; and some assistive technologies will require access to a power source. Having such accommodations in place prior to the start of the test avoids placing undue pressure on the test taker to work out such details at exam time.

Additionally, many learners with attention deficit disorders and those using amanuenses benefit from testing in a room separate from other test takers.

Two common accommodations are the provision of extended time and extra breaks in the testing session (Thompson et al., 2002). Extended time may be required not only to address the needs of those with cognitive processing disorders, but also those whose manner of text requires more time to decode. Allman (2009) explains that students with visual impairments usually require extended time during testing because using braille, large print, and audio formats requires more time to process than does reading print with acceptable visual acuity. Research into the amount of extra time required is inconclusive, ranging from Wetzel and Knowlton's (2000) suggestion that experienced adult braille readers may need no more than 50% more time than the stated duration to Morris's (1974) conclusion that braille readers require 2.5 times the duration of sighted readers (as cited in Allman, 2009).

Additional time will also be needed for the manipulation of an audio device, the marking of an answer sheet, or amanuenses or transcriptionist procedures. Cambridge Michigan Language Assessments' procedures for amanuenses allow time for the test taker to spell content words, indicate capitalization and punctuation, and for the amanuensis to read back the essay, allowing the test taker to indicate necessary revisions (Banerjee et al., 2013).

The inclusion of rest breaks may also be appropriate for test takers who have difficulty concentrating for long periods of time, who have repetitive strain injuries requiring frequent breaks in the dominant hand, or to combat the fatigue of an extended testing session.

Tindal and Haladyna (2002) recommend that a well-designed test for standard administration be untimed (as cited in Allman, 2009, pp. 63–64); however, if automaticity or ability to write under speeded conditions is part of the construct measured, this cannot be allowed as it provides an unfair advantage to the accommodated test taker. This is supported by Sireci et al.'s (2005) findings that extended time advantages all test takers.

Allman (2009) notes that several current researchers suggest lessening the emphasis on designating a uniform, "one size fits all" duration of extended time as an accommodation. Rather, these researchers suggest that the accommodation of extended time consists simply of "adequate time." That is, it should be a specified length of time, which must be determined through careful assessment of the individual learner's physical disability, skills, and needs.

Scoring

As writing exams are accommodated to meet learner needs, the needs of the end score user—be they employers, sponsors, or educational institutions—are also significant. That is, they must be able to trust that the scores reported for all test takers measured the same construct and are of equivalent meaning. Key to this is employing the same standard for all test takers.

Same Scale

Until as late as 2004, Cambridge English undertook the practice of "separate marking" of written responses produced by test takers with dyslexia. These responses were scored to a different principle than other responses, with mistakes in spelling disregarded. Following investigations into the validity, reliability, and practicality of this practice, it was discontinued. Rather, the exam board determined that extra time is the most appropriate provision, as although it is common practice to disregard form-focused features of writing, such as spelling, in content-based tests such as history, in an assessment in which the focus is language itself, such features ought not be ignored (Shaw & Weir, 2007).

Same Meaning

To avoid misleading the end score user about the test taker's written proficiency, it is critical that the score issued to test takers provide appropriate meaning. Whenever accommodations are made, examination boards need to consider their impact in terms of the test construct. The guiding principle must remain that the validity of the test should not be compromised by any accommodations that are made, and that no unfair advantages or disadvantages result from the accommodations (Shaw & Weir, 2007).

This brings forward debate surrounding the contentious practice of "flagging" test scores of those who have taken a test with accommodation. Flagging is the policy of annotating test scores, typically in the form of a footnote indicating the test was not administered under standard conditions, or otherwise reporting scores in a manner that indicates the exam was taken with an accommodation. Opponents argue that doing so announces to those receiving the scores that the test taker has a disability, and may call into question the validity of the score. This practice may also discourage test takers from requesting accommodation for fear of discrimination. Taylor and Chen (2016) address this matter:

> In some cases it may be appropriate to add an endorsement (or "flag") to a test taker's certificate indicating that some objectives of the test could not be assessed due to the candidate's disability in some respect. However, this approach raises other ethical issues and needs careful handling to ensure that it does not unduly or unfairly label test takers as having taken a modified test and thus lead to them suffering subsequent discrimination.

(pp. 390–391)

The *Standards for Educational and Psychological Tests*, which guide professional test developers, indicate

> when there is credible evidence of score comparability across regular and modified administrations, no flag should be attached to a score. When such evidence is lacking, specific information about the nature of the modification should be provided, if permitted, by law, to assist test users properly to interpret and act on test scores.
>
> *(AERA, 1999)*

The legality of such a practice was put to the test in the 2000 case of *Breimhorst v. Educational Testing Service* (as cited in Sireci, 2005, p. 1), during which a student with a physical disability who took the computerized Graduate Management Admissions Test (GMAT) with the accommodations of extended time and a trackball sued ETS because his score was flagged as a nonstandard administration. ETS settled the case by agreeing to stop flagging GMAT scores, as well as scores on TOEFL (Sireci, 2005). In rare instances, ETS will flag a score report as a "nonstandard administration" only if the test is significantly altered, such as if a test taker has been exempted from taking an entire section of a test for which a total score is reported (ETS, 2017).

Chase (2005) notes that for deaf or hard of hearing test takers to respond to writing prompts in sign language to a scribe alters the construct measured. Others disagree, suggesting that a student's communication mode must be based on what works for him or her (Allman, 2009). That is, students should not be penalized for use of approved accommodations that do not change the test construct and do not provide an unfair advantage to the test taker. Reporting of scores should be a consideration during the test development phase so that all parties understand the purpose of the testing and how the results will be reported and used (Allman, 2009).

Conclusion

In daily interaction, second language learners with disabilities may be doubly challenged as strangers assume a deficit in both capability and language proficiency. Opportunities to prove these skills can be especially consequential, and succeeding on a high-stakes writing test is one manner by which one's abilities are validated. As such, it is the responsibility of test developers to employ UD principles from the earliest stages of test design, considering the accessibility of content, administration, and score use. This allows for effective participation of the widest possible range of learners.

Limitations do arise, however, in the ability to include that range in meaningful pilot testing because of the low incidence of test takers with disabilities in high-stakes language tests (Chase, 2005) and the wide range of disabilities repre-sented. In such cases, assessment professionals must rely on their informed and educated professional judgment and regularly review policy and practice in this area to confirm the suitability of particular accommodations, as well as to identify where improvements must be made (Shaw & Weir, 2007).

Chase (2005) describes the goal of these activities as "a way of leveling the playing field on high-stakes assessments. If chosen wisely, accommodations provide students with access to showing what they know without affecting the validity of the test results." It is, therefore, the legal and ethical responsibility of assessment professionals in the United States and beyond to make every effort to accom-modate examinations accordingly.

References

AERA, APA, NCME (American Educational Research Association, American Psychological Association, & National Council on Measurement in Education). (1999). *Standards for educational and psychological tests.* Washington, DC: American Educational Research Association.

Allman, C. (2009). *Making tests accessible for students with visual impairments: A guide for test publishers, test developers, and state assessment personnel* (4th ed.). Louisville, KY: American Printing House for the Blind.

American Speech-Language-Hearing Association. (2015). *Audiology information series: Type, degree, and configuration of hearing loss.* Retrieved from asha.org/uploadedFiles/AIS-Hearing-Loss-Types-Degree-Configuration.pdf

Americans with Disabilities Act of 1990, Pub. L. No. 101–336, 104 Stat. 328 (1990).

Association of Language Testers in Europe (ALTE). (1994). *Code of practice.* Retrieved from alte.org

Banerjee, J., Chen, N. N., & Dobson, B. (2013). Special needs test forms: Levelling the playing field for test takers with disabilities. In D. Tsagari & G. Spanoudis (Eds.), *Assessing L2 students with learning and other disabilities* (pp. 253–270). Newcastle upon Tyne, UK: Cambridge Scholars Press.

British Council. (2017). *Special requirements.* Retrieved from https://takeielts.britishcouncil.org/book-your-test/special-arrangements

Cambridge English Language Assessment. (2017). *Special requirements.* Retrieved from www.cambridgeenglish.org/help/special-requirements/

Cambridge Michigan Language Assessments. (2013). *Special accommodations.* Ann Arbor: Cambridge Michigan Language Assessments.

Cambridge Michigan Language Assessments. (2017). *Special accommodations.* Retrieved from www.cambridgemichigan.org/test-takers/policies-principles/special-accommodations/

Chase, B. J. (2005). *Accommodations to improve instruction and assessment of students who are deaf or hard of hearing.* Retrieved from www.images.pearsonassessments.com/images/tmrs/tmrs_rg/Deaf.pdf

Commonwealth Consolidated Acts. (1992). *Disability discrimination act.* Retrieved from www.austlii.edu.au/au/legis/cth/consol_act/dda1992264/

Educational Testing Service. (2017). *Disabilities and health-related needs.* Retrieved from www.ets.org/disabilities/test_takers

Elliot, M. (2013). *Examining listening: Research and practice in assessing second language listening.* Cambridge, UK: UCLES/Cambridge University Press.

International Language Testing Association (ILTA). (2000). *Code of ethics.* Retrieved from http://www.iltaonline.com/page/CodeofEthics

Jernigan Institute. (2009). *The Braille literacy crisis in American: Facing the truth, reversing the trend, empowering the blind.* Retrieved from https://nfb.org/.../word/The_Braille_Literacy_Crisis_In_America.doc

Khalifa, H., & Weir, C. J. (2009). *Studies in language testing: Examining reading.* Cambridge, UK: Cambridge University Press.

Mariga, L., McConkey, R., & Myezwa, H. (2014). *Inclusive education in low-income countries: A resource book for teacher educators, parent trainers and community development workers.* Cape Town, South Africa: Atlas Alliance and Disability Innovations Africa.

Ministry of Law, Justice, and Company Affairs. (1996). *The persons with disabilities (equal opportunities, protection of rights and full participation) act.* Retrieved from www.disabilityaffairs.gov.in/upload/uploadfiles/files/PWD_Act.pdf

Morris, J. E. (1974). The 1973 Stanford Achievement Test Series as adapted for use by the visually handicapped. *Education of the Visually Handicapped, 6*(2), 33–46.

National Federation of the Blind. (2017). *General braille education center.* Retrieved from https://nfb.org/braille-general

National Research Council. (1999). *High stakes: Testing for tracking, promotion, and graduation* (J. Heubert & R. Hauser editors, Committee on Appropriate Test Use). Washington, DC: National Academy Press.

Neuhaus, R., Smith, C., & Burgdorf, M. (2014). Equality for people with disabilities, then and now. *GPSolo Magazine, 31*(6). Retrieved from https://americanbar.org/publications/gp_solo/2014/november_december/equality_people_disabilities_then_and_now.html

Nguyen, P. T. (2010). *The law on persons with disabilities.* Retrieved from https://web.archive.org/web/20140201230039/ and www.drdvietnam.org/nguoi-khuyet-tat/494-the-law-on-persons-with-disabilities-.html

Shapiro, J. (2015, July 24). How a law to protect disabled Americans became imitated around the world. *National Public Radio.* Retrieved from https://npr.org/sections/goatsandsoda/2015/07/24/425607389/how-a-law-to-protect-disabled-americans-became-imitated-around-the-world

Shaw, S. D., & Weir, C. J. (2007). *Examining writing: Research and practice in assessing second language writing.* Cambridge, UK: UCLES/Cambridge University Press.

Sireci, S. G. (2005). Unlabeling the disabled: A perspective on flagging scores from accommodated test administrations. *Educational Researcher, 34*(1), 3–12. https://doi.org/10.3102/0013189X034001003

Sireci, S. G., Scarpeti, S. E., & Li, S. (2005). Test accommodations for students with disabilities: An analysis of the interaction hypotheses. *Review of Educational Research, 75,* 457–490. https://doi.org/10.3102/00346543075004457

Starr, J. (2016). Life before the ADA: A brief history of disability in America. *The Odyssey Online.* Retrieved from theodysseyonline.com/life-before-ada

Taylor, L. (2012). Accommodations in language testing. In C. Coombe, P. Davidson, B. O'Sullivan, & S. Stoynoff (Eds.), *The Cambridge guide to second language assessment* (pp. 307–314). Cambridge, UK: Cambridge University Press. http://dx.doi.org/10.1515/9781614513827-025

Taylor, L., & Chen, N. N. (2016). Assessing students with learning and other disabilities/special needs. In D. Tsagari & J. Banerjee (Eds.), *Handbook of second language assessment* (pp. 377–396). Boston/Berlin: Walter de Gruyter.

Thompson, S. J., Johnstone, C. J., & Thurlow, M. L. (2002). *Universal design applied to large scale assessments* (Synthesis Report 44). Minneapolis, MN: National Center on Educational Outcomes. Retrieved from https://nceo.info/Resources/publications/OnlinePubs/Synthesis44.html

Tindal, G., & Haladyna, T. M. (Eds.). (2002). *Large-scale assessment programs for all students: Validity, technical adequacy, and implementation.* London: Lawrence Erlbaum Associates.

U.S. Department of Justice Civil Rights Division. (n.d.). *Testing accommodations.* Retrieved from https://ada.gov/regs2014/testing_accommodations.html

Wetzel, R., & Knowlton, M. (2000). A comparison of print and braille reading rates on three reading tasks. *Journal of Visual Impairment & Blindness, 94*, 146–154.

17

E-PORTFOLIO PROJECT

Assessing Language Teacher Learning in the Chilean Desert

Betsy Gilliland, Katterine Pavez Bravo, and Andrea Muñoz Galleguillos

University students preparing to teach English as a foreign language (EFL) in Chilean schools must demonstrate not only their language proficiency, but also their pedagogical content knowledge in order to receive their teaching licenses. Recent reforms in both English language and pre-service teacher education policy have created a dynamic opportunity for curriculum and assessment development in Chile, the site of this project. The South American nation has spent the 30 years since emerging from dictatorship reshaping its image into an active member of the global community. A 2004 policy, *Programa Ingles Abre Puertas* (PIAP, English Opens Doors), expanded English language education and established standards for English learning that added productive language, including writing (Ministerio de Educación de Chile, 2016). The policy also created funding opportunities for teacher professional development, with a goal of technical and educational support, collaboration and networking, and ongoing professional development (Ministerio de Educación de Chile, 2016).

Along with the school curriculum, the Chilean government has further reformed teacher education policy to increase accountability while allowing individual institutions flexibility in implementation. Between 1997 and 2002, the Ministry of Education introduced a new system of teacher evaluation and improved the quality of teacher education, including more and earlier in-school practical experiences and the beginning of national standards for teacher preparation (Avalos & Aylwin, 2007). Obligatory standards for pedagogical careers emphasizing disciplinary content and pedagogical knowledge were delivered in 2014, including an expectation that English teaching candidates should have language proficiency at the CEFR C1 level[1] by graduation (Gobierno de Chile,

2014). Accreditation of teacher education programs, determined in part by graduates' meeting of the new standards, was made compulsory in 2006, but accrediting bodies allowed individual institutions to determine how they demonstrate competencies (Avalos, 2014).

Preparing language teachers to implement curriculum requires balancing national expectation with local needs. Because incoming language teacher candidates often have low levels of English proficiency (Avalos, 2014), most Chilean programs separate English language learning—both linguistics and teachers' own proficiency development—from pedagogical learning (Abrahams & Farias, 2010; Barahona, 2014, 2016). After intensive language study, teacher candidates begin multiple field placements in schools while taking courses in language teaching methodology (Barahona, 2014). Barahona (2016) found that teacher candidates reported feeling overwhelmed by written assignments they had to complete while simultaneously preparing lessons for their teaching placements. In this chapter, we describe how teacher educators in one Chilean university, Universidad de Atacama (UDA), used their knowledge of the local context to develop a program-wide electronic portfolio (e-portfolio) assessment documenting student teachers' pedagogical and linguistic development across their four years of study.

Context of the Project

Universidad de Atacama was founded in Copiapó, in the northern desert of Chile, in 1857 as the Escuela de Minas (School of Mines), whose purpose was to train workers for the recently discovered silver mines in the area. Over the twentieth century, enrollment expanded and the institution became part of the national university system under the Ministry of Education of Chile. In 1981, State Technical University, campus Copiapó, became Universidad de Atacama. Presently, UDA's main goal is to prepare professionals in areas such as Engineering, Education, Technology, Law, Science, and Medicine.

UDA's English Pedagogy teacher education program started in 1991 to meet a need for English teachers in the Atacama region. Most entering freshmen say that they want to study English primarily because they like the language and only secondarily because they want to become teachers. Between 20 and 24 students come to the English department each year to study pedagogy, and a similar number enter the translation program; due to money and family problems, however, only some finish their education. Each year between eight and 15 teachers graduate from the program and take jobs in local schools.

High school graduates entering the program are evaluated on all four language skills, using the CEFR levels as reference. Having spent seven to 12 years learning English as a foreign language in school, most students can read and write adequately but still have problems communicating orally. Although entering

Pedagogy and Translation students' scores increased slightly from 2008 to 2015, with a few reaching B1 level in the latest assessments, they have an enormous gap to fill as they must develop their English abilities to reach the Ministry of Education's graduation expectation of a C1 level while also learning how to teach the language.

Recognizing the need to document program outcomes for accreditation while also supporting formative assessment, instructors in the English department sought an assessment that would allow students to showcase their development both as language teachers and language users. As this chapter describes, the faculty developed a program-wide e-portfolio allowing students to exhibit progress throughout their studies at the university. By writing their reflections in English, students demonstrate their growth and learning as teachers of English as a foreign language.

UDA E-Portfolio Development Process

Previous Forms of Assessment

Portfolio assessment had been tried previously at UDA, but with mixed results. The English Pedagogy program used a paper portfolio until 2008, in the form of a binder divided among four categories: values, culture, pedagogical area, and subject matter. Each category included indicators that students demonstrated through evidence such as written reports, videos of their teaching, and lesson plans. This portfolio, however, had too many indicators (four areas, each divided into standards, with a total of 75 indicators), making it almost inconceivable for students to address even a majority of them. For example, one standard stated that students should be responsible, neat, and punctual, but no clear artifact could illustrate this. Assessors had individual views about appropriate artifacts or evidence, causing conflict among evaluators and instructors. Language and Communication professors further requested fourth-year students to create separate portfolios to showcase their language development. One year, however, was too little time for students to show progress.

In addition to the above-mentioned portfolios, the English Pedagogy program assessed pre-service teachers' overall language proficiency with a diagnostic test administered annually. Test results were used to place students into classes focused on improving their individual English language needs. With respect to writing, students were retaught their specific grammar weaknesses as identified in the diagnostic test and other coursework. Writing was primarily assessed through in-class sentence and paragraph writing. Increased national pressure for accountability for students' language proficiency and pedagogical aptitude, however, made it necessary to develop a new approach to documenting undergraduate students' ongoing learning.

Developing an E-Portfolio

Given the problems of the old portfolio system and limitations of the annual language proficiency assessments, as well as increased national attention to accreditation of teacher education programs, in 2014 the English Pedagogy program recognized the need for a new approach to assessing teacher candidates' learning. Analyzing the advantages and disadvantages of the old portfolio system, they decided to improve on it by building an electronic version using available technology that could allow standardizing procedures among the five careers in the Faculty of Humanities. After reviewing information from the old portfolio system, Katterine and Andrea (teacher educators in English Pedagogy appointed as directors of the portfolio revision process) drafted a manual organized in four areas, each with standards and indicators to guide students' gathering of evidence.

E-portfolios have been used worldwide for student assessment since the 1990s. Though they have been implemented in different ways, e-portfolios generally maintain the goal that students should *collect* artifacts created during the program or course, *select* those that they feel best represent their performance of course objectives, and *reflect* on how the artifacts represent what they have learned. Hawisher and Selfe highlighted e-portfolios as "an online collection of student work that will ultimately be evaluated by an audience of some type" (1997, p. 308), suggesting a broader potential readership than paper portfolios may have. Although not all e-portfolios are intended as assessment, in educational settings such as teacher education and writing programs, their most common use is to evaluate student learning over a period of time ranging from a single instructional unit to a four-year degree program. E-portfolios support students to integrate multiple forms of reflection, including on their writing processes, identity development, and presentation of their work for specific audiences (Yancey, 2015).

E-portfolio implementation in language teacher education has found both benefits and challenges. Language teachers' e-portfolios may contain video of their teaching, lesson plans, textbook evaluations, materials they created, evidence of language proficiency, documentation of professional development, or job application materials (Dhonau & McAlpine, 2005). Assessment activities can be designed specifically to address evaluation standards: artifacts such as teaching videos show not only pedagogy but also the teacher's language proficiency, and the e-portfolio allows teacher candidates to demonstrate technology skills that are also in the standards (Dhonau & McAlpine, 2005). Hung (2012) found that e-portfolios implemented in one course in an EFL teacher education program in Taiwan promoted positive washback in the form of a community of practice among teacher candidates, who reported learning from their peers, understanding course content better, and seeing connections between the course and classroom practice.

In initiating the project, the UDA team focused on reviewing published literature on the topic and talking with experienced teachers in Chile and abroad who had worked with e-portfolios. Scholars offer recommendations to programs wishing to implement e-portfolios. On a practical level, all users (both students assembling portfolios and faculty evaluating them) must be familiar with the technological aspects (Brown, 2015; Dhonau & McAlpine, 2005). Faculty evaluators must also be comfortable teaching students how to use the technology and how to incorporate multimodality into instruction (Brown, 2015; Hawisher & Selfe, 1997). To make the e-portfolio process a learning experience, instructors must think about their instructional practices more deeply as well. The process should allow students to choose artifacts that represent their learning and their desired identities (Brown, 2015; Jenson & Treuer, 2014). Peer response to artifact selection, portfolio design, and reflection supports students to think broadly about their audiences (Yancey, 2015).

Much information is available on the importance of portfolios and their advantages and disadvantages as alternative assessments; few publications, however, related to what the UDA instructors wanted to do in integrating an e-portfolio throughout a complete four-year program. Katterine and Andrea therefore reached out to others who had developed e-portfolios similar to what they envisioned. In talking to teachers in the south of Chile who shared their work, they learned that in single courses, most used open source platforms because they were free and offered adequate tools, but none of the existing platforms completely met the UDA team's goals.

Early studies of e-portfolios found that technology challenged both students, who felt rushed trying to complete portfolio tasks while doing other assignments, and evaluators, who had difficulty accessing artifacts and felt it redundant to score coursework that had already been graded by instructors (Banister, Vannatta, & Ross, 2006; Grier, Denney, & Clark, 2006). Grier et al. recommended that programs carefully consider how e-portfolios integrate with program instruction and assessment, as well as how portfolio elements will be assessed. To facilitate access for students and evaluators, Banister et al. (2006) suggested developing an in-house platform customized to program needs.

With respect to program needs, UDA students in English Pedagogy wish to become English teachers or translators. They should know not only about grammar but also how to reflect on their initial teacher/translator learning process in order to improve while they are still in the university and to overcome difficulties after they graduate (Farrell, 2015). Rather than assuming students already had skills for reflecting, Katterine and Andrea realized that students needed to learn *how to reflect*. As a result, they determined to teach students how to reflect through the e-portfolio.

Learning to reflect takes time and needs to be taught as more than just reporting on what students learned in creating an artifact (Jenson & Treuer, 2014). The medium of e-portfolios allows teacher candidates to extend their reflection process by thinking about how the connections they describe among their selected artifacts contribute to the overall messages they want to convey about their learning (Norton-Meier, 2003). Hawisher and Selfe (1997), however, cautioned that the electronic format may encourage students' collection of artifacts without thinking about which best represent messages they want to convey. As a solution, Yancey (2015) recommended considering reflection as more than a stand-alone item on a single assignment, but rather as integral to the overall curriculum.

With an interest in understanding e-portfolio use in other contexts, Katterine and Andrea contacted Betsy. She organized their visit to the University of Hawai'i at Mānoa to meet with faculty members using e-portfolios in language programs, including the Second Language Studies BA degree capstone e-portfolio. They observed the final products and interviewed students about the advantages and disadvantages of the process. One feature they remarked on was the Philosophy of Teaching, in which students reflected on their beliefs regarding teaching and learning. They also noticed how the e-portfolio process enabled students to compare their writing skills across their years in the program. Drawing on what they had learned from the literature and others, the UDA professors shifted their attention to their specific context.

Context-Specific Assessment Development

Having established goals for the project, Katterine and Andrea formed a committee including professors from the other participating departments (Pre-School Pedagogy, Physical Education Pedagogy, and Elementary Pedagogy). Each representative discussed with their department the evidence and artifacts students would include in their e-portfolios. For the purposes of this chapter, we will focus on the English Pedagogy and Translation e-portfolio.

To ensure consistency in the e-portfolio design, the professors described the following:

- *Subject* related to this evidence
- *Professor* who assigned the artifact or evidence
- *Year and semester* of the course
- *Standard* from the Ministry of Education for English Pedagogy programs
- *Indicator* from the Ministry of Education for English Pedagogy programs
- *Evidence or artifact* directly related to the standard and indicator
- *Guiding reflection questions* for students

The guidelines enabled the e-portfolios to meet national standards while fitting within the local program's expectations. The e-portfolio covers the main subjects of the Ministry of Education's national standards and indicators for pedagogy careers: *Language and Communication in English, Teaching Methodology,* and *Literature.* There are no nationally established standards or indicators for the translation career, so the professors in charge of the career developed their own, covering the subjects *Language and Communication in English*, *Introduction to Translation*, and *Human Science*.

In 2014 the UDA team received a grant from the Chilean government's *Programa Ingles Abre Puertas* (PIAP) to fund technology innovations. With grant funding, the project hired a dedicated programmer to collaborate with UDA technology staff for the web platform design, paying special attention to recommendations from the committee discussions and local needs assessment. The technology experts designed a site-specific e-portfolio platform that avoided some of the pitfalls other programs had experienced to maximize the experience for UDA professors and students.

E-Portfolio Classroom

Consideration of local needs also led the UDA team to innovate with respect to the physical context of the e-portfolio process. With PIAP grant funding, they established a dedicated classroom for the purpose of supporting students' work on their e-portfolios. Located in the UDA Technological Learning Center, it has an area where students can sit on comfortable sofas to work on their tablets as well as a computer room with 43 computers, scanners, and lockers. In an effort to preempt technical issues noted in earlier work with electronic portfolios (Banister et al., 2006; Grier et al., 2006; Thang, Lee, & Zulkifli, 2012), such as students' unfamiliarity with the platform or limited access to reliable Internet, students can visit the portfolio room at any time during school hours to write reflections and upload artifacts.

First-year students in all departments are assigned a two-hour period once a week in the e-portfolio classroom to work on their portfolios. An English teacher is in the room 22 hours per week to support students' portfolio development and writing process. During the first class session, she introduces students to the purpose and advantages of the e-portfolio and reasons why they should make use of the classroom. In subsequent classes, students get to know the Ministry standards and then start drafting their philosophies of teaching/translating. Students in the e-portfolio classroom also peer review their classmates' philosophies and begin collecting other evidence. Although attendance is mandatory, students have some flexibility in choosing when to attend during the week.

Assignments

Taking into account both national requirements and local needs, e-portfolio assignments reflect the UDA professors' vision of how student teachers and translators will demonstrate their personal and professional learning. Aligned with a central competency from UDA's institutional learning objectives, "Capacity to be lifelong learners," the e-portfolio serves as a vehicle through which students can identify their learning needs through a strategic and critical analysis of their professional development; they set goals for lifelong learning as they transfer knowledge and skills acquired in initial teaching formation to imagined future scenarios as teachers. The goal is for students to reflect upon their professional development throughout their four years in the program.

When the assessment is fully implemented, students will select two artifacts per semester to include in their e-portfolios, based upon the program curriculum. The English department decided that students in their first year should evidence their work in the courses *Language and Communication in English I* and *Methodology I*, while second year students should evidence their work in *Language and Communication in English II*, *Methodology II*, and *Children's Literature*. The instructors in charge of those subjects will grade and give feedback to the students' work.

Through the written reflections, professors can observe students' writing processes as well as their subject-matter learning. The first reflective writing assignment students complete is a Philosophy of Teaching/Translating, written in English. The writing process is scaffolded through a worksheet explaining what a Philosophy of Teaching is and guiding idea development and organization through questions. During the first semester, students also record a video in which they discuss why they want to be teachers, which they will contrast with another recording on the same topic during their final semester of the program. It is expected that the students' writing and discourse in the e-portfolio will document how much they have grown during their years at UDA.

Writing is an important part of the process. Evaluation criteria address both language and content in students' e-portfolio submissions. The main goal is that the students demonstrate critical thinking skills in selection of high-quality artifacts and reflection on their meaning. Reflections allow professors to witness students' critical thinking skills during their initial teaching formation. Use of written language, however, also counts in scoring, since it is the form in which students convey their ideas. It is possible for teacher candidates to have high quality artifacts but get low scores due to poor quality English in their reflections. Students may think critically as expected, yet limited control of language prevents them from displaying what they understand. Evidence and reflection, therefore, cannot be assessed separately. In order to overcome this difficulty, cohort teachers and the e-portfolio teacher will monitor students' writing process and provide feedback on draft reflections to allow students to demonstrate clear critical thinking skills through accurate language use.

Rubric Development

At the time of this writing, first- and second-year students have worked on their e-portfolios for one semester. The committee is still in the process of establishing evaluation guidelines. To create assessment rubrics, Katterine and Andrea first presented a proposal to the e-portfolio committee, and then each department provided feedback for improvement. The committee organized the suggestions to create rubrics that were tested in December 2016 when the instructors evaluated the students' philosophy statements and artifacts. A revised rubric was introduced in April 2017 for the purpose of giving revision-focused feedback to students' philosophy statement drafts. Another group of instructors developing a postgraduate program will contribute to improving the rubrics as well.

Besides UDA's institutional learning objective "Capacity to be lifelong learners," additional factors considered in the rubric development process included the choice of evidence, reflection content, use of language in the reflection writing, and APA style. In general, the committee considered the evidence itself as well as the different aspects coming from it. It is thought that the more demanding the expectations, the better the students will perform in the required tasks. The English Pedagogy program is going through a redesign of the curriculum. As a result, new rubrics are being discussed in order to fit this competency-based curriculum model. These rubrics will be used with freshmen and sophomores who started the academic year in March 2017.

Pilot Testing

The e-portfolios were pilot tested with the English Pedagogy and Pre-School Pedagogy groups during the second semester of 2016. In total, 78 students from the first two years of those programs participated in the pilot study. During the last week of September 2016, students received training and the corresponding worksheet listing the expected forms of evidence requested by their instructors. Rubrics were also shared with them, so they could know how their work would be evaluated. The students also started to attend weekly sessions in the e-portfolio classroom, where they learned about the Ministry standards, the e-portfolio project, and how to use the platform. They then focused on writing their philosophy statements and collecting evidence.

During the semester of pilot testing, the e-portfolios were expanded to the whole Faculty of Humanities and Education, adding Physical Education Pedagogy and Elementary Pedagogy. To date, 242 students (almost 90% of students enrolled in the platform) have created portfolios, uploading 175 artifacts to the platform for different subjects. Students were asked to upload two artifacts per subject, but as of December 2016, most students had just one artifact plus their philosophies and peer review. They explained that they lacked time (the process started midway through the semester) and thought participation was optional because it was a pilot study. Starting in March 2017, students will be required to include work based on the competencies established in the e-portfolio model.

Qualitative Outcomes

In January 2017, English Pedagogy instructors evaluated the philosophies of teaching/translating and the artifacts that the students had uploaded to the platform. Most evaluators said that it was enlightening to read students' thoughts on why they chose the career, although it was more difficult to check first-year students' philosophies than those of second-year students. Evaluators observed that first-year students had problems with organization of ideas, vocabulary, and focusing on a topic. Second-year students' writing was more comprehensible, and even though they lacked paragraph-writing techniques, they were able to organize their ideas. We noted an improvement in accuracy and the amount of new words used. Having evaluated the students' philosophy statements, instructors will know on what areas of language to focus their teaching in the next semester's Language and Communication classes. Some professors plan to employ a self-assessment checklist so students can reflect on their writing and identify which aspects they need to improve.

To evaluate the students' experiences with this first semester of the e-portfolio project, Katterine and Andrea surveyed students about their experiences, asking them to discuss their process of writing their philosophies of teaching/translating, the peer review experience, and the process of creating and uploading artifacts to the platform. Students were asked to reflect upon writing in English and the mechanisms they used to get their ideas together. First-year Pedagogy students said that they lacked the necessary words and struggled with grammar, so it was difficult to express their ideas in the foreign language. Nevertheless, evaluators felt that their ideas could be read without difficulty. Second-year students said that while vocabulary and writing skills did not hinder their reflection writing, they struggled with some specific grammar mistakes, paragraph format, and time constraints. First-year Translation students said that it was difficult to write because they had problems organizing their ideas, they lacked vocabulary, and they made minor mistakes in grammar. Second-year Translation students said that they had problems conveying their ideas and lacked vocabulary to express what they wanted.

Explaining their writing process, most first-year Pedagogy students brainstormed following the guiding questions provided; they wrote several drafts and did some research to support their ideas. Second-year Pedagogy students also brainstormed by reflecting on their strengths and teaching experiences, using guiding questions, and focusing on the main ideas of the assignment. Most first-year Translation students used the assignment guiding questions to focus on required ideas; they employed brainstorming, drafts, and what they had learned in class. Second-year Translation students also used the guiding questions, Spanish-English translation, and brainstorming, as well as prioritizing important information.

When asked what they could do to improve their writing, all four groups suggested that they needed to increase their vocabulary and grammar knowledge as well as to be more organized and efficient in the work. First-year Pedagogy and Translation students were also concerned with improving their reading skills, while second-year Pedagogy students wanted to learn how to self-regulate to avoid grammar mistakes, use short sentences to express ideas, and integrate more references and quotations. Second-year Translation students also wanted to learn more about translating and language and to be more creative.

With respect to the effects of writing in a foreign language on their ability to reflect on their teaching, students universally expressed value in the process in spite of some difficulties. First-year Pedagogy students said it was sometimes hard because they lacked the words, but writing their reflection in English helped them correct their mistakes, learn more vocabulary, organize their ideas, and improve their critical thinking. Second-year Pedagogy students said that writing the reflection helped them improve their English and learn more about the language so that they could express their ideas. One student commented: "It will be interesting to read what I wrote in two years. All I wrote is part of what I want to become and it is a process that started the day I decided to study English pedagogy." This statement reflects what the professors had hoped to achieve in implementing the e-portfolio system: that students see the process of growing as professionals through the reflections and artifacts uploaded to the platform through the years that they spend in the university.

Translation students were similarly positive about the experience, seeing it as an opportunity to apply and reflect on what they had learned in their classes. First-year Translation students said that it was not a problem to write the reflection in English, as it helped them to improve grammar and spelling and think about writing more in English. A few students said that it was challenging to translate ideas from Spanish to English, as they lacked precise vocabulary. Another student said it was difficult because he did not have his ideas in order. Second-year Translation students felt that expressing their ideas was straightforward and writing in English helped them realize what they should improve. One student noted: "When you start using a different language in your life, you actually change on the inside; so that could help in a professional environment."

Students were honest about the challenges of the writing process. The majority thought it was difficult, but considered it an impetus to keep improving. Others reflected that they could easily convey the ideas they wanted in writing. Concerning teaching, they mused that they were convinced they chose the appropriate program since they were attracted to the teaching vocation. They were also motivated by innovation they might accomplish when working as teachers. Writing their initial philosophy statements motivated some students to see their teaching as a service to the community, particularly in changing English language learning from their experiences in school. These future English teachers felt comfortable and able to face the upcoming challenge of English teaching in Chile.

These findings will be shared with the language and communication professors so they will be able to give feedback on the common problems students find when they have to write multi-paragraph texts. Students will also have the support of the English teacher in the e-portfolio classroom. The e-portfolio class will address weaknesses noted in students' writing, so during the first semester of 2017 and before they start working with the artifacts, professors will develop a plan to address these problems. Students will have the opportunity to revise the philosophies and reflections they wrote the previous year and further demonstrate how much they have improved.

Conclusions

At the time of writing, the UDA e-portfolio has only been in place for one full semester, so we cannot make any definitive statements about its overall success. Judging by the students' work so far, however, we believe it is serving its purpose in allowing students to showcase their learning not only of individual course goals, but of their overall knowledge of foreign language pedagogy and their abilities to write in English as well. While the purpose of this e-portfolio is more than just a writing assessment, it has allowed teachers to evaluate what their first- and second-year Pedagogy and Translation students have mastered and where they are struggling with written English. Further, it is already showing its potential as documentation of student teachers' achievement of Ministry of Education standards as well as the university and the English department's goals for lifelong learners.

Requiring students to write about their teaching/translation philosophies in English did to some extent affect their performance, since they lacked adequate vocabulary to express what they really meant. Nevertheless, they acknowledged that the assessment served as an impetus to acquire more vocabulary and use it in context in their future work as English teachers and translators. As they noted in the survey summarized earlier, students perceived that writing in English somewhat hindered their opportunity to demonstrate their knowledge of pedagogy, but at the same time, they regarded it as a learning opportunity. Consistent with the university's mission, they conceive of themselves now as constant learners.

Regarding the process of using the platform to upload the philosophies and artifacts, the electronic nature of the e-portfolio did not affect what the students created. The platform supported their representation of their teaching and English abilities. Similar to Hung's finding (2012), the reflection writing process promoted positive washback among the students. This can be seen in the peer review that students did concerning their philosophies of teaching/translating. They also learned from their peers. Unlike Hung's students, however, the UDA students did not report anxiety related to sharing their e-portfolios with their classmates.

As the students progress through the rest of their teacher education program, we will continue to track their e-portfolio process. Future research will address changes in their reflection writing, documented through their Philosophies of Teaching/Translating and other artifacts, as well as how they grow as teachers and translators over their four years in the program.

In terms of policy, students will face high-stakes evaluation once they finish their program, as they will be tested on their English language proficiency and achievement of standards from the Ministry of Education. Reflection permits an ongoing improvement process that students will be used to, particularly if they know their own needs. We feel that as long as the students are able to reflect on their strengths and weaknesses, they will continue learning and improving. After reading students' appraisals regarding their writing process, we think they considered this an opportunity to enhance learning from difficulties they might find on the way.

Note

1 The Common European Framework of Reference for Languages (CEFR) serves as a comparative proficiency scale for 40 languages while also providing guidelines for language curriculum development and language teacher education (Council of Europe, n.d.). The six levels range from A1 (lowest proficiency) to C2 (highly proficient).

References

Abrahams, M. J., & Farias, M. (2010). Struggling for change in Chilean EFL teacher education. *Colombian Applied Linguistics Journal, 12*(2), 110–118.

Avalos, B. (2014). La formación inicial docente en Chile: Tensiones entre políticas de apoyo y control. *Estudios Pedagógicos, 40*(1), 11–28. https://doi.org/10.4067/S0718-07052014000200002

Avalos, B., & Aylwin, P. (2007). How young teachers experience their professional work in Chile. *Teaching and Teacher Education, 23*(4), 515–528. https://doi.org/10.1016/j.tate.2006.11.003

Banister, S., Vannatta, R. A., & Ross, C. (2006). Testing electronic portfolio systems in teacher education: Finding the right fit. *Action in Teacher Education, 27*(4), 81–90. https://doi.org/10.1080/01626620.2006.10463404

Barahona, M.A.M. (2014). Exploring the curriculum of second language teacher education (SLTE) in Chile: A case study. *Perspectiva Educacional, 53*(2), 45–67.

Barahona, M.A.M. (2016). *English language teacher education in Chile*. London: Routledge.

Brown, S. (2015). The impact of the ePortfolio tool on the process: Functional decisions of a new genre. *Theory into Practice, 54*(4), 335–342. https://doi.org/10.1080/00405841.2015.1077618

Council of Europe Language Policy Unit. (n.d.). Common European framework of reference for languages: Learning, teaching, assessment. Retrieved from www.coe.int/lang-CEFR

Dhonau, S., & McAlpine, D. (2005). An electronic portfolio for the ACTF/NCATE teacher program standards in the second language methods course. *Foreign Language Annals, 38*(1), 69–76. https://doi.org/10.1111/j.1944-9720.2005.tb02454.x

Farrell, T. S. C. (2015). *Promoting teacher reflection in second language education: A framework for TESOL professionals*. New York: Routledge.

Gobierno de Chile. (2014). *Estándares orientadores para carreras de pedagogía en inglés*. Santiago: Ministerio de Educación-República de Chile. Retrieved from www.cpeip.cl/

Grier, J. M., Denney, M. K., & Clark, M. M. (2006, April). *A tale of two programs: A comparative study of electronic portfolio assessment in teacher education*. Paper presented at the American Educational Research Association, San Francisco. Retrieved from http://files.eric.ed.gov/fulltext/ED494953.pdf

Hawisher, G. E., & Selfe, C. L. (1997). Wedding the technologies of writing portfolios and computers: The challenges of electronic classrooms. In K. B. Yancey & I. Weiser (Eds.), *Situating portfolios: Four perspectives* (pp. 305–321). Logan, UT: Utah State University Press.

Hung, S.-T. A. (2012). A washback study on e-portfolio assessment in an English as a foreign language teacher preparation program. *Computer Assisted Language Learning, 25*(1), 21–36. https://doi.org/10.1080/09588221.2010.551756

Jenson, J. D., & Treuer, P. (2014). Defining the e-portfolio: What it is and why it matters. *Change: The Magazine of Higher Learning, 46*(2), 50–57. https://doi.org/10.1080/00091383.2014.897192

Ministerio de Educación de Chile. (2016). *Programa Inglés Abre Puertas (PIAP).* Retrieved from http://ingles.mineduc.cl/programa-ingles-abre-puertas/

Norton-Meier, L. A. (2003). To efoliate or not to efoliate? The rise of the electronic portfolio in teacher education. *Journal of Adolescent & Adult Literacy, 46*(6), 516–518.

Thang, S. M., Lee, Y. S., & Zulkifli, N. F. (2012). The role of electronic portfolio in enhancing information and communication technology and English language skills: The voices of six Malaysian undergraduates. *Computer Assisted Language Learning, 25*(3), 277–293. https://doi.org/10.1080/09588221.2012.655299

Yancey, K. B. (2015). Grading ePortfolios: Tracing two approaches, their advantages, and their disadvantages. *Theory into Practice, 54*(4), 301–308. https://doi.org/10.1080/00405841.2015.1076693

18

THE VALUE OF USAGE-BASED APPROACHES TO DIAGNOSTIC PLACEMENT ASSESSMENT IN GRADUATE EAP

Megan M. Siczek and Natalia Dolgova

Large-scale and commercialized assessment measures (e.g., TOEFL, IELTS) are routinely critiqued for being imprecise and ill-fitted for predicting academic success and/or the task readiness of specific student populations, yet they form the basis of a great number of policies that influence students' admission to universities and placement into classes. Though all institutions are under pressure to assess second language (L2) students' language proficiency appropriately and efficiently, there is little evidence that placement measures—even direct ones—necessarily align with institutional curricula and pedagogy. Furthermore, these assessments rarely address functional adequacy, which is increasingly considered a crucial component of L2 performance (Kuiken & Vedder, 2014). Thus, in line with the overall purpose of this volume, this chapter is premised on the limitations of generic and a contextual assessment and placement practices. As administrators and educators, it is critical that we realize the "pedagogical, social, and political implications of the tests we administer to our students" (Crusan, 2002a, p. 21).

This chapter documents the evolution of a targeted usage-based diagnostic assessment procedure strategically developed and implemented within the particular institutional and curricular context of a private East Coast university's graduate level English for Academic Purposes (EAP) program. Conceptualized in line with recent research supporting the value of contextually grounded assessments over standardized/generic ones (Plakans, 2013), our approach aimed to ensure that L2 graduate students were being assessed and placed appropriately and ethically (Cumming, 2002; Silva, 1997) and that the administration of the diagnostic procedure did not overwhelm the program's already strained capacity. Based on the development, refinement, and assessment of this method, we conclude that locally developed and functional mechanisms for placement are valuable tools for ethically and efficiently placing students in appropriate writing classes.

Description of Institutional and Program Context

The EAP program at the George Washington University, a research-intensive private university on the East Coast of the United States, is housed in the College of Arts and Sciences and primarily teaches required academic writing courses to students who have matriculated in degree programs. The mission of the program is "to socialize international students [. . .] into our academic discourse community [and] to prepare students to meet academic expectations for written communication at a university level" (https://eap.columbian.gwu.edu). EAP's pedagogy draws on academically purposed content and materials using a task-based approach. The requirement to take EAP is based on long-established university policy: International students who are admitted to the university with TOEFL (or equivalent) scores below 100 are required to register for an EAP academic writing and research course during their first semester of study. There are two levels of graduate-level EAP courses, and most admitted students are required to complete only one. While both levels offer scaffolded instruction involving academic content, tasks, and skills, the lower-level class targets foundational skills, including rhetorical and genre awareness, working with academic sources, the process of drafting and revising written work, and grammatical accuracy. The upper-level class, for students with higher proficiency, focuses on research paper writing, critical reading and analysis of academic discourse, small-group work, and oral presentations on research.

The program has experienced particularly explosive growth at the graduate level in the last several years. For example, in 2008–2009, 69 students were enrolled in graduate-level EAP classes, and all sections were taught by a single full-time faculty member. By 2013–2014, there were 391 graduate EAP students; and in 2016–2017, enrollments reached nearly 600 students, taught by two full-time faculty members and as many as ten part-time instructors. This growth aligns with overall increases in the number of international students pursuing higher education in the United States, as well as the university's own strategic internationalization agenda, which involves increasing international student enrollments at the graduate level to 25–30% of the student population by 2021. Despite this incredible growth, the EAP program remains constrained in terms of its infrastructure, adjunct status of the majority of instructors, relatively large class sizes, insufficient administrative support, and limitations of space and budget—all of which limit its capacity to engage in comprehensive proficiency assessment.

Assessing Writing in Context

This chapter is centrally informed by the need for thoughtful and ethical approaches to assessment in L2 writing contexts. As stakeholders in the process, both administrators and faculty should take responsibility for reflecting critically on status quo approaches and improving them where possible (Crusan, 2010;

Huot, 2002). This criticality derives from both a knowledge of theoretical principles of assessment and a situated awareness of the contexts in which assessment occurs. As Crusan (2010) noted, "critical decisions" are made as a result of institutional assessment practices, and placement into writing classes has a number of pedagogical, ethical, political, psychometric, and financial implications (pp. 7–8). As a result, we should not leave assessment to entities outside of the context, or even to institutional policy makers and administrators who may have little understanding of the program and its curriculum.

Developing placement assessment *within* local contexts—particularly direct assessment that involves student production of written text that is evaluated by faculty—offsets a number of limitations to commercialized assessment measures or institutional approaches that rely on indirect measures (CCCC, 2009; Crusan, 2002a, 2010; Huot, 2002). First, it gives programs control, instead of ceding control to outside forces. Second, it reflects the actual curriculum within a specific institution; in other words, "practice defines assessment" (Crusan, 2010, p. 15), a contention that is consistent with the Conference on College Composition and Communication (CCCC, 2009) recommendation to ground writing assessment in the context of the program. Such curricular alignment can in turn be used to improve teaching and learning in a given context (Huot, 2002). Third, it offers a set of evaluative tools that are grounded in the accumulated experience that program administrators and faculty have acquired through direct experience with the program's student population, curriculum, and pedagogy (CCCC, 2009; Huot, 1996; James & Templeman, 2009). Finally, the insights gained from documenting and analyzing data from institutional placement can help develop a scholarly body of empirical work that drives best practice in the field, contributing to what Huot (1996) would call a theory of assessment.

The literature has noted the ethical imperative of placing students appropriately in writing classes (Crusan, 2002b; Cumming, 2002; Silva, 1997) and emphasized the fact that decisions on placement have notable consequences for students, faculty, programs, and even institutions (Fox, 2009; James & Templeman, 2009). It is clear that scholars in the field continue to advocate for assessment situated in local contexts and supported through the collaborative effort of program administrators and faculty, but translating this into systematic practice depends on a narrower understanding of ethical and appropriate placement policies within particular L2 writing environments.

Functionally and Contextually Based Aspects of Assessment

Functional, dynamic, and communicative dimensions of L2 production have been gaining greater attention in the field of second language acquisition in the past several decades (Tyler, 2010). In particular, the concept of dynamically situated L2 production—functional adequacy, which emphasizes socio-pragmatic appropriateness or successful task completion—has been increasingly recognized as an essential component of L2 proficiency (Kuiken & Vedder, 2014). However, if we consider the notion of functional adequacy in relation to large-scale, generic assessments, it appears that the latter largely ignore it. To illustrate, Matsuda and Jeffery (2012) found that large-scale standardized assessments disregard the notions of *voice* or *stance* that are bound to capture functional adequacy of L2 written production.

To compensate for this drawback of standardized assessments, researchers and practitioners in EAP settings have designed complementary assessments reflecting the local context and addressing the functional adequacy of obtained L2 samples. For instance, Kim (2011) led the development of an empirically derived and descriptor-based diagnostic checklist, which proved to be almost equivalent statistically to a larger-scale standardized assessment, but its key benefit was that it captured the characteristics of the assessed writing skills and indicated which may be more difficult to master in the EAP context. Plakans (2013) described the process of bottom-up creation and validation of a writing test in a large ESL program, demonstrating the superiority of such assessment to generic, large-scale tools. Hill (2015) found that integrating curriculum and assessment through a curriculum-based assessment (CBA) approach proved a more beneficial practice for learners than the use of a standardized/generic assessment approach alone. Another successful example of a targeted/localized assessment is Lockwood (2017), who described the process of creating tasks and validating rubric descriptors for different levels in a Hong Kong EAP program, emphasizing the importance of context for discipline-specific EAP.

Implementing and exploring the usefulness of contextually and functionally relevant assessment tools complements a general call for "establishing a body of practice-oriented research" (Wette, 2010, p. 158). Previous research has documented positive changes associated with contribution and participation of local resources, such as faculty, students, and policy makers. Fox (2009) documents one EAP program's bottom-up involvement in diagnostic assessment of their students, which prompted institutional collaboration in policy and renewal of curriculum. James and Templeman (2009) strongly suggest that EAP faculty involvement is crucial for the success of diagnostic placement. In sum, existing research provides plentiful evidence supporting the importance of contextualized assessments and suggests benefits that extend beyond the immediate assessment purpose.

In light of these findings, our action research project aimed to document the process of creating a locally relevant diagnostic assessment that would allow for greater integration of standardized assessment practices with functional aspects of our context. As noted previously, this response is shaped in large part by the broader institutional environment, whereby administrators have strategically increased international student enrollment with little input from the units that will be impacted by such increases, notably EAP. Not surprisingly, the revenue from these enrollments likewise does not flow to the program level, so EAP has been forced to adapt to these increasing enrollments with little additional resourcing beyond a growing pool of part-time faculty hires. At the same time, our EAP program enjoys relative autonomy in its policy and curricular decisions, as well as a certain amount of institutional legitimacy because it is housed in the College of Arts and Sciences and its courses are offered for academic credit. Further, because EAP is a little-understood academic unit on campus, the expertise of its faculty—particularly full-time faculty—remains relatively unquestioned at the university. These politically situated aspects of our work enabled us to play an active role in evolving the placement process for EAP graduate students and further legitimizing our institutional position.

The Evolution of the EAP Placement Procedure

Using Large-Scale Proficiency Results for Pre-Placement

As noted above, our graduate EAP program includes two levels separated by a proficiency threshold. A decade ago, when enrollments were quite small, placement of students was managed by two full-time faculty, who proctored, distributed, and evaluated a timed "blue book" essay on a general topic and reported placement results in person to students the following day. As program enrollments grew and these faculty gained a more situated awareness of appropriate assessment practices for their instructional context, the placement mechanism became more complex; migrating to an Internet-based platform (quia) and involving several components (summary of an academic lecture, topical essay, multiple-choice vocabulary assessment, and open-ended question about academic skills). This assessment format required significant logistical coordination within an already constrained program context, including scheduling and reserving computer classrooms, registering students, arranging proctors and qualified evaluators, and managing the reporting of results—all of which needed to happen before the semester even began. Despite the relative robustness of the newer model, it nevertheless created instability for program administrators, faculty, and students because students could not officially register for their EAP class until the placement procedure was complete.

In order to provide more timely placement of students into EAP classes and enable the program to consider a greater range of information when making placement decisions, the EAP director proposed a new two-phase placement model to the university administration, involving pre-placement based on TOEFL subscores followed by an in-class diagnostic writing assessment. An analysis of existing program data was used to determine correlations between TOEFL score components, EAP placement test components, EAP placements, and students' point scores in EAP classes and to establish a cut-off score for pre-placement into an EAP level. It was found that the productive modalities (speaking and writing) had a higher correlation with the EAP-specific data than the receptive modalities (listening and reading). Further tests were run to determine that, when using a combined TOEFL speaking and writing score, a cut-off of 41.5 accurately placed more than two thirds of EAP students in an appropriate level. Because the EAP program had a certain amount of institutional legitimacy and the policy modification proposed was supported by quantitative analysis, the university agreed with EAP's proposal to use TOEFL subscores to pre-place international graduate students into one of two EAP levels, enabling students to register for their classes before the semester began. While the TOEFL pre-placement procedure proved to be fairly straightforward, the EAP part of the diagnostic assessment presented a number of challenges in line with existing circumstances.

Development of a Functional Diagnostic Writing Sample

During the first use of TOEFL pre-placement, the diagnostic assessment repeated the pre-TOEFL pattern and included a multi-component computer-based assessment. However, this arrangement presented a number of challenges that stemmed from the program's limited capacity and heavy dependence on part-time instructors, who comprise approximately 75% of its teaching force. Dealing with multiple components led to a complicated grading process, which was logistically difficult to handle due to staffing, space, and budget constraints. In consequence, evaluation sometimes lacked clarity and consistency, and communicating the test results to students led to frequent confusion about the final placement. In addition, this complicated process sometimes resulted in students taking a long time to switch levels, which affected class organization and created additional challenges for faculty.

To resolve these problems—and relying on EAP's relative institutional autonomy—the next phase of diagnostic assessment shortened the placement test to two parts: a cloze test (C-test) focused on general proficiency and a writing sample eliciting a standard five-paragraph essay. Both were administered on the first day of class by individual instructors, who then graded the two test components, reported the results to the level coordinator (who made placement decisions), and then communicated the final placement decision to the students who needed to switch levels. This approach had the benefit of engaging instructors more fully in the process and was more straightforward and logistically simpler than the previous version; however, the process of dealing with multiple components was still fairly labor-intensive for instructors and level coordinators. Also, a question remained as to whether this reduced approach was fully reliable in terms of level placement and whether the construct of a C-test, aiming at general proficiency, was valid in the context of academic tasks (Van den Branden, Bygate, & Norris, 2009).

With these concerns in mind, the practicality and feasibility of this testing approach was assessed using correlation analysis, which demonstrated that C-test scores had high correlations with the TOEFL total and production scores (r=.80,[1] p<=0.001), signaling that the C-test was duplicating previously available information on proficiency. Another potential shortcoming of the C-test was that it did not address the students' specific task readiness for each EAP level or the functional adequacy of produced writing.

Similarly, the writing assessment also had a strong correlation with the initially assigned level (.570), reflecting that it was capturing similar skills to those used for the placement decision (i.e., the TOEFL production scores—writing and speaking). It was thus determined that the C-test could be eliminated and the writing test alone could be used as the primary/main diagnostic placement tool. Such a move appeared to be statistically justified, and made the overall administration of the placement procedure less cumbersome and more efficient for both faculty and students. This streamlined procedure further opened the door for program leadership to think more strategically about developing a modified writing assessment that captured students' readiness for the academic tasks taught in the EAP program more directly. Because university administrators were comfortable with this streamlined procedure and saw decisions about level placement and curriculum as within the domain of the EAP program, we were able to move forward with a functional writing assessment, which was piloted in spring 2015.

Program Assessment Study

Conceptualized in line with recent research supporting the value of contextually grounded assessments over standardized/generic ones (Plakans, 2013), a functional writing assessment was developed and administered on the first day of class during the following semester. Because TOEFL scores were found to serve as a good predictor of the students' proficiency, the writing assessment had a more distinct focus on identifying clear "misfits" who should take a different EAP level.

Piloting

The first version of the writing assessment was piloted during spring and summer semesters when overall EAP enrollments are lower and the majority of classes are taught by full-time or highly experienced part-time faculty. The writing sample alone was used for program placement in spring 2015 (n=70) and summer 2015 (n=50). The piloting process included a preliminary faculty training; after administering the test on the first day of class, faculty also participated in a moderated discussion of results. Later on, both faculty and students were asked to provide feedback regarding usefulness and potential modifications to test forms and the assessment rubric, which underscores the value of local contributions to assessment frameworks and processes. The final, improved versions of the test and assessment rubric were used in the full-scale assessment and corresponding action research study the following fall semester, when program constraints and challenges were much more visible due to the high number of students the university admits for fall semester.

Materials: Writing Test Forms

In the writing test, students were asked to provide their own position towards an issue using synthesized findings from academic sources, with production assessed along five categories, including author's stance and functional awareness of sources. The target production genre was a source-based essay (rather than a generic topical essay) that required summarizing, synthesizing, and citing. The writing prompt asked students to skim, use for informing their argument, and cite several excerpted academic texts in their written response. Topics of source texts were easily relatable for students from a variety of disciplines (e.g., use of technology for education, phenomenon of study abroad, use of alternative energy sources) and came from reputable academic sources. In other words, the task students had to complete for the diagnostic assessment was more authentic than a generic five-paragraph essay because it emphasized skills relevant for an EAP instructional context. To ensure academic integrity, three different test forms were created for use on different starting days (e.g., Monday, Tuesday, Wednesday).

Materials: Assessment Rubric

The rubric included five categories: (1) content and author's stance; (2) discourse organization; (3) vocabulary and tone; (4) grammar and punctuation; (5) awareness of sources. Despite the fact that it is absent from many large-scale assessment instruments such as TOEFL or IELTS (Matsuda & Jeffery, 2012), author's stance or voice was established as an important feature contributing to the quality of L2 writing (Zhao & Llosa, 2008). The descriptors explicitly targeted observable and documented EAP level-specific linguistic behaviors (based on qualitative analysis of writing data from the pilot phase). The two EAP levels were separated based on the following criteria: language proficiency, awareness of academic process/standards, and presence of own "voice." A rubric and guidance on scoring guidelines was provided to instructors for calculating total scores, with scores in the 5–6 range placing students in the lower-level and scores in the 8–10 range placing students in the upper-level EAP writing class. The writing samples that were rated "in between" required a second rating and possible subsequent negotiation by raters/instructors.

Procedure

Following the pilot study, student score data was collected over the course of three consecutive semesters. The goal of the study was to validate the functional writing assessment procedure; the main research question addressed whether the functional writing approach to EAP diagnostic testing could predict students' fit with either of the two class levels. The data analyzed included three sets of scores (n=292; from three consecutive semesters) including initial (TOEFL-based) and adjusted (post-diagnostic) placement, rubric category scores plus total score, and final grades. The purpose behind including final grades was to ensure that students who placed in one or the other level did not experience difficulty meeting the class requirements for either level. Linear regression was applied to determine how multiple constructs within the functional diagnostic test may have predicted the students' linguistic performance in their recommended EAP classes.

Study Results

The results of statistical analyses demonstrated that the relationship between the *adjusted (post-placement) level* and *final grades* was statistically significant at $p<0.001$, $R=0.411$, showing a medium effect size. The relationship between the *initial level* and *final grades* was not statistically significant ($p=0.1$), signaling that the initial, proficiency-only based assessment was not sufficient for predicting students' success and that a diagnostic procedure is indeed necessary. Finally, the relationship between the *total score* on diagnostic test and *final grades* was statistically significant at $p<0.001$, $R=0.382$ (medium effect size), suggesting that diagnostic placement results had a medium-strength correlation with the respective final grades; in other words, the diagnostic test was a generally appropriate measure for students to be placed into a level they could handle academically (i.e., not fail). Furthermore, the scores in rubric categories of "vocabulary and tone" and "grammar and punctuation" were statistically significant (with small effect sizes) in relation to adjusted level, suggesting that these categories were particularly important for determining the adjusted level; the remaining rubric categories, however, did not exhibit statistical significance.

Table 18.1 demonstrates correlations between rubric components and EAP final grades. The results suggest that all rubric components were in statistically significant relationship with EAP final grades, but grammar and punctuation and content and author's stance had the highest effect sizes.

In sum, analyses of data from the three consecutive semesters suggest that the usage-based procedure was successful in determining students' readiness

TABLE 18.1 Rubric Components in Relation to EAP Final Grades

Criterion	Significance/effect size
Content and author's stance	$p<0.001$, $R=0.301$ (medium)
Discourse organization	$p<0.001$, $R=0.239$ (small-to-medium)
Vocabulary and tone	$p<0.001$, $R=0.165$ (small)
Grammar and punctuation	$p<0.001$, $R=0.358$ (medium)
Awareness/use of sources	$p<0.001$, $R=0.196$ (small)

for a particular EAP level, and the results obtained through this assessment complemented the general proficiency information provided by the TOEFL production scores (cf. Hill (2015) on the value of integrating assessments). The materials were designed in consideration with the local context and specific learners' needs, which is admitted to be a recommended practice in EAP (cf. Dunworth, 2008). This conclusion is consistent with the argument of Crosthwaite (2016), who emphasizes the need for analyzing learner production for making curriculum decisions based on data-driven evidence rather than holistic evaluations.

Conclusion: Benefits, Challenges, and Recommendations

This chapter emphasizes the importance of developing streamlined placement and assessment procedures targeted to local institutional, curricular, and pedagogical contexts. At this particular university, even though EAP is considered vital to—and is even cited in—the university's strategic plan, very little investment has been made in building its instructional capacity long-term. At the same time, because of this strategic importance and its position within the university's academic structure, EAP has had a certain amount of leverage on an institutional level, with school and provost-level administrators showing openness toward policy changes and curricular innovations, as well as respecting the expertise of EAP faculty in aligning the program with best practices in the field.

In the case of this EAP program, the local placement approach has had clear benefits on a number of levels. On an institutional and program level, this targeted placement assessment serves as a valuable complement to the existing pre-placement standardized test measure and also values the EAP program's faculty expertise and awareness of student needs. Such local assessment methods can be considered a signal of institutional or programmatic values toward writing (Crusan, 2002b), a value that is clearly messaged at our institution through the enduring policy mandating an EAP writing course and the frequency with which high-level administrators reference EAP as a key support for international students. The program further benefited from increased efficiency in the administration and evaluation of students' writing samples and could more confidently attest to the appropriateness of students' level placement. Not only was the assessment itself grounded in research but systematic analysis of the procedure and outcomes also allowed for refining the approach over time and provided the means for validating the approach both institutionally and more broadly within the field of L2 writing assessment (Huot, 1996).

In addition, the entire exercise of developing and offering the functional level assessment improved the instructional approach for graduate level EAP in several key ways. First, on a foundational level, because the assessment was locally developed, site-based, and evaluated by teachers themselves, it reflected what teachers "know about writing and the curriculum of the courses they teach" (Huot, 1996,

p. 554). Second, the process of developing the assessment allowed program administrators and level coordinators to reflect on the distinction between the two levels of instruction, which not only shaped and defined the student writing task and rubric but also led to refining the syllabi and learning objectives for both EAP levels, in line with the best practices covered in the Conference on College Composition and Communication (2009) position statement on writing assessment. Similarly, in being trained to administer and evaluate the students' writing samples, all faculty—both new and returning—gained a clearer understanding of the delineation between levels. This was particularly important in our EAP program due to its heavy reliance on existing part-time faculty who may have taught only one of the two levels and its frequent need to hire new faculty to accommodate growing program enrollments.

Similar benefits were visible at the level of teaching and learning. Situating assessment in a local curricular context gave faculty and program leadership a sense of ownership over the process of placement and more continuity at the classroom level. Though not all placements were perfect, faculty had a much better chance of teaching a group of students with similar levels and needs than they had previously had, and perhaps more importantly, the faculty themselves played a role in determining how these placements came about. For students, a key benefit was being placed in a learning environment that matched their skill set coming in, which in turn positioned them better for success in meeting their course's learning objectives.

However, some caveats and recommendations should also be mentioned, particularly for programs considering adopting similar locally developed placement tools for their curricular contexts. In terms of logistics, this classroom-based approach had clear advantages: i.e., there was no need to schedule placement tests, find classrooms, register students, hire proctors/evaluators, or ask faculty to come early and do more than what they were compensated for. That said, a placement procedure like this requires strong logistics behind the scenes. For example, decisions about how many sections to offer and how many faculty are needed must be made based on the information available (previous enrollments and placement results, projected enrollment based on initial TOEFL placement, etc.), and disruption from switching levels needs to be minimized/mitigated through a specially arranged schedule of classes. Our approach to the latter was implementing a parallel structure for each level, i.e., each lower-level EAP class had a corresponding upper-level class scheduled for the same time band. As a result, students who needed to switch levels could do so with no disruption to their schedule. However, we still had to respond flexibly as rosters remained unstable during the early part of the semester, and sometimes the movement of students caused imbalance in class sizes.

Though there were clear benefits for teaching and learning, faculty had to assume considerable responsibility in supporting this placement procedure. They had to "give up" their first day of class to the writing assessment, commit to understanding the process (including scoring the writing samples), and then assess and submit results promptly to facilitate students' joining the "correct" EAP level by the second class meeting. These expectations were sometimes challenging for both the new/contingent and veteran faculty. In addition, the rubric was sometimes interpreted subjectively by different faculty, and some found it challenging to assign a definitive score and wanted to "hedge" with a 1.5 score. Some of these scoring concerns were offset by involving a second reader (e.g., a level coordinator) in making a final level determination for borderline cases.

On a student level, however, we acknowledge that one-shot, one-draft, timed direct assessments such as this may be perceived as "inauthentic" (cf. Crusan, 2002a). However, this is partially offset by our two-phased approach and how the placement assessment is framed: Rather than determining whether students should be waived from the institutional requirement, this process was designed to ensure that students are placed in an *appropriate* level of EAP. Additionally, some students may feel disadvantaged if a placement result recommends movement to another level, taught by a different instructor, when they have a preference for a particular instructor or section of the class. Also, for various reasons, some students prefer not to switch levels at all. Thus, we would recommend that programs implementing similar approaches make sure that students understand the purpose of and reasons behind (i.e., improved learning experiences and outcomes) the diagnostic writing sample.

In conclusion, developing and refining this placement procedure at our institution was systematic and driven by both program data and an awareness of context-specific conditions, including an institutional legitimacy that facilitated our autonomy in evolving this procedure. Though large-scale proficiency assessment is key for students' admission to the university and pre-placement into an EAP level, this functional placement mechanism complements this and has been refined to "serve [our] own needs" (Crusan, 2002a, p. 41). We plan to continue collecting placement-related data and consider ways to further improve our approach, including exploring Internet-based options for assessment and reporting of placement results and collecting data on student perspectives.

Note

1 r levels signal the degree and strength of a linear relationship between two variables. r values between 0.5 and 1 signal strong correlation levels, 0.3–0.49 signal medium range, while 0.1–0.3 indicate low correlation.

References

Conference on College Composition and Communication. (2009). *Writing assessment: A position statement*. Retrieved from www.ncte.org/cccc/resources/positions/writingassessment

Crosthwaite, P. (2016). A longitudinal multidimensional analysis of EAP writing: Determining EAP course effectiveness. *Journal of English for Academic Purposes, 22*, 166–178. https://doi.org/10.1016/jjeap201604005

Crusan, D. (2002a). An assessment of ESL writing placement assessment. *Assessing Writing*, *8*(1), 17–30. https://doi.org/10.1016/s1075-2935(02)00028-4

Crusan, D. (2002b). The quagmire of assessment for placement: Talking out of both sides of our mouths. *TESL Reporter*, *35*(2), 37–48.

Crusan, D. (2010). *Assessment in the second language writing classroom*. Ann Arbor: University of Michigan Press. https://doi.org/10.3998/mpub770334

Cumming, A. (2002). Assessing L2 writing: Alternative constructs and ethical dilemmas. *Assessing Writing*, *8*(2), 73–83. https://doi.org/10.1016/s1075-2935(02)00047-8

Dunworth, K. (2008). A task-based analysis of undergraduate assessment: A tool for the EAP practitioner. *TESOL Quarterly*, *42*(2), 315–323. https://doi.org/10.1002/j1545-72492008tb00126x

Fox, J. (2009). Moderating top-down policy impact and supporting EAP curricular renewal: Exploring the potential of diagnostic assessment. *Journal of English for Academic Purposes*, *8*, 26–42. https://doi.org/10.1016/jjeap200812004

Hill, K. (2015). Integrating instruction, curricula, and assessments in the L2 classroom. *TESL-EJ*, *19*(2), 1–22.

Huot, B. (1996). Toward a new theory of writing assessment. *College Composition and Communication*, *47*(4), 549–566. https://doi.org/10.2307/358601

Huot, B. (2002). Toward a new discourse of assessment for the college writing classroom. *College English*, *65*(2), 163–180. https://doi.org/10.2307/3250761

James, C., & Templeman, E. (2009). A case for faculty involvement in EAP placement testing. *TESL Canada Journal*, *26*(2), 82–99. https://doi.org/10.18806/teslv26i2416

Kim, Y.-H. (2011). Diagnosing EAP writing ability using the Reduced Reparameterized Unified Model. *Language Testing*, *28*(4), 509–541. https://doi.org/10.1177/02655322 11400860

Kuiken, F., &Vedder, I. (2014). Rating written performance: What do raters do and why? *Language Testing*, *31*(3), 329–348. https://doi.org/10.1177/02655322145261

Lockwood, J. (2017). Towards a specific writing language assessment at Hong Kong universities. In J. Flowerdew & T. Costley (Eds.), *Discipline-specific writing: Theory into practice* (pp. 196–215). Oxford/New York: Routledge.

Matsuda, P. K., & Jeffery, J. V. (2012). Voice in student essays. In K. Hyland & C. Sancho-Guinda (Eds.), *Voice and stance in academic writing* (pp. 151–165). New York: Palgrave Macmillan.

Plakans, L. (2013). Writing scale development and use within a language program. *TESOL Journal*, *4*(1), 151–163. https://doi.org/10.1002/tesj66

Silva, T. (1997). On the ethical treatment of ESL writers. *TESOL Quarterly*, *31*(2), 359–363. https://doi.org/10.2307/3588052

Tyler, A. (2010). Usage-based approaches to language and their applications to second language learning. *Annual Review of Applied Linguistics*, *30*, 270–291. https://doi.org/10.1017/s0267190510000140

Van den Branden, K., Bygate, M., & Norris, J. (2009). *Task-based language teaching: A reader*. Amsterdam: John Benjamins. https://doi.org/10.1075/tblt1

Wette, R. (2010). Evaluating student learning in a university-level EAP unit on writing using sources. *Journal of Second Language Writing*, *19*, 158–177. https://doi.org/10.1016/jjslw201006002

Zhao, C. G., & Llosa, L. (2008). Voice in high-stakes L1 academic writing assessment: Implications for L2 writing instruction. *Assessing Writing*, *13*(3), 153–170. https://doi.org/10.1016/jasw200810003

19

VIGNETTE

Challenging the Deficit Mindset: The WIDA Can Do Philosophy in a Second Language Writing Context

Mark Chapman, Ahyoung Alicia Kim, Jing Wei, and Tanya Bitterman

In our experiences of working with English language learners in both educational and assessment contexts, we observe that students from linguistically and culturally diverse backgrounds have unfortunately and all too often been subject to a deficit mindset view. This deficit mindset is unfortunate and can be potentially harmful to students' academic and linguistic development if they are characterized by what they cannot do, rather than by their strengths and potential. In contrast to the deficit mindset is a Can Do Philosophy that articulates and values the assets, contributions, and potential of students from culturally and linguistically diverse backgrounds. The WIDA Consortium promotes such a philosophy and believes that all students bring important and valuable resources to the educational community (WIDA, 2014).

In this chapter, we describe the WIDA Can Do Philosophy, in the context of English language learners (ELLs) in U.S. PreK–12 schools, and draw concrete examples from our experiences as researchers and test developers to explain how this philosophy is operationalized within a large-scale, high-stakes assessment that measures ELLs' academic English language development.

The WIDA (2014) Can Do Philosophy states:

> Linguistically and culturally diverse learners, in particular, bring a unique set of assets that have the potential to enrich the experiences of all learners and educators. As these young children and students learn additional languages, educators can draw on these assets for the benefit of both the learners themselves and for everyone in the community. By focusing on what language learners can do, we send a powerful message that students from diverse linguistic, cultural, and experiential backgrounds contribute to the vibrancy of our early childhood programs and [Pre]K—12 schools.

Table 19.1 demonstrates how culturally and linguistically diverse students' assets, contributions, and potential can help support a vibrant education system.

Supported by research, a central tenet of the WIDA Can Do Philosophy is that students' academic language development in their native language facilitates and supports their academic language development in English (August & Shanahan, 2006; Escamilla & Hopewell, 2010; Schleppegrell & Colombi, 2002; Tabors, 2008). Students' varied linguistic resources, beyond their proficiency in the English language and their knowledge of other cultures, are valuable assets that may be tapped into and incorporated into schooling (Escamilla & Hopewell, 2010; Freeman, Freeman, & Mercuri, 2002; García, 2005; Goldenberg & Coleman, 2010; González, Moll, & Amanti, 2005). Students' home, school, and community experiences influence their language development (Collier, 1995; Nieto, 2008). This philosophy emphasizes the importance and educational benefits of a diverse and multilingual school population, a stance consistent with WIDA's promotion of social justice and desire to challenge linguistic discrimination, cultural biases, and racism in education.

TABLE 19.1 Assets, Contributions, and Potential of Linguistically and Culturally Diverse Students

Assets	Contributions	Potential
Linguistic	Knowledge of multiple languages, varying representation of ideas, metalinguistic and metacognitive awareness, diverse strategies for language learning	Bi- or multilingual practices, abilities that learners utilize to communicate effectively across multiple contexts, multiple ways of expressing their thinking
Cultural	Different perspectives, practices, beliefs, social norms, ways of thinking	Bi- or multicultural practices as well as unique and varied perspectives, ability to develop relationships in a global society, ability to navigate a variety of sociocultural contexts
Experiential	Varied life and educational experiences, exposure to unique topics, diverse approaches to learning and expressing content knowledge	Enrichment of the school curriculum, extracurricular, and community opportunities, success in school and beyond
Social and Emotional	Personal interests and needs, awareness of/empathy for diverse experiences, knowledge and enrichment of community resources	Ability to form and sustain positive relationships, and broker meaningful interactions among peers and others within and beyond school

Can Do Philosophy in the Second Language Writing Assessment Context

The ACCESS for ELLs 2.0 assessment of English language proficiency operationalizes the WIDA Can Do Philosophy, and that approach has influenced the design of the writing test. We draw on students' experiences in academic contexts and aim to elicit written language that demonstrates students' highest abilities while minimizing other factors such as affect, background knowledge, computer or typing skills, and reading or listening proficiency.

We develop writing tasks that target different levels of language proficiency. The construct of writing proficiency in the K–12 academic context is operationalized through the five WIDA Standards (Social and Instructional Language, The language of Language Arts, The language of Mathematics, The language of Science, and The language of Social Studies) in the WIDA Standards Framework. Each writing task targets one or more standards, and has a unique theme drawn from topics in the relevant academic content area(s).

Tasks targeting lower levels of language proficiency consist of two or three sub-tasks, all connected to the same theme (see Figure 19.1). Through such a design, we aim to provide multiple opportunities for students to write, producing single words, phrases, and/or simple sentences before producing a short paragraph. Our goal is to provide an opportunity for students who can produce minimal written language in English to demonstrate what they "can do."

In addition, writing tasks are developed with the understanding that students have diverse backgrounds, and that the academic content knowledge necessary

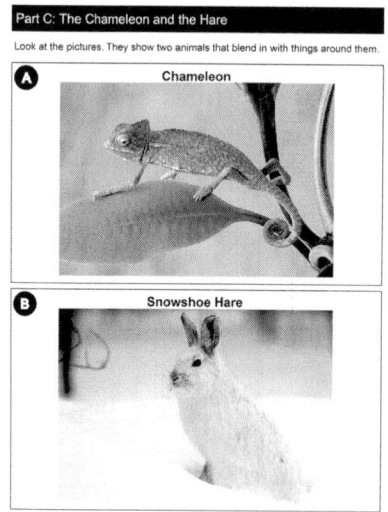
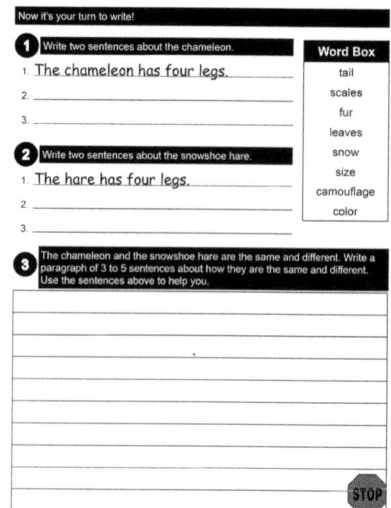

FIGURE 19.1 Sample Writing Task Designed for Lower Proficiency Students in Grades 2–3, Targeting the Language of Math and Language of Science

for producing a written response may be unfamiliar to some. Thus, we design task input to support understanding of the content that is needed to complete the writing task, ensuring that students from diverse backgrounds have the opportunity to demonstrate what they "can do." Task input utilizes graphics or other visual support, allowing the test input to support academic content concepts without the need to process complex language that might otherwise hinder the ability of the task to effectively distinguish between students at different levels of language proficiency.

In order to ensure that modes of task presentation and student response do not prevent students from demonstrating their language proficiency, we allow students in grades 4 and higher to view task input on a computer and to have the option of either keyboarding their response or writing in a paper booklet. Students in lower grades (grades K, 1, 2, and 3) complete writing tasks on paper, both viewing the task and writing their responses in the booklet. This design allows students whose typing skills are still developing the opportunity to respond on paper, minimizing the construct-irrelevant variable of typing facility.

Can Do Philosophy and the Scoring of the Writing Assessment

The WIDA Can Do Philosophy is reflected in the development of the WIDA writing rubric and rater training materials. One of the functions of scoring rubrics is to distinguish test takers into different levels. In the domain of writing, rubric descriptors often capture differences in written responses in terms of the number and severity of errors. In other words, they often distinguish test takers by what "they cannot do," rather than what "they can do." By doing so, the scoring rubrics reinforce a deficit view of ELLs, particularly when they are directly used by educators to interpret students' writing performance and inform instruction. In contrast, we designed the WIDA writing rubric to capture differences in written responses in terms of positive attributes, reinforcing the Can Do Philosophy in both the scoring of student responses and score interpretation.

In the discourse dimension, we observe that writing at lower proficiency levels is often characterized as being seriously disorganized or underdeveloped by other rubrics. In contrast, in the WIDA writing rubric, we emphasize that responses at that level, albeit minimal, still represent one idea or more. Similarly, in the sentence dimension, beginner writing is typically described as having serious or frequent errors in structures or usage. However, the WIDA writing rubric focuses on the length and complexity of sentence structures, rather than on the severity and frequency of grammatical errors. Finally, in the vocabulary dimension, other rubrics describe writing at lower levels as having inappropriate word choice, whereas in the WIDA writing rubric we use neutral terms to describe the type of vocabulary used (e.g., usage of highest frequency vocabulary, distinguishable English words).

The WIDA Can Do Philosophy is also reflected in the materials that are used to train raters. In these training materials, raters are instructed to focus on students' abilities to demonstrate communicative competence and to integrate content and language in their writing rather than to identify whether students lack discrete point abilities that underlie the construct of writing proficiency in a K–12 academic context (Mohan, 1986). In practice, this means that raters are trained to prioritize communicative competence over grammatical competence (Bachman, 1990) and that raters focus on three core dimensions of written language (word, sentence, and discourse dimensions) rather than on a lack of control over spelling, punctuation, and grammar (Bailey & Huang, 2011; Gottlieb, Katz, & Ernst-Slavit, 2009).

Can Do Philosophy and Score Reporting

The WIDA Can Do Philosophy is embedded in the ACCESS for ELLs 2.0 score reports and their supporting resources. Students' writing performance on ACCESS for ELLs 2.0 is reported to students, teachers, and families via an *Individual Student Report*. It includes information about each student's scores in four language domains (listening, reading, speaking, and writing) and four composites: oral language (listening and speaking), literacy (reading and writing), comprehension (reading and listening), and overall score (all domains).

In addition, the Individual Student Report features detailed descriptions of what individual students *can do* at each proficiency level within the four test domains, including writing. This *Description of English Language Proficiency Level* aligns with the WIDA Can Do Descriptors and the WIDA English Language Development Performance Definitions, and explains the students' level in detail. It reflects the Can Do Philosophy by specifically using Can Do language when describing the students' proficiency levels. For example, a student who receives a score of proficiency level 3 in writing is described in the Individual Student Report as being able to "communicate in writing in English using language related to common topics in school." We suggest that they would be able to:

- describe familiar issues and events
- create stories or short narratives
- describe processes and procedures with some details
- give opinions with reasons in a few short sentences.

To enhance the interpretation of writing scores, we have created a number of score report resources: (1) *Interpretive Guide for Score Reports*, a technical document that provides detailed information about what the scores mean, (2) score report translations in multiple languages to promote the interpretation of scores, and (3) parent resources (e.g., *Parent Guide for ACCESS for ELLs 2.0 Score Report*, *Parent Handouts for ACCESS for ELLs 2.0*) that describe the purpose of ACCESS for ELLs 2.0 and how to interpret scores on the Individual Student Report in straightforward, non-technical language.

These resources are designed to make students' performance on the test as accessible as possible to families from diverse linguistic and cultural backgrounds. By designing these interpretive materials in multiple languages and presenting scores and reports in a non-technical way, we aim to increase the opportunities for families to process and act on information provided by the test, supporting the view that families are essential for successful student learning.

Contrary to a more punitive perspective on score use, students' writing scores are intended to initiate conversations among educators, families, and students. For instance, language educators may meet with content teachers to promote instruction. Educators may meet with students to discuss their current writing ability and set goals for further improvement. Moreover, educators may meet with students' family members during teacher conferences to discuss students' writing performance. During these conversations, having a score report that uses Can Do statements allows the stakeholders to view ELLs from a positive perspective rather than through a deficit lens.

Summary

We have described how a large-scale, high-stakes writing test can apply a Can Do Philosophy that impacts all facets of the assessment. This Can Do Philosophy helps ensure that the writing test is designed in such a way that all students may meaningfully engage with the writing tasks and show what they can do, regardless of their background. The scoring and reporting processes also reflect the Can Do Philosophy in that students receive credit for all written language they produce and educators and families receive meaningful and understandable information about the writing proficiency demonstrated on the assessment. Overall, by applying this approach to second language writing assessment, we treat the student as a valued stakeholder in the assessment process and as the most important agent in any educational context.

References

August, D., & Shanahan, T. (Eds.). (2006). *Developing literacy in second-language learners: Report of the National Literacy Panel on language-minority children and youth*. Mahwah, NJ: Lawrence Erlbaum Associates, Inc.

Bachman, L. F. (1990). *Fundamental considerations in language testing*. Oxford: Oxford University Press.

Bailey, A. L., & Huang, B. H. (2011). Do current English language development/proficiency standards reflect the English needed for success in school? *Language Testing, 28*(3), 343–365. https://doi.org/10.1177/0265532211404187

Collier, V. P. (1995). Acquiring a second language for school. *Directions in Language & Education, 1*(4), 1–10.

Escamilla, K., & Hopewell, S. (2010). Transitions to biliteracy: Creating positive academic trajectories for emerging bilinguals in the United States. In J. Petrovic (Ed.), *International perspectives on bilingual education: Policy, practice, controversy* (pp. 69–93). Charlotte, NC: Information Age Publishing.

Freeman, Y. S., Freeman, D. E., & Mercuri, S. (2002). *Closing the achievement gap: How to reach limited formal schooling and long term English language learners.* Portsmouth, NH: Heinemann.

García, E. E. (2005). *Teaching and learning in two languages: Bilingualism and schooling in the United States.* New York: Teachers College Press.

Goldenberg, C., & Coleman, R. (2010). *Promoting academic achievement among English learners: A guide to the research.* Thousand Oaks, CA: Corwin Press.

González, N., Moll, L. C., & Amanti, C. (Eds.). (2005). *Funds of knowledge: Theorizing practices in households, communities and classrooms.* Mahwah, NJ: Lawrence Erlbaum Associates, Inc.

Gottlieb, M., Katz, A., & Ernst-Slavit, G. (2009). *Paper to practice: Using the English language proficiency standards in PreK–12 classrooms.* Alexandria, VA: Teachers of English to Speakers of Other Languages.

Mohan, B. (1986). *Language and content.* Reading, MA: Addison-Wesley.

Nieto, S. (2008). *Affirming diversity: The sociopolitical context of multicultural education* (5th ed.). New York: Allyn & Bacon.

Schleppegrell, M. J., & Colombi, M. C. (Eds.). (2002). *Developing advanced literacy in first and second languages: Meaning with power.* Mahwah, NJ: Lawrence Erlbaum Associates, Inc.

Tabors, P. O. (2008). *One child, two languages* (2nd ed.). Baltimore, MD: Paul H. Brookes.

WIDA Consortium. (2014). *The WIDA can do philosophy.* Retrieved from WIDA Web site www.wida.us/aboutUs/AcademicLanguage/

AFTERWORD

Christine Pearson Casanave

I found it a most interesting decision on the part of the editors of this volume, both dear friends and colleagues in the field of second language writing, to choose me to write an afterword to this volume on the politics of writing assessment. In most ways, I am an outsider to the world of writing assessment, except that sometimes I do just enough "homework" on the topic to justify to myself my occasional rants and critical commentaries and to put me into a state of depression about some of the more nefarious practices and consequences of L2 writing assessment. But maybe this was in fact a sensible choice: An outsider's view will not be overly clouded or crowded with the views of others or with mounds of scholarly work on the topic; an outsider will nevertheless surely have had experience (decades' worth in my case, much of it in Japan) with writing assessment in all contexts she or he has worked in; and an outsider can sometimes see and say things that are invisible, or politically incorrect, to those with deep insider knowledge and experience.

I therefore accepted this invitation, read the chapter drafts by authors from different parts of the world with interest, and found myself making notes and comments on themes and issues that jumped out at me as I read. Some of these themes comprise the sections of this afterword, which contains no summaries of individual chapters (not needed; read the book!) and no extensive citations of literature on assessment (see the cited works in the introduction to the book and in its chapters and the work of editor Deborah Crusan (2010) in particular). The afterword is therefore a partial and biased reflection by just one reader. I first discuss cultures of testing and the pernicious influence of high-stakes writing assessments, followed by shorter comments on purposes of assessment and on our continued obsession in L2 writing assessment with formal accuracy. I then present a perspective-taking aside on the need for L1 English writing instructors to experience what it is like to have their own L2 writing assessed in various ways. My rather pessimistic concluding section asks where change and reform might come from.

Cultures of Testing and Assessment

This book is filled with descriptions (exposés?) of a culture of testing and assessment in schools and universities in many parts of the world. The stories are both familiar and distressing, given the life-consequences of a high-stakes test on students, including entrance into and exit from domestic and international schools. This expanding testing culture is undermining good writing instruction and development and discouraging the local and context-based assessment practices that should accompany contextualized writing instruction.

Exam-driven, at institutions nationally and internationally, the testing culture inspires fear in students and teachers, unhealthy competitiveness among teachers, students, and whole institutions, and the ambitions of administrators and politicians who care more about school rankings than about the educational benefits of learning to write in an L2. Indeed, many of the authors in this book comment on the paucity of writing instruction in their countries and institutions beyond exam preparation. Why should students in Poland or China or Vietnam or Iran or other places in the Middle East learn to write in English, beyond learning to pass discrete point tests of formal accuracy or constructing a brief formulaic essay? The points are what count (literally and figuratively). They determine entrances to and exits from schools, grades and rankings of students, rankings of institutions themselves, and ultimately students' futures. Will institutions be able to resist the cultures of testing that generate the scores they need for their competitive rankings?

From my experience in Japan, a country famous for its culture of testing, like China and Korea, I noted that, as in many other parts of the world as documented in these chapters, there is a great deal of English teaching, but not much teaching of English L2 writing or even of L1 writing. Hence, there is not much direct assessment of writing per se. As documented in some chapters in this book, formal tests might incorporate aspects of writing in English, such as a brief essay component of an otherwise traditional test of reading and grammar. Long ago when I worked in Japan, many Japanese teachers of English were not confident to teach or test writing, or even to assess the essays that were part of major exams (entrance tests; program wide placement tests). The "foreign teachers" were assigned to review such tests, and most of those teachers had had little experience or training in the teaching and assessing of writing. Many of the chapters in this volume confirm that serious attention to the teaching and assessment of L2 writing has yet to evolve, even though cultures of testing of English are widespread. At the same time, some authors point to promising changes in their institutions.

Cultures of testing and assessment are also about money. They feed the corporate textbook and testing companies, who have little reason to support local materials and assessment tools. For example, a whole industry of automated essay scoring tools has sprung up, to the horror of some and the praise of others (Condon, 2013; Dikli & Bleye, 2014; Shermis & Burstein, 2013; Weigle, 2013). Of course, Japan is not unique in the way that corporate money drives whole industries of English language testing, and in the ways that politics and these industries are entangled. Therefore, as L2 English writing is increasingly incorporated into national and international tests, the testing industries are likely to expand into areas of writing that previously were not assessed at all or that were covered by discrete point methods. Perhaps a separate book is needed to cover the for-profit testing, textbook, and cram school industries devoted to English language standardized exams, but I wish there had been more attention to them here. I hope that readers of this collection, and the authors themselves, will be inspired to continue work in this area.

In cultures of testing, whether students or teachers in various parts of the world will have time or motivation to engage in English language writing activities that are unrelated to high-stakes exams remains a question for further inquiry. I find it difficult to envision how the for-profit world of testing will loosen its grip on how L2 writing is taught, learned, and assessed. Profits are too great and continue to grow. Will teachers, in the privacy of their own classrooms, and administrators of departments and institutions be able to resist political pressures from the industry, and indeed from students and parents themselves, who might insist that instructors teach to high-stakes tests that could determine students' futures? Some examples in this volume depict the high emotional cost to students and their teachers of a mandate that traps everyone in competitive testing. Still, localized activities in writing classrooms and attempts by some instructors to resist and negotiate with national assessment mandates show what is possible, as described in some of the chapters in this book, but also how risky and challenging such local pedagogical solutions are. It seems that trends continue in many countries toward more standardization than ever, particularly as class sizes continue to increase, and that purposes for studying L2 writing too often revolve around test preparation.

Purposes of L2 Writing and Writing Assessment

Teachers of L2 writing in a culture of testing are trapped: Although they may hold strong beliefs about the many intellectual, personal, and professional purposes for learning to write in both L1 and L2, they probably dare not refuse to help students with test preparation. It will look bad for the students, who might not achieve the scores they need; it will look bad for teachers themselves, who might be evaluated poorly or accused of holding students back from passing an all-important test. Writing activities and assessments of a more sophisticated kind—ones that help students and teachers develop and monitor progress, identify areas for improvement, and even promote creativity—fall by the wayside in a testing culture that does not or cannot make time for them.

It is thus difficult not to feel cynical on reading some of the chapters in this volume about the stunted and misguided purposes of L2 writing that are described or implied: to attain a score on a required test that will allow a student to enter or exit an institution, department, or class. Of course, my reaction is that of someone who feels strongly that the worldwide testing culture has derailed the likelihood that students will develop a love of writing and come to understand its many possibilities in work and personal life. Overwhelmingly, the chapters in this book depict narrow purposes of learning to write in English as learning to pass a required exam, even when some higher-minded purposes are evident in individual classrooms and when authors themselves are committed to doing the best they can for their students. The "best" might just have to be exam preparation.

As I realized when I was teaching in Japan, where all students were required to study English whether they wanted to or not, I found myself asking why anyone should be forced to take high-stakes writing tests in English who does not need or want English in his or her personal or professional life. Even for those students who need English, why should their futures depend on an English essay and grammar test when there are so many other wonderful literacy activities they could engage in? Writing in English as both an L1 and an L2 can be an eye-opener, a life-changer, a creative and intellectual experience, a pleasurable exercise in learning to craft language into beautiful strings of words—this is what it should be. Cynical as I am, I also am an idealist, and glimmerings of idealism come through some of the chapters in this book.

One question that has been actively addressed in L2 writing studies, and that by implication affects purposes of and views on assessment, asks whether a major purpose of L2 writing instruction is to help students with the formal accuracy of their writing. If high-stakes writing exams are graded for formal accuracy, or if subject matter faculty do likewise, then the problems of error correction and feedback on writing do indeed play into the politics of assessment. The controversial topic, especially of error correction in writing, has been covered in books and articles for many years (see, e.g., Bitchener & Ferris, 2012; Bitchener & Storch, 2016; Casanave, 2017; Ferris, 2011; Truscott & Hsu, 2008), but the tensions continue.

In English-dominant settings or courses, conflicts arise between subject matter faculty who may know little about L2 writing and so are not prepared to assist L2 writers, and L2 writing teachers who know that it is impossible for even the best of them to "perfect" L2 students' language to a native speaker's level within a semester or a year of writing instruction. Indeed, writing instruction and writing assessment continue to be interpreted or practiced as grammar instruction and grammar correction rather than as the construction and revision of interesting and comprehensible writings that show knowledge of topics and readings, critical thinking, and creative use of language and rhetorical structures.

Yet it is understandably difficult for many subject matter teachers and evaluators to reenvision the purposes of L2 writing instruction and assessment so as to see past the language level errors, just as it is difficult and time consuming to provide feedback to students, especially substantive commentary beyond the visible surface errors. As some of the authors in this book indicate, class sizes of 50 or more students make anything but the most speedy and superficial error correction impossible. Such problems will not be solved without greater training of L2 writing instructors and vastly reduced class sizes in many parts of the world. But such changes require money, commitment, and planning from the top and joint efforts by subject matter faculty, L2 writing specialists, and informed and cooperative administrators. One take-away message from this book is that there is still a great deal of work left to do, and that moving beyond error correction to substantive feedback and assessment cannot happen without structural, institutional, and educational changes.

A Perspective-Taking Aside

I include a brief perspective-taking commentary in this afterword as a way of helping L1 English users in particular comprehend what it could feel like to have one's L2 writing assessed in various ways that could affect one's life. For those L1 English users who have written in an L2 and received feedback, critique, and correction, I will not be offended if you just skip this section. But I am not sure if many L1 English users who teach L2 writing have experienced what it is like to be evaluated on a high-stakes piece of L2 writing, particularly in an advanced academic setting or for purposes of public consumption. After all, English is the privileged academic and professional language worldwide. Scholars like me are not forced to write in an L2. Hence, my overarching question is: Have we ever done what we expect our L2 writing students and colleagues to do? How would our understanding of L2 writing and assessment differ if we did?

I wrote about this not too long ago as I reflected on my experiences writing for publication (Casanave, forthcoming) and on the fact that I often help L2 and other writers prepare manuscripts for publication in my role as a manuscript reviewer for journals and as a doctoral dissertation advisor, but that I have never done this myself in my strong L2, Spanish. I was struck by my own presumptiveness—that I could possibly understand what my L2 colleagues and graduate students go through as they draft their own manuscripts, receive corrections and responses from me and others, and revise multiple times. Of course, I receive collegial assessments on my own writing that is submitted for publication and I too revise multiple times (my record is 20), but reviewers respond to me as an L1 user of the language I am writing in. I don't receive the kinds of corrections and commentaries on language use that L2 writers do.

If I were to draft an academic article for publication in a Spanish language journal, I would need to do everything that I expect from my L2 colleagues and students when they write in English. I would need to choose an appropriate journal, to read and critically synthesize relevant academic articles in Spanish, to draft with the help of dictionaries and of terminology and formulaic phrases plucked from the articles I read, to get corrections and comments from "a native speaker," assuming that my reviewers adhere to this myth, and to prepare for rejection by reviewers who were overly distracted by my language errors to see the substance of the paper. If my career depended on such publications or on a thesis in Spanish, rejections based on inadequate academic language proficiency in Spanish would be especially devastating. Similarly, if I had to pass an essay exam in Spanish in order to enter or exit from a school—the high-stakes writing assessment that many of the authors in this edited volume discuss—I too might spend vast amounts of money and time trying to prepare for such an exam. Just the thought that a single-score exam written in my L2 might determine my future would likely create such a block that I would undermine my own efforts just out of nervousness. And dare I suggest that many politicians and administrators throughout the world have also never undertaken the kinds of L2 English writing tasks that they expect their faculty to provide evidence of on CVs and annual reports and to teach their students.

And why should they, if they do not need English in their work? Similarly, if scholars and students in Iran, Poland, Thailand, and many other places use English writing tests only as a status symbol, why should there be a national or institution-wide requirement? How might change and reform happen?

Where Might Reform and Change Come From?

It is gratifying to see in this volume that so many people, including some new scholars from around the world, are working to expand what we know about and do with L2 writing assessment. The burdens are heavy for teachers who work in states or nations with standardized assessments for all aspects of English language education, and in particular with high-stakes English writing assessments. L2 writing scholars and teachers know that assessments of writing are needed to further and to monitor students' improvement, assuming that students have meaningful reasons to learn to write in English. However, the good intentions are often co-opted by power and money—the desire of nations, states, and institutions to control and compete, the continued expansion of English linguistic imperialism (Phillipson, 2009), and the desire of testing companies, textbook publishers, and for-profit schools to pocket what they can from customers who fear being left behind. The suggestions for change and reform that the chapters in this book offer may therefore be more idealistic than realistic. As I read, I tried not to feel too discouraged, but it was difficult. Here are a few of my thoughts, as I conclude this afterword.

Curricular reforms are often mentioned as a way that positive washback onto testing and assessment practices can help redirect the negative path that the testing mania has led us down. But teachers and institutions resist change. Moreover, teachers with huge numbers of students are justified to some extent in resisting changes that will require more work for them, such as actually designing interesting locally relevant writing topics and then reading their students' writing rather than marking discrete point tests quickly. It is not clear whether curricular reforms throughout the world will ever result in smaller classes that would allow the kinds of L2 writing instruction and assessment that we know are needed. Economic pressures, lack of understanding by politicians and administrators of how writing is best taught and assessed, and unclear purposes in many contexts for why L2 writing (English or any other L2) should be taught work against top-down changes.

It is thus difficult to envision how change will happen from the top in this heavily politicized and competitive academic world, and if it doesn't happen from the top, how will it happen at all, except in the secret spaces behind closed classroom doors? Nevertheless, the chapters in the volume speak to the power of localized practices, often just within a teacher's own classroom, especially when English writing ability is not valued highly in the broader educational system. Teachers who can singly or collectively learn and enact sensible L2 writing instruction and assessment practices, and who *write about their experiences* in volumes like this one, may be able to influence other teachers and their students even within a high-stakes assessment culture, and possibly even reach a few politicians and administrators who are willing to listen. Learning to write in any L2, and to write for purposes that are meaningful to the writer beyond passing a test, are small miracles of education within any context. If change does not come easily from the outside-in, then what choices do we have except to work from the inside-out? Teachers who write and speak publicly about their experiences and beliefs about good L2 writing assessment practices—in other words, teachers who become authors and presenters—can put some needed critical perspective on the proliferation of high-stakes standardized testing. They can also bring to light some of the small miracles that happen every day in many L2 writing classrooms. But even without speaking and writing publicly about these matters, teachers can resist within their own classrooms, enacting their agency behind closed doors.

References

Bitchener, J., & Ferris, D. R. (2012). *Written corrective feedback in second language acquisition and writing*. New York: Routledge.

Bitchener, J., & Storch, N. (2016). *Written corrective feedback for L2 development*. Bristol, UK: Multilingual Matters.

Casanave, C. P. (2017). *Controversies in second language writing: Dilemmas and decisions in research and instruction* (2nd ed.). Ann Arbor: University of Michigan Press.

Casanave, C. P. (forthcoming). Does writing for publication ever get easier? Some reflections from an experienced scholar. In P. Habibie & K. Hyland (Eds.), *Novice writers and scholarly publication: Authors, mentors, gatekeepers*. New York: Palgrave Macmillan.

Condon, W. (2013). Large-scale assessment, locally-developed measures, and automated scoring of essays: Fishing for red herrings? *Assessing Writing, 18*, 100–108. doi: 10.1016/j.asw.2012.11.001

Crusan, D. (2010). *Assessment in the second language writing classroom*. Ann Arbor: University of Michigan Press.

Dikli, S., & Bleye, S. (2014). Automated essay scoring feedback for second language writers: How does it compare to instructor feedback? *Assessing Writing, 22*, 1–17. https://dx.doi.org/10.1016/j.asw.2014.03.006

Ferris, D. R. (2011). *Treatment of error in second language student writing* (2nd ed.). Ann Arbor: University of Michigan Press.

Phillipson, R. (2009). *Linguistic imperialism continued*. New York: Routledge.

Shermis, M. D., & Burstein, J. (Eds.). (2013). *Handbook of automated essay evaluation: Current applications and new directions*. New York: Routledge.

Truscott, J., & Hsu, A. Y. (2008). Error correction, revision, and learning. *Journal of Second Language Writing, 17*(4), 292–305. https://doi.org/10.1016/j.jslw.2008.05.003

Weigle, S. C. (2013). English language learners and automated scoring of essays: Critical considerations. *Assessing Writing, 18*(1), 85–99. https://dx.doi.org/10.1016/j.asw.2012.10.006

AUTHOR BIOGRAPHIES

Muhammad M. Abdel Latif is a lecturer of English language teaching in the Faculty of Graduate Studies in Education at Cairo University, Egypt. He has also taught at the University of Essex, UK and Al-Imam University, Saudi Arabia. His PhD research received some prestigious international research awards, and he has published in ranked international journals.

Solange Aranha is Associate Professor of English in the Department of Modern Languages at São Paulo State University, São José do Rio Preto. She advises master's and doctoral students. Her research focuses on English for Academic Purposes (EAP), genres, and learning through telecollaboration.

Hadi Banat is a PhD student in Second Language Studies at Purdue University. He has taught in Lebanon, the United Arab Emirates, and the U.S. His research interests are in the intersections between second language writing and composition studies, writing assessment, cross-cultural composition, WAC/WID, and writing center studies.

Mira Bekar is Assistant Professor of Applied Linguistics at Ss. Cyril and Methodius University, Macedonia. She obtained her PhD at Purdue University, USA, and has taught English and writing to Macedonian and international students. Her research interests include the teaching of writing and online written communication understood in a sociocultural context.

Tanya Bitterman is a language testing specialist at the Center for Applied Linguistics. She has a master's degree in TESOL and a bachelor's degree in linguistics, and previously taught ESL in New York City schools. Her current work focuses on the development and refinement of a writing test for K–12 ELLs.

Christine Pearson Casanave is affiliated with Temple University's Japan campus and the Middlebury Institute of International Studies at Monterey. She advises Temple doctoral students on their qualitative dissertations, helps organize writing retreats at MIIS, and writes and publishes on topics related to second language writing, dissertation writing, and writing for publication.

Bee Chamcharatsri is a joint appointed assistant professor in the Department of Language, Literacy, and Sociocultural Studies and the Department of English. His research interests include emotions, language learning and teaching, and arts-based research methods. His publications can be seen in *L2 Journal*.

Mark Chapman directs test development at WIDA and his work involves leading new test development projects. His research interests focus on writing assessment, particularly the relationships between task design, written product, and writing process. He holds a PhD in writing assessment from CRELLA at the University of Bedfordshire.

Natalie Nordby Chen is an educator and assessment professional, having taught in the U.S. and Taiwan, and working 25 years in the testing industry at ETS, CaMLA, and Questar. She serves as president of the MidWest Association of Language Testers, and is committed to ensuring access and accommodation for all learners.

Deborah Crusan is Professor of Applied Linguistics at Wright State University. Her work has appeared in academic publications including *Assessing Writing* and *TESOL Quarterly*. Her research interests include writing assessment, particularly for placement of second language writers, writing teacher education, and the politics of assessment. Her book, *Assessment in the Second Language Writing Classroom*, was published by University of Michigan Press.

Luciana C. de Oliveira is Chair and Professor in the Department of Teaching and Learning in the School of Education and Human Development at the University of Miami, Florida. Her research focuses on issues related to teaching English language learners (ELLs) at the K–12 level.

Natalia Dolgova (née Jacobsen) is Teaching Assistant Professor of EAP at the George Washington University. She holds an MA in English Linguistics (with a TESOL certificate) and a PhD in Applied Linguistics. Her research interests include task-based language teaching, applying usage-based linguistics to L2 instruction, and second language writing.

Kathrin Eberharter attained an MA in Language Testing from Lancaster University and worked as a test moderator for the Austrian school-leaving examination. Kathrin is a member of the Language Testing Research Group at the University of Innsbruck and is enrolled in Lancaster University's Applied Linguistics PhD program.

Estela Ene is Associate Professor and Director of the English for Academic Purposes Program at Indiana University—Purdue University Indianapolis. Her publications on L2 writing have appeared in *Assessing Writing, System, ELTJ, CALICO, the Wiley Encyclopedia of Applied Linguistics*, and *the International Journal of Applied Linguistics—ITL*.

Betsy Gilliland is an associate professor in the Department of Second Language Studies at the University of Hawai'i Mānoa. Her research addresses the intersections of adolescent L2 literacy, writing teacher education, and teachers' classroom research. She teaches undergraduate and graduate classes on second language writing and qualitative research approaches.

Abdelbaset Haridy is a PhD candidate in TESOL at the University of New Mexico (UNM). He also works as a TA at UNM. Abdelbaset was granted several academic awards, including the 2011 Fulbright FLTA award, the 2015/2016 UNM Outstanding TA Award, and the 2016/2017 William and Roberta Fellowship. His research interests include language testing and assessment, World Englishes, and psycholinguistics.

Mojtaba Heydari is a PhD candidate of Applied Linguistics at Allameh Tabataba'i University. His research interests include second language assessment in general and assessing writing in particular. He has worked as an EFL teacher and teacher educator over the past eight years and is currently a lecturer at Allameh Tabataba'i University.

Katarzyna Hryniuk is Assistant Professor at the Institute of English Studies at Warsaw University, Poland. Her main research interests in Applied Linguistics include EFL learning and teaching, academic writing, psycholinguistics, corpus linguistics, and discourse analysis. Her publications have appeared in *International Journal of Applied Linguistics* and *Applied Linguistics Review*.

Chenchen Huang is a PhD student of English at The Pennsylvania State University. Her research interests include multilingual writing, comparative rhetoric, and Asian American rhetorics. Her work has appeared in *English for Specific Purposes*.

Hee-Seung Kang is Assistant Professor of ESL/TESOL at Sheridan College, Canada. Before teaching at Sheridan, she served as Director of the ESL Writing Program at Case Western Reserve University. Her research interests include multilingual students' academic writing socialization, writing teacher education, and qualitative research methods.

Aleksandra Kasztalska is Assistant Professor of English at Southern Arkansas University in Magnolia, Arkansas, where she teaches courses in composition, linguistics, and TESOL. Her research interests include applications of World Englishes for teaching composition, non-native and multilingual teacher identity and EFL writing assessment and English in Poland.

Ahyoung Alicia Kim is a researcher at WIDA, University of Wisconsin-Madison, where she conducts research on language assessment and development of PreK–12 English language learners. Her research interests include language assessment, child bilingualism, language literacy, and computer-assisted language learning. Alicia holds an EdD in Applied Linguistics from Teachers College, Columbia University.

Benjamin Kremmel researches and teaches language testing at the University of Innsbruck, Austria, and is a PhD student at the University of Nottingham, UK. He was involved in the Austrian SRP project, which developed standardized national school-leaving exams for the modern languages. He is the recipient of the 2013 Caroline Clapham IELTS Masters Award 2013 and the Robert Lado Memorial Award 2015.

Fahimeh Marefat is Associate Professor of Applied Linguistics at Allameh Tabataba'i University, Iran. Her research program focuses on writing, assessment, CALL, and recently she is working on English for research publication purposes.

Michael Maurer holds an MA in Language Testing from Lancaster University, UK and in English & American Studies from the University of Innsbruck, Austria, and was involved in the development of the Austrian school-leaving exam. He is a certified teacher for German as a FL and currently develops teaching material.

Xuan Minh Ngo is a TESOL lecturer at the University of Languages and International Studies, Vietnam National University, Hanoi. Besides his extensive experience in training pre-service and in-service English teachers, Minh was a member of the team responsible for developing the country's first CEFR-aligned standardized English test.

Andrea Muñoz Galleguillos is an instructor professor in the Language Department of University of Atacama, Chile. Her research aims at creating a mentoring-like plan for English collaborating teachers in order to guide future English teachers during Teaching Practicum Process. She teaches English as a foreign language to freshmen and sophomore students.

Theresa A. Orlovsky holds a master's in TESL/Applied Linguistics. In addition to teaching in university and community settings in the U.S., she has also served as a visiting lecturer at the Tecnológico de Monterrey in Querétaro, Mexico. Her research interests include balanced literacy and second-language writing pedagogy.

Katterine Pavez Bravo is an assistant professor in the Language Department at the University of Atacama, Chile. Her research addresses the field of mentoring and how to include culture when teaching English as a foreign language. She teaches undergraduate classes on Didactics and Teaching methodologies for TEFL students.

Todd Ruecker is Assistant Professor of English at the University of New Mexico. His research focuses on investigating issues surrounding the increasing linguistic and cultural diversity of education systems and making institutions and classrooms more welcoming spaces for all students. He has published four books as well as articles in respected composition, education, and applied linguistics journals such as *TESOL Quarterly* and *College Composition and Communication.*

Renée Saulter is an assessment developer at Cambridge Michigan Language Assessments (CaMLA), working with the creation of accommodated forms for test takers with special needs and the scoring of constructed responses. She holds MAs in Arabic for Professional Purposes and TESOL and has taught ESL/EFL in the U.S. and Oman.

Megan M. Siczek is Assistant Professor and Director of the EAP program at the George Washington University. She has a master's degree in TESOL and a doctorate in Educational Policy Studies, and her research interests include second language writing, global English, and the internationalization of higher education.

Pornpimol Sukavatee is a professor in the Faculty of Education, Chulalongkorn University, Bangkok, Thailand. Her research interests include technology and blended learning environment in language teaching. Her publications can be found in *Asian EFL Journal* and *Rangsit Journal of Arts and Sciences.*

Aleksandra Swatek is a PhD student in the Second Language Studies program at Purdue University, where she has taught courses in the introductory composition program, as well as the Oral English Proficiency Program. In her research she focuses on second language writing, rhetoric and composition, corpus linguistics, and writing assessment.

Bala Thiruchelvam is a professor of TESOL at Sookmyung Women's University. He mainly teaches Methodology and Reading in the in-service English teacher training program. His research interests include methodology, teacher education, and reflective teaching practices.

Jing Wei is a language assessment specialist on WIDA assessment series and a project director on STARTALK program evaluation at Center for Applied Linguistics. She received her PhD from New York University in 2015. Her current research interests include World Englishes assessment as well as writing rubric development and validation.

Gordon Blaine West is Assistant Professor of TESOL at Sookmyung Women's University. He teaches primarily in the Young Learner TESOL program. His research interests include critical literacy, teacher education, and narrative research.

Xiaoye You is Associate Professor of English and Asian Studies at The Pennsylvania State University, USA and a Yunshan Chair Professor at Guangdong University of Foreign Studies, China. He is interested in comparative rhetoric, translingual writing, and English as a cosmopolitan language.

Fernando Zolin-Vesz, PhD, is Assistant Professor in the Department of Linguistics at the Universidade Federal de Mato Grosso (UFMT), Brazil. His research focuses on issues related to teaching and the decoloniality of the conception of language.

A FEW KEY TERMS

analytic rating: rating used in the scoring of writing, which offers a detailed analysis of a highly contextualized checklist of prominent features or characteristics of a specific writing assignment.

centralized examination: a standardized examination set at a local or national level to be used as a selection tool for matters such as college admission and/or employment. These examinations are often the driving force behind secondary education in many countries.

continuous assessment: often referred to as formative assessment, continuous assessment includes a range of formal and informal assessments used by teachers to determine what and when students are learning and ways in which that data informs classroom activity in order to improve student learning.

direct assessment: particularly in writing assessment, direct assessment refers to testing writing through actual writing rather than through the analysis of the subskills of writing.

discrete-point items: discrete-point items test one component at a time, item by item. For instance, a test might assess a **series** of items that related to a particular grammatical structure, such as present perfect.

high-stakes assessments/tests: tests that are often used as the sole measure upon which to make important and often life-altering decisions.

indirect assessment: rather than test a skill such as writing directly, an indirect assessment, usually in multiple-choice format, tests the subskills of that skill. In writing, those subskills might include elements such as spelling, word choice, correct verb tense, syntax, and punctuation.

reliability: a test that is reliable is consistent and stable in measuring what it intends to measure. For instance, a student who takes different forms of a standardized exam multiple times should be able to perform consistently. Concern with reliability is one reason why writing does not play a large role in many standardized assessments.

validity: generally, validity refers to the degree to which a test actually measures what it purports to measure. Threats to validity include cultural bias, lack of motivation to take the test seriously, and knowledge of test questions.

INDEX

Page numbers in italics indicate figures and in bold indicate tables on the corresponding pages.